JAPANESE INDUSTRIALIZATION AND THE ASIAN ECONOMY

Much has been made of the post-war Japanese economic miracle. However, the origins of this spectacular success and its effect on the region can actually be traced back to an earlier period of Asian history. In *Japanese Industrialization and the Asian Economy* the authors examine the factors which contributed to the period of major industrialization from 1870–1940. They trace the roots of this growth back to seventeenth-century rivalry between Japan and China and how this acted as a spur to the expansion of Japanese manufacturing skills. They go on to examine how the development of the Asian market was an important pre-condition of Japanese economic growth but was, in turn, fostered by that growth. The volume comprises nine chapters by eminent economic historians. While the style is non-technical, details are backed up by diagrams and graphs. *Japanese Industrialization and the Asian Economy* offers a valuable guide to the origins of economic dynamism in the Pacific Rim.

A.J.H. Latham is Senior Lecturer in International Economic History at University College, Swansea. He has written widely on market forces in international economic history.

Heita Kawakatsu is Professor of Economics at Waseda University, Japan.

JAPANESE INDUSTRIALIZATION AND THE ASIAN ECONOMY

Edited by
A.J.H. Latham
and
Heita Kawakatsu

London and New York

First published 1994
by Routledge
11 New Fetter Lane, London EC4P 4EE

Simultaneously published in the USA and Canada
by Routledge
29 West 35th Street, New York, NY 10001

© 1994 this volume A.J.H. Latham and Heita Kawakatsu;
individual chapters: the contributors

Typeset in Scantext September by Solidus (Bristol) Limited

Printed and bound in Great Britain by
Biddles Ltd, Guildford and King's Lynn

British Library Cataloguing in Publication Data
A catalogue record for this book is available from the British Library.

Library of Congress Cataloging in Publication Data has been applied for.

ISBN 0–415–11501–9

CONTENTS

CONTENTS

FIGURES

TABLES

CONTRIBUTORS

Dennis O. Flynn is Professor and Chairperson of the Department of Economics, University of the Pacific. He has published on various aspects of early-modern monetary history since 1978. The theoretical basis of his work can be found in 'A microeconomic quantity theory of money and the price revolution', in E. Van Cauwenberghe (ed.) *Precious Metals, Coinage and the Changing Structures in Latin America, Europe and Asia* (1989). A recent application can be found in 'Comparing the Tokugawa shogunate with Hapsburg Spain: two silver-based empires in a global setting', in J. Tracy (ed.) *The Political Economy of Merchant Empires* (1991).

Arturo Giraldez is Assistant Professor of Spanish in the Modern Language Department and in the School of International Studies, University of the Pacific. He received his MA at UNED (University of Madrid Complutense) in 1980, and a PhD in Spanish Literature at the University of California, Santa Barbara, in 1990. He is currently completing a PhD dissertation in History at UNED on the Philippines trade in the early modern period.

Takeshi Hamashita is Professor at the Institute of Oriental Culture, University of Tokyo. His main publications in Japanese are *The Economic History of Modern China, with Special Reference to Maritime Customs Finance and Open Port Market Zones in Late Ch'ing China* (1989), and *Modern China in International Perspective* (1990). His publications in English include 'The tribute trade system and modern Asia', *The Toyo Bunko* (1988).

Chuimei Ho is a research associate at the Anthropology Department of the Field Museum, Chicago. Her main interest is in ceramic archaeology and its role in early trade between East and South-East Asian countries.

xiii

Her publications include *Minnan Blue-and-White Wares: An Archaeological Survey of Kiln Sites of the 16th–19th Centuries in Southern Fujian, China* (1988) and she is editor of *New Light on Chinese Yue and Longquan Wares* (1993).

Heita Kawakatsu received his DPhil from the University of Oxford, and is Professor of Economics at Waseda University, Tokyo. His main publication in English is 'International competition in cotton goods in the late nineteenth century', in W. Fischer *et al.* (eds) *The Emergence of a World Economy, 1500–1914* (1986). His publications in Japanese include *Japanese Civilization and the Modern West* (1991), and he has edited *The Asian Trading Sphere and Japan's Industrialization 1500–1900* (1991) and *A New Asian Drama: Five Hundred Years' Dynamism* (1994).

Hajime Kose is a lecturer at Ryukoku University, Kyoto. His main publication in Japanese is 'The structure of Chinese inter-port trade in the late nineteenth century', *Shakai-Keizai Shigaku*, 54 (1989).

A.J.H. Latham is Senior Lecturer in International Economic History at University College, Swansea. He is the author of *Old Calabar, 1600–1891: The Impact of the International Economy upon a Traditional Society* (1973), *The International Economy and the Undeveloped World, 1865–1914* (1978; in Japanese 1987), and *The Depression and the Developing World, 1914–39* (1981). He was co-editor of *The Market in History* (1986), and co-author of *Decline and Recovery in Britain's Overseas Trade, 1873–1914* (1993). He is currently working on the history of the international rice trade.

Eiichi Motono is a lecturer at Tokyo University of Fisheries, and his main publications include 'The traffic revolution: remaking the export sales system in China, 1866–1875', *Modern China*, 12 (1986), and 'A study of the legal status of the compradors during the 1880s, with special reference to the three civil cases between David Sassoon Sons & Co., and their compradores, 1884–1887', *Acta Asiatica*, 62 (1992).

Peter Schran is Professor of Economics and Asian Studies at the University of Illinois, Urbana-Champaign, where he was also for many years director of the Center for East Asian and Pacific Studies. He received a diploma in political economy from the Free University of Berlin in 1954, and then studied economics and Chinese at the University of California, Berkeley. Later he taught at both Berkeley and Yale. His research focuses on China's economic development since the mid-nineteenth century and he is the author of many articles and three books, including *Guerrilla Economy: The Development of the Shensi-Kansu-Ninghsia Border Region, 1937–45* (1976). He is a regular visitor to the People's Republic of China.

Sakae Tsunoyama received his PhD from Kyoto University, and is Emeritus Professor of Wakayama University and also Professor at Nara Sangyo University, Nara. His main work in English was published in Bombay, *A Concise Economic History of Modern Japan* (1965), and he has published numerous books in Japanese including *A History of Tea* (1980), *A Social History of Clocks* (1984) and *Information Strategy of the Commercial State of Japan* (1988). He is also editor of *A Study of the Japanese Consular Reports* (1986).

PREFACE

Most of these papers were originally presented at the Tenth International Economic History Congress held at Leuven in 1990. They marked a continuation of a theme explored at the Ninth International Economic History Congress at Berne in 1986.

Papers at the Berne Congress drew attention to the stirrings of economic growth in East Asia during the nineteenth century. One pointer to this was the international rice trade. Rice exports from Burma, Siam and French Indo-China increased rapidly, much of the rice going to Singapore and Hong Kong. The Singapore rice was transhipped to the Malay Peninsula and the Dutch East Indies, whilst the Hong Kong rice was sent to the Southern Provinces of China, and even Japan. Rice was also shipped direct from Indo-China to the Philippines. Some of this rice went to mine and plantation workers, but the flow of rice into China suggested something more fundamental was taking place: there were no mine or plantation workers there (Latham, 1986).

Heita Kawakatsu drew attention to the fact that, contrary to Marxist theorizing, textiles imported from Britain did not prevent the industrialization of the Asian cotton industry. This was because Asia industrialized by producing cheap down-market yarn and textiles for the peasantry, whereas Britain supplied expensive up-market goods (Kawakatsu, 1986). Another paper linked these two themes together, and suggested that rice and textiles were the opposite sides of the same coin. Rice-exporting peasants used the cash they obtained to buy Asian yarn and textiles, facilitating industrialization. In return, Asian millworkers bought imported rice (Sugihara, 1986). In this way an internal dynamism was generated in the Asian economy.

So the purpose of the session in Leuven was to explore further the intricacies of intra-Asian trade. Scholars working on these issues were invited to contribute and the following papers resulted. At the session there were about forty people, including K.N. Chaudhuri, Wolfram Fischer, David Landes and Angus Maddison, and there was substantial discussion, much of which has been incorporated into the final versions of the papers. The only papers not presented at Leuven are those by Chuimei Ho, and Dennis O. Flynn with Arturo Giraldez, but we have made a special point of including them because they draw attention to some of the earliest and most important items of intra-Asian trade, namely ceramics and silver.

A.J.H. LATHAM
HEITA KAWAKATSU

REFERENCES

Fischer, W., McInnis, R. M. and Schneider, J. (eds) (1986) *The Emergence of a World Economy, 1500–1914*, Wiesbaden: Franz Steiner Verlag.

Kawakatsu, H. (1986) 'International competition in cotton goods in the late nineteenth century: Britain versus India and East Asia', in Fischer *et al.* (1986): 619–43.

Latham, A.J.H. (1986) 'The international trade in rice and wheat since 1868', in Fischer *et al.* (1986): 645–63.

Sugihara, K. (1986) 'Patterns of Asia's integration into the world economy', in Fischer *et al.* (1986): 709–28.

INTRODUCTION

A.J.H. Latham

The first papers in this collection are by Heita Kawakatsu. He argues that Tokugawa Japan saw herself as the land of gods. When she adopted the Confucian idea that she was the central kingdom in creation, surrounded by barbarians, she refused to enter the Chinese tribute system and cut herself off from the rest of the world. Now she had to produce for herself things she had previously imported, including cotton goods. But Japanese cottons, like those in Asia, were thick fabrics for working clothes and winter wear, taking the place that woollens filled in the West. They were made from short-staple Old World cottons, quite different from those of the New World. It was with these heavy fabrics that Japan industrialized and made such inroads into the Asian market after the opening of her ports in 1859. China was her main competitor, not Britain.

Chuimei Ho's paper draws attention to the fact that in the seventeenth century the ancient intra-Asian ceramic trade of East Asia moved into a period of rapid change, with Japan emerging as a rival supplier to China, and Europe and the Americas becoming major purchasers. However, the overall ceramic market within Asia was not greatly affected by the development of the new Western markets. But the development of a new and wealthy foreign market for fine-quality wares did make a difference to some kiln areas, and encouraged further specialization among producers.

Dennis O. Flynn and Arturo Giraldez concentrate on the little-studied flow of silver from America to China, by way of Manila. The collapse of the paper monetary system in China created a substantial and growing demand there for silver through the seventeenth century. The main sources of silver were Peru, Mexico and Japan, the supplies being controlled by the Spanish Emperor and the Shogun. The trade was carried on by European and private Chinese merchants, with Manila

1

and Nagasaki as key trade centres. Chinese silk was important as an exchange item.

Takeshi Hamashita deals with the trade and tribute system centred on China, mentioned previously by Kawakatsu. This, he suggested, created an Asian sense of unity. Satellite countries paid tribute and received imperial gifts in return, but over the years this provoked nationalism, as the act of paying tribute defined the separate identity of countries within the system. The tribute trade area formed an integrated 'silver zone' which was linked to neighbouring trade zones in India, the Islamic region and Europe.

Eiichi Motono presents a very different paper, which concentrates on the decline of the British cloth trade in Shanghai. After complicated negotiations between the Lancashire merchants and the Chinese dealers, the Manchester men were forced to charge gold prices to protect themselves from the falling price of silver. This resulted in rising silver prices for their goods in China, and the decline in their trade. It is clear that the Westerners and the Chinese were equal participants in these dealings, and the failure of China to modernize cannot be attributed to foreign influence, the Quing government itself being much to blame.

China's inter-port trade is the subject of Hajime Kose's paper, and he argues that internal trade and foreign trade were interdependent. There were two main linkages, Shanghai with Central and North China, and Hong Kong with South China and South-East Asia. Foreign trade did not damage internal trade, and the fact that the domestic trade network remained in the hands of Chinese merchants prevented Japanese merchants penetrating to any great extent.

A.J.H. Latham examines the trade of Asia's two great entrepôts, Singapore and Hong Kong, before the First World War. If there was dynamism in intra-Asian trade, surely it must have been manifest here? But he comes to the conclusion that although Singapore's trade grew at about 4 per cent per annum, the dynamic element was Western purchases of tin and rubber which passed through Singapore from Malaya and the Dutch East Indies. Much of the purchasing power from the West was retained in Asia, where it was spent by mine and plantation workers on rice, foodstuffs and the manufactures of Asia's emergent industries. But Hong Kong was different. First, the trade figures for Hong Kong had to be reconstructed from those of her trade partners, as they had never been recorded in Hong Kong itself. From this exercise it emerges that China was the biggest trading partner, imports growing at over 4 per cent per annum. China was also the largest destination for Hong Kong's exports, leading to the suggestion that Hong Kong was simply a Chinese port which happened to be administered by the British. Even rice was imported from Siam and French Indo-China, to be sent on into China. Singapore was the second most important destination for Hong Kong exports. Japan's exports to Hong Kong grew quickly during the period and she had a useful surplus on her trade there. The implication of this paper is that within China specialization of function by producers, and interchange of goods by the market, was creating increased productivity and growth, and this was reflected in her trading relationship with Hong Kong.

In the next paper Sakae Tsunoyama asks how the Japanese could industrialize in the late nineteenth century, when they had no tariffs to protect them from the impact of British Free Trade. His answer is that the Japanese understood the structure and needs of the Asian market better than the British did and successfully industrialized by making cheap copies of Western smallwares. These suited the pockets of the ordinary people of Asia better than expensive Western goods.

Peter Schran is also interested in Japanese industrialization, but he argues that Japanese imperialism was a crucial part of the process. By the eve of the Pacific War in 1941, Japan had transformed most of East Asia into a set of colonies, formal and informal. Their external trade was regulated to ensure flows towards and in favour of Japan. But it meant an Empire-wide market for Japanese consumer and capital goods. The capital goods improved the productivity of the Empire countries, and as a result of the Japanese investment which took place, production and processing of primary products benefited, ensuring that the economies of the colonies grew nearly as fast as Japan itself, at about 4 per cent per annum.

The overall conclusion of this set of papers is that there does seem to have been an internal dynamic in intra-Asian trade, and that it centred in particular on China, which was such a large part of the East Asian economy. Japanese industrialization was also fed by this dynamism, and in its turn contributed to it.

HISTORICAL BACKGROUND
Heita Kawakatsu

The historical background against which Japan industrialized needs some examination. Recently, scholars and laymen have tended to associate the rapid economic growth of Japan and countries such as Taiwan, Korea, Hong Kong and Singapore with their common cultural heritage of Confucianism (Morishima, 1982). But despite this common heritage, East Asian countries had very different historical experiences before 1914. In the age of 'Imperialism' China became politically and economically unstable largely due to foreign interference, and it finally collapsed. Korea and Taiwan came under Japanese rule, Hong Kong and Singapore under British rule, and Vietnam fell under French control. Only Japan successfully maintained political independence, to become the first industrialized nation in Asia. Taking these facts into account, the common cultural experience of East Asian countries should not be overemphasized as an explanation for their recent economic development.

Economic historians have argued that the Tokugawa period in Japan provided the preliminary conditions for the later economic development of the country. This was the period which saw Confucianism become the state ideology, so clearly a link between Confucianism and economic development can be argued. Bellah (1957) suggests that a merchant ethic established by Ishida Baigan (1685–1744) was akin to Calvinism and the protestant work ethic, but in fact Baigan's influence faded long before the end of the Tokugawa period. In the preface to the Japanese edition of his book, Bellah accepted that his view was not sustainable.

Morishima (1982) has similarly argued that Japanese group orientation and loyalty was in some way equivalent to Calvinist frugality and the work ethic, and dates back to the seventh century. However, he does not explain why the existence of this ethic from such

4

an early time suddenly led to economic development in the late nineteenth century. He also argues that Tokugawa Japan closed the country to outside trade in the 1630s to protect inefficient handcraft industries from Western competition, and save the country from becoming an agricultural and mining primary producer (Morishima 1982: 59–60). But the leading industrial products of the West in the seventeenth century were woollens and guns, and woollens were not suited to the Japanese market, which used cotton, hemp and silk fabrics. As for guns, the Japanese were already masters of gun-making in the late sixteenth century and could more than hold their own in the arms trade (Perrin 1979: 4, 70). What is more, Japan was a prosperous country, well-endowed with natural resources such as timber, iron ore, gold, silver and copper.

Yet the fact remains that it was during the Tokugawa period that the Japanese version of Confucianism became the dominant ideology. Although it was brought to Japan in the mid-sixth century, it was not until the seventeenth century that Confucianism played a significant role in the country. Up until then Buddhism had dominated Japanese intellectual life. But Confucianism became the official learning in Tokugawa Japan as the shogunate needed to bring peace and order after the prolonged period of war. Confucianism, then, had a political rather than a moral purpose.

The social order of the Confucian Tokugawa state was hierarchical, with four distinct classes: samurai, peasants, craftsman and merchants. Externally, Japan had relations only with those countries which would abide by regulations imposed by the Tokugawa shogunate. So Ryukyu (Okinawa) came to pay tribute to Japan. The activities of Dutch and Chinese merchants were confined to Nagasaki, although the Dutch had to report to the authorities all the news of the outside world, and send an emissary to the capital every year, where they were sometimes mockingly humiliated by the shogun court. Korean embassies were regarded by the Japanese as tributary missions.

Clearly, Japanese external relations were influenced by the Confucian view that there was a division between the civilized and the barbarian world. Prior to the Tokugawa period East Asia had been dominated by the Chinese world order, which assumed that the ethical norm of Confucianism constituted civilization, and this norm was embodied in the Chinese state and personified by the Chinese emperor. Non-Chinese states could bring their countries into the Chinese world order by proclaiming themselves subjects of the Chinese emperor. But events in China, particularly the conquest of China by the barbarian

Manchurians, damaged China's claim to superiority and domination over the rest of the East. For they had had to accept barbarians as their rulers, something the Japanese had never done. The political and ideological map of East Asia was transformed. Japan's indigenous view of herself was that she was the land of gods. When this was linked to the Confucian idea of a central kingdom surrounded by barbarians, the idea was generated of Japan, rather than China, being the central kingdom surrounded by barbarians. She persuaded Korean kings to stop using the Chinese calendar in correspondence with Japan after 1645, and issued trade credentials to Chinese merchants dated in the Japanese calendar from 1715. So Tokugawa Japan rejected the idea of China being the central kingdom, and installed herself in that position (Toby, 1984).

The economic implications of this change are clear. One reason for participating in the China-centred world order was trade, because it was necessary to accept the Chinese tribute system to trade with China. So before the Tokugawa period some Shoguns accepted the Chinese world order so that they could participate in commerce. But Tokugawa Japan adopted its policy of isolation in order to reject Chinese dominance. Previously the Japanese had actively traded throughout both the New and the Old Worlds, and particularly China, exchanging gold, silver and copper for foreign goods. Cotton goods, silk, porcelain, dyestuffs, sugar, and so on, came into the country from China and abroad, and, of course, new ideas, such as Confucianism. But Japan seemed to have nothing to offer China in exchange, except metals. But the outflow of metals could not be sustained and caused domestic shortages. So the shogunate attempted to stimulate the production of goods in Japan which had previously been imported. Japan was trying to become a mini-China both ideologically and materially.

During the Tokugawa period Japan produced goods similar to those in China, but there was little competition between the two economies because of the regulations enforcing isolation. Competition only came to the surface when the Western powers came to East Asia and introduced free trade. During the seclusion period, Japan continued to import things which she found she could not produce herself. Pepper, spices, drugs, tea, coffee, sugar, cotton textiles, silk fabrics, indigo and other dyestuffs, porcelain and saltpetre came through the strictly regulated ports at Nagasaki, Tsushima and Ryukyu (Okinawa). At the same time Europe imported these same goods and, like the Japanese, paid for them with precious metals. But the Japanese were successful in transplanting to her soil most of the agriculture-based products she had previously imported. This was possible because of the climatic conditions she shared with other Asian countries. Europe could not do this so easily and had to continue importing from abroad, in particular from the Americas. Sugar, coffee and rice were established there, and a new and different indigenous cotton plant discovered. The Japanese could run a closed economy effectively, whereas the Europeans were forced to continue importing tropical products and therefore operate an open trading system, leading eventually to free trade.

These circumstances even linked into different economic revolutions within the two different economic systems. In Britain there was a manufacturing industrial revolution, which used more capital and less labour, resulting in higher labour productivity; whereas in Tokugawa Japan there was an agricultural industrious revolution, which raised land productivity by using more labour and fertilizer. Each economic revolution was a rational economic response, given the respective factor endowments involved (Hayami, 1992). The Japanese industrious revolution enabled the Japanese economy to be more efficient than the Chinese economy, and this proved crucial when the two countries were brought into competition by the opening up of trade.

When Japan opened her ports, goods came not only from the West but also from other Asian countries. By and large, Western goods were new to the Japanese, so there was very little competition with indigenous products. The competition came from Asia in those goods which Japan had introduced from Asia itself, such as cottons, silks, sugar, etc. As a result a new intra-regional division of labour emerged in Asia. Production of raw cotton in Japan was wiped out by the importation of cheaper Chinese and Indian raw cotton. Japan specialized in cotton spinning, with the help of machinery imported from Britain. Success in this area instigated a sequence of mechanization in several other Japanese industries. Japan also competed with China for the world market in tea and silk. Intra-Asian competition was seen in sugar, indigo and rice as well. In the West, Japan found the technologies to produce these products more efficiently than other Asian countries. Japanese industrialization was not so much a process of catching up with the West, but more a result of centuries-long competition within Asia (Kawakatsu, 1986).

REFERENCES

Bellah, R. (1957) *Tokugawa Religion: The Values of Pre-Industrial Japan*, Glencoe, Ill.: Free Press.

Fischer, W., McInnis, R.M. and Schneider, J. (eds) (1986) *The Emergence of a World Economy, 1500–1914*, Weisbaden: Franz Steiner Verlag.

Hayami, A. (1992) 'The industrious revolution', *Look Japan*, 38, no. 436: 8–10.

Kawakatsu, H. (1986) 'International competitiveness in cotton goods in the late nineteenth century: Britain versus India and East Asia', in Fischer *et al.* (1986): 619–43.

Morishima, M. (1982) *Why Has Japan Succeeded?: Western Technology and the Japanese Ethos*, Cambridge: Cambridge University Press.

Perrin, N. (1979) *Giving Up The Gun*, Boston, Mass.: D.R. Godine.

Toby, R. (1984) *State and Diplomacy in Early Modern Japan: Asia in the Development of the Tokugawa Bakufu*, Princeton, N.J.: Princeton University Press.

1

THE EMERGENCE OF A MARKET FOR COTTON GOODS IN EAST ASIA IN THE EARLY MODERN PERIOD

Heita Kawakatsu

INTRODUCTION

Cotton was grown in India for several thousands of years before Christ and for a long time India monopolized the product. By the time Europeans and Japanese launched out into the so-called 'East Indies', cotton textiles were being used by the people of East Africa, the Middle East and South and South-East Asia, not only as clothing materials but also as a means of exchange. In the course of history from the Middle Ages to the early modern period, as trade began between the East Indies and the two extremities of Eurasia, cotton products found their way from India to the East and the West via various routes.

As indicated in my historical background note, two economic revolutions took place in Britain and in Japan: the industrial revolution in Britain, and the industrious revolution in Japan. These revolutions created an import-substitute industry for cotton goods: the British industry copied Indian goods, whereas the Japanese copied Chinese goods. As a result, what emerged were two markets for cotton products with distinct qualities, in the West and in the Far East respectively (Table 1.1).

The following account describes when and how a particular type of cotton plant spread eastward, resulting in the creation of this market in East Asia.

Table 1.1 Two markets for cotton products

	Raw cotton	Cotton yarn	Cotton cloth
Western type	Long-stapled cotton	Fine yarn	Thin and light texture
Far Eastern type	Short-stapled cotton	Thick yarn	Thick and heavy texture

CLASSIFICATION

The cotton plant belongs to the genus *Gossypium*, of the Hibiscus genus of the Mallow family. From the beginning of the study of *Gossypium* considerable difficulty was encountered in attempting to draw up the classification of its species. In early studies, Linnaeus, Parlatore (*Le Specie dei cotoni*, 1866), Bowman, Forbes Royle (*Illustrations of Botany and Natural History of Himalayan Mountains*, 1839) and Todaro (*Relazione sulla culta dei cotoni*, 1877–78) were notable botanists.[1] These scholars differed greatly in the number of species they recognized. 'The number of species from a botanical point of view', wrote Brooks in 1898, 'is variously stated as from four to eighty-eight'.[2] This disagreement took place because, during the period in which the cottons had been cultivated, selection had occurred, either consciously or unconsciously, resulting in the appearance in different places, but probably from the same stock, of well-marked forms which, in the absence of the history of their origins, must be regarded as different species.[3] The most elaborate attempt at classification by the morphological approach was made by Watt in 1907.[4] His main subdivisions of the species were largely based upon the presence or absence of fuzz on the seeds. This character, however, is inherited in simple Mendelian fashion, and it can be associated with any other group of characteristics. It is not strange, therefore, that of two forms otherwise similar, one may have very fuzzy and the other may have naked seeds. Classification on this basis is necessarily artificial. But the following two decades did not see any significant contribution to the taxonomy comparable to his.[5]

In 1928, the appearance of an article entitled 'A contribution to the classification of the genus *Gossypium*', written by a Russian botanist G.S. Zaitzev, brought a revolution in the taxonomy of *Gossypium*.[6] Zaitzev, who made use of discoveries concerning the minute structure of the reproductive cells, adopted a genetic approach for the first time, a very different form of analysis from the morphological approach employed so far. What Zaitzev discovered was as follows:[7]

(a) The cotton forms of the Old World (Asia and Africa) have a haploid (in the sexual cells) number of chromosomes, 13; the corresponding diploid number in the somatic cells is 26. The cotton forms of the New World have a haploid chromosome number of 26; the corresponding diploid number is 52.

(b) Crosses between the cotton forms of the Old World and those of the New fail almost completely; when such crosses are effected, in a natural or an artificial way, they are, first, very rare; and second, the hybrids obtained from such crosses in the first generation are completely sterile in spite of their normal appearance. Because of such genetic differences, any interaction between the forms of the Old World and those of the New is entirely excluded (in spite of the statements of some botanists, especially Watt) and they are entirely isolated from one another.[8]

Furthermore, based on the experimental results that hybrid forms obtained from cotton plants belonging to different sub-groups were of only transitory importance and sooner or later died out or reverted to the ancestral forms, a fact showing the steadiness and independency of the sub-groups, he discovered that the cotton group of the New World and that of the Old World could be divided into two sub-groups respectively. Each of these two sub-groups had its own geographical distribution. Accordingly, he subdivided the Old World and the New World cottons into the African and the Indo-China (Asiatic) sub-groups of the former, and the Central American and the Southern American sub-groups of the latter.[9] The cytological, morphological and physiological data which he collected, together with the genetic investigations of the genus *Gossypium*, also supported the fact that the genus *Gossypium* falls phylogenetically into the above four groups.[10]

Successive analyses by botanists have corroborated Zaitzev's findings in respect of the genetic nature of the species, that is, only four species embrace the whole vast diversity of cultivated cottons. Zaitzev followed his predecessors' (particularly Watt's) nomenclature. His followers found the original species of each sub-group.

S.G. Harland, among others, who worked on the New World cotton with 26 chromosomes, established that:

(a) two species, namely *G. barbadense* and G. hirsutum are good taxonomic species;

(b) in these two species, long separation had produced profound genetic change;

(c) *G. hirsutum* and *G. barbadense* possess relatively few genetic attributes in common;

(d) geographical isolation over a long period of time had resulted in the production of new alleles at most loci and in a characteristic distribution of the differing alleles between the two species;

(e) although *G. hirsutum* and *G. barbadense* were so closely related that their first-generation hybrids were fully fertile, sterile and unviable types appeared in their second generation;

(f) the discontinuity between these entities in nature, even in the areas where their ranges overlapped, was taken to indicate that they were good taxonomic species.[11]

R.A. Silow made extensive investigations into the genetic aspects of taxonomic divergence in the diploid Asiatic cottons, and found that two cultivated Asiatic species, *G. arboreum* and *G. herbaceum* diverge in their genetic composition. He maintained that:

(a) taxonomically the relationship existing between *G. arboreum* and *G. herbaceum* was similar to that between the New World cultivated species, with full fertility in the first generation and partial sterility and disintegration in later generation;

(b) the separation of *G. herbaceum* from *G. arboreum* was not only by a genetic barrier, but also by ecological adaptabilities.[12]

Three independent lines of evidence confirm Silow's findings:

(a) the species integrity was maintained when cultivated cottons were grown mixed in commercial crops; mixtures of *G. arboreum* and *G. herbaceum* were grown commercially in western India and in parts of Madras for many years without breakdown of the species distinction;[13]

(b) before the distinction between *G. arboreum* and *G. herbaceum* was worked out genetically, comprehensive and long-continued efforts were made in South India to breed commercially acceptable cottons from *G. arboreum* × *G. herbaceum* hybrids. These consistently failed to give material of agricultural value, and it was remarked that 'the better the single plant selection in any generation, the worse the segregates that appeared in its progeny';[14]

(c) in crosses made for the genetic analysis of species difference, there arose a wide range of unbalanced and unthrifty types in segregating generations.[15]

THE OLD WORLD COTTONS

Origin and spread

According to Watt, 'no species of *Gossypium* is known, in its original habitat, to be annual.'[16] Historical and botanical evidence is equally emphatic that the primitive cottons were perennial.[17] Since cotton plants were originally long-lived perennials, the natural limits of distribution of the genus were fixed by climatic conditions favourable to this habit of growth.[18] The earliest civilization to spin and weave the perennial cotton seems to have been that of the Indus Valley. The fragments of cotton fabrics found at Mohenjo-Daro have been dated at approximately 3000 BC.[19] As mentioned above, differentiation in the Old World complex of cultivated cottons led to the establishment of two clearly defined species, *G arboreum* and *G. herbaceum.* Concerning the origin of both species, one conjecture is that the collapse of the Indus civilization in the middle of the third millennium BC effectively divided the area which formed the primary centre of origin (Sind) into two, because of the absence of a well-organized community to maintain irrigation facilities. Sind and Rajputana present an almost complete desert barrier between Persia and peninsular India. The isolation so established produced the conditions under which genetic divergence took place and led to the establishment of the species distinction between *G. herbaceum* and *G. arboreum.*[20] How they spread to other places is shown in Figure 1.1. This ended the first phase of the evolution of the cottons.

A radical transformation of cotton cultivation then occurred as a consequence of the intensification of agriculture: the establishment of the supremacy of annual cropping. Selection by man of early-maturing forms suitable for cultivation as an annual crop made possible a great extension of the original limits.[21] However, 'in the thirteenth century all Indian cottons were perennials'.[22] The geographical distribution of these two species in the same period – about the time when Marco Polo was travelling – is shown in Figure 1.2. As indicated in the figure, by that time *G. herbaceum* cotton had already spread to Persia and Central Asia, where the spread of the perennial cotton crop must have been very sharply limited by the severity of the winter season.

The sequence of development of annual varieties of *G. herbaceum* presents no difficulty once an annual type, able to crop and complete its growth cycle before the onset of cold winters, had been established. In Persia, the annual variety *persicum* was developed to meet the

13

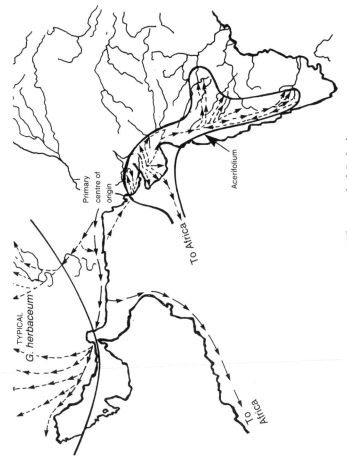

Figure 1.1(a) The spread of *G. herbaceum*

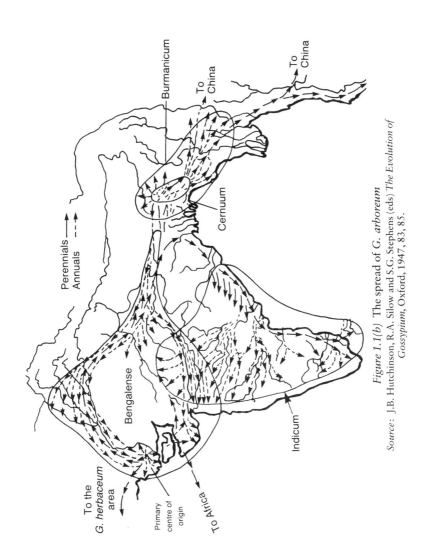

Figure 1.1(b) The spread of *G. arboreum*

Source: J.B. Hutchinson, R.A. Silow and S.G. Stephens (eds) *The Evolution of Gossypium*, Oxford, 1947, 83, 85.

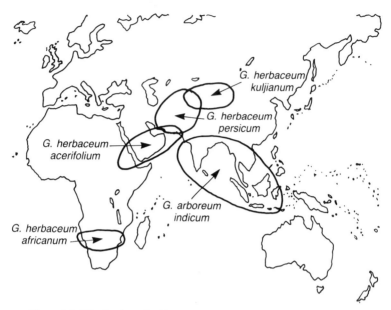

Figure 1.2 Distribution of Old World cottons at the time of Marco Polo
(thirteenth century)
Source: Sir Joseph Hutchinson, 'The history and relationships of the world's cottons',
Endeavour, 21 (1962): 7.

limitations imposed by such cold winters, and further north the very
short season variety *kuljianum* arose in response to selection in an area
of short, hot summers and long, cold winters. Later, when the
advantages of the annual varieties became apparent in India, annual
herbaceum was carried south to replace perennial *arboreum* and gave
rise to the variety *wightianum* in western India.[23] The geographical
distribution of five varieties of G. *herbaceum* in the modern age is
shown in Figure 1.3(a).

It was first believed that G. *arboreum* arose in cultivation by
differentiation from a cultivated stock of G. *herbaceum*,[24] partly
because G. *arboreum* was never truly wild,[25] and partly because
G. *herbaceum* is cytologically more primitive than G. *arboreum*.[26] This
idea is now rejected, and what is now accepted is that the two species
were separately adopted from the wild.[27] According to Hutchinson,
G. *arboreum* cottons were first domesticated in Gujerat.[28]

G. *arboreum* developed into six geographical varieties: *soudanense*
in Africa, *indicum* in western India and the peninsula, *burmanicum* in

16

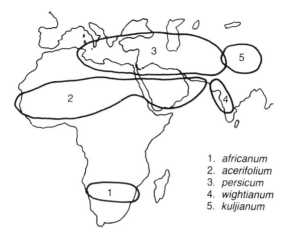

1. africanum
2. acerifolium
3. persicum
4. wightianum
5. kuljianum

Figure 1.3(a) Distribution of G. *herbaceum*

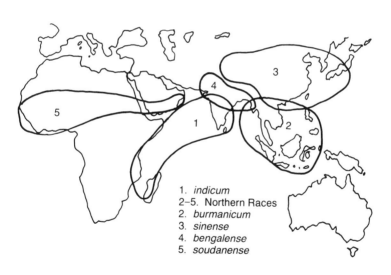

1. indicum
2–5. Northern Races
2. burmanicum
3. sinense
4. bengalense
5. soudanense

Figure 1.3(b) Distribution of G. *arboreum*
Source: J.B. Hutchinson, 'New evidence on the origin of Old World cottons', *Heredity*,
8(2), (1954): 235–6.

17

eastern Bengal, Assam and Burma, *sinense* in China, and *bengalense* in northern and central India. This distribution is mapped in Figure 1.3(b). The species can be divided into two groups, namely, the *indicum* cottons and the *burmanicum* cottons. From the latter two annual varieties, *bengalense* and *sinense*, arose.[29] A comparison between Figure. 1.1(b) and Figure. 1.3(b) shows immediately that *sinense* was the last variety of the three to be developed.

Levant cottons

The so-called Levant cotton belonged to the typical form of *G. herbaceum*, called *persicum*.[30] The characteristics of the crop are described thus:[31]

> Small, annual sub-shrubs, with stiff stems and few or no vegetative branches. Twigs and leaves sparsely hairy or glabrous. Leaves large, almost fleshy, very broad lobed (not more than half cut), flat. Bolls usually rather large and round, sometimes tapered and prominently shouldered; pale green, generally only cracking and remaining closed when ripe, sometimes opening widely. Seeds large, fuzzy. Lint copious, and of fair quality. Distribution: Iran and Baluchistan, Afghanistan, Russian Turkestan, Iraq, Syria, Turkey, Greece and the Mediterranean islands. It was widely spread round the Mediterranean by the Moslem invasion and was the earliest cotton cultivated in the Nile delta in Egypt.

Indian cottons

The botanical study of cottons in India provides a clear indication that the former status of the ancient Indian cotton plant underwent a change from the eighteenth century. This change in essence was that the old fine cottons (*G. arboreum* var. *neglectum* forma *indica*) were replaced by coarse, high-ginning types of *G. arboreum* var. *neglectum* forma *bengalensis*.[32]

Marco Polo referred to the perennial cotton plant in Gujerat: 'The growth of these trees is such that up to twelve years they produce for spinning, but from twelve to twenty an inferior fibre only.'[33] The incentive to grow annuals was much less in India than in more northern countries and until the advent of the British in India there appears to be no record of the cultivation of annual types.[34]

The fine spinning and weaving commonly associated with Dacca muslins was made possible by the selection of fine-quality types among perennials. These cottons were all forms of G. *arboreum*. The cotton from which the famous Dacca muslins were made was fine in staple, and seems to have been triennial, as Price reported in Dacca in 1844: 'I found the triennial kind scarcely able to bear the weight of boll that was on it; it has a fine silky staple, and the *riots* informed me that they get from twelve annas to a rupee per maund more for it than for the annual kind.'[35] Referring to tests carried out on Dacca muslin, Ahmad stated that the mean fibre length of the cotton used in the manufacture of this fine material was found to be just about an inch, the fibre-weight per inch was 0.12 to 0.15 × 10 oz. and the yarn was so fine that there were only ten to fifteen fibres in a cross section of the yarn.[36] Though the Dacca muslins were the best known of India's fine textiles, fine spinning and weaving was carried on in all parts of India, and fine cottons, some of which were exported to Dacca, were grown to meet the demand. These cottons were the cottons of old Hindu India.

But a change occurred in the Indian cotton crop. The introduction of an annual variety of G. *herbaceum* cotton into India, probably from Iraq, stimulated by a developing interest in the potential of growing cotton as an annual, marked 'the beginning of the second phase in the development of the Indian crop'.[37]

In general, the northern cottons were short and coarse, but they possessed a high ginning out-turn, whereas the *indicum* cottons were comparatively fine in staple, but low in ginning out-turn.[38] The selection of annual types of G. *arboreum* cottons gave rise to the annual *bengalense* of northern India. It was a variety of the northern cottons and was 'a rather uniform group of early, high ginning, relatively coarse cottons';[39] the invasion of *bengalense* into all parts of India took place as a result of the demand for a high ginning percentage, but produced a deterioration in quality.[40] The reasons for this change are: (a) a large export trade in raw cotton to China created preference for quantity over quality;[41] (b) cheap machine-made cotton goods from England began to compete successfully with the fine hand-made local muslins, resulting in a reduction in the cultivation of fine cottons. In 1844, Price, an American planter engaged by the government to investigate the state of cotton cultivation in Bengal, reported:

> Sonergong, which is one of the principal manufacturing places in this district of the fine muslin fabrics, and, I am informed, at one time cultivated a considerable quantity of the Dacca *Kuppas*, but whether for the loom becoming more profitable than the plough,

or for the want of demand for that article, can not say, but the *riots* appear to have entirely neglected cultivation as the lands on which they cultivated cotton at one time, are now, and have been for a length of time, a dense jungle.[42]

Moreover, (c) the mill industry in India which was concerned with coarse counts led to the development of a marked premium for ginning percentage as against the comparatively small advantage of high quality. Since there were no safeguards against adulteration, the cultivator in self-defence grew the high-ginning coarse cottons in place of the low-ginning types.[43]

The coarse stapled *bengalense* spread in northern India during the nineteenth century, and was widely extended at the expense of finer *indicum* in the Central Provinces and northern Dacca, and they displaced *herbaceum* cottons in parts of western India, too.[44] It also spread south into the peninsula, invading the *indicum* areas of Maharashtra and Andhra Pradesh at the expense of the *indicum*.[45] The area covered by *bengalense* was very greatly increased in the nineteenth century, and a great cotton-growing tract changed over from medium-stapled to coarse-stapled. At the beginning of the twentieth century the northern *bengalense*, which had displaced the southern *indicum* so successfully in the Central Provinces and Khandesh, was introduced into the *herbaceum* tract of Kathiawar; under the name of Matthio, it spread until it contributed a very large proportion of the Dholleras crop. In the Punjab the development of the canal irrigation system resulted in a great increase in the area under cotton, and this is where the northern *bengalense* spread. These extensions all involved an increase in the amount of coarse-stapled Indian cottons, and constituted a source of serious weakness to India's position in the cotton markets of the West.[46] There were attempts at hybridization between short-stapled Indian cottons and American uplands. But because of the sterility barrier that we mentioned earlier, these were abortive. After the failure of the attempt to introduce American cottons at the time of the cotton famine, 'for the next half-century the Indian crop was grown virtually entirely from *G. arboreum* and *G. herbaceum*'.[47]

The Far Eastern cottons

Sinense

Of the Far Eastern countries, China was among the first to develop annual forms of *arboreum*, since most of the crop was grown in areas where winter cold would preclude the growing of perennials on a field scale. *Sinense* varieties are the earliest-fruiting forms of the species and developed a distinctive character that marked them off the two main Indian types, *bengalense* and *indicum*.[48]

Silow first noted the botanic classification of the Far Eastern cottons: that in their extreme earliness and their glabrous tendency the Far Eastern cottons were 'establishing a norm distinct from that for the species in general, and they might well be separated under the name *sinense*'.[49] Distribution was confined to China, Japan, Manchuria and Formosa. No perennials survived in this area. Though a wide range of variation developed within the limits of the early habit imposed by a short growing season, *sinense* continued to be a new and extremely important source of variability, which led to the eventual establishment of a full varietal distinction within *G. arboreum*.[50] In China, Manchuria, Korea and Japan only early annual cottons could survive, and the spread of cotton into that region followed the development of the early annual habit characteristic of *sinense*.[51]

THE SPREAD OF COTTON EASTWARDS

At the end of the Middle Ages, Old World cotton which originated in India reached its maximum historical extent in the Eurasian continent, stretching from Spain to China, and on to Japan. The following pages will briefly describe when and how it took place in the Eastern half of Eurasia.

China

China had cold winters where only annual types of cotton could survive. According to Watt, cotton was grown in Chinese gardens as an ornamental shrub towards the end of the seventh century. But in fact long before then *G. herbaceum* var. *kuljianum* had been grown in western China. The utilization of this cotton can be dated back to as early as the second century. This type was adapted to the climate of Central Asia where the summers are short and the winters cold. *Kuljianum* could 'mature a small crop in three months from sowing',[52] though the cotton fibre was 'scanty and of low quality'.[53] This *G. herbaceum* var. *kuljianum* was diffused across China along the famous 'silk road' but in the reverse direction. In its eastward movement, the further cotton went, the stronger the competition it would encounter. Shensi was the terminal point for cotton coming from Chinese Turkestan, for the city of Sian in Shensi province was one of the major centres of the silk industry from the Han period (BC206–AD220). The quality of this cotton species, however, was not good enough to break the barrier: the *G. herbaceum* type was not the one that eventually spread throughout the Far East.[54]

China was the first country among the three Far Eastern countries into which cotton was introduced (China, Korea and Japan). During Marco Polo's stay in China during the period 1271–92, he observed that the people's clothing was made not of cotton but silk. He mentioned only one place in which cotton goods were manufactured, namely, the city of Kien-ning-fu in Fukien, stating 'they have no lack of silk', and at the same time, 'so much cotton cloth is woven here of dyed yarn that it supplies the whole province of Manzi'.[55] Therefore, by the end of the thirteenth century cotton had been established as a commercial crop. Indeed, in the last quarter of the century, cotton inspectors were set up in the province of Fukien and a few other provinces, each of which owed an annual tribute of 100,000 pieces of cloth.[56] This crop is now known as *G. arboreum* var. *sinense*. This new type of cotton was initially thought to have been introduced from India by the following routes: carried overland from Bengal and Assam and/ or brought by sea from Indo-China.[57] The first route is now accepted as more probable than the second on the authority of Chinese literature,

Table 1.2 Chronology and path of diffusion of cotton cultivation in southern China

Name of book	Period referred to (AD)	Place
Wu-lu	AD 220–280	Yungch'ang (Yunnan)
		Chiaochou (Indo-China)
Nan-chou i-wu chih	220–280	Nanchou (Kwangsi)
Nan-shih	420–588	Linyi (Indo-China)
Liang shu	502–556	Linyi (Indo-China)
Pai Chu-i's Poems	772–846	Kuei (Kwangsi)
Wen ch'ang tsa-lu	1085	Kwangsi and Kwangtung
Meh-keh hui-si	1023–1064	Kwangsi and Kwangtung
Kuei-hai yu-heng chih	1126–1193	Kueilin (Kwangsi)
Ling-wai tai-ta	1174–1190	Kwangsi and the Hainan Island
Chu-fan chih	1174–1190	Fukien
P'o-tse pien	1180–1200	Fukien and the Hainan Island

Figure 1.4 Introduction and diffusion of cotton cultivation in China
Source: Kang Chao, *The Development of Cotton Production in China*, Cambridge, Mass.,
1977, 17.

which indicates the chronology and the path of diffusion of cotton
cultivation in southern China (Table 1.2).[58] It is obvious from the
chronology that cotton growing spread from Yunnan to the adjacent
districts of Kwangsi and Indo-China, then to the Kwangtung coast and
Hainan Island, and finally to Fukien province. This is mapped in Figure
1.4.

By a century after Marco Polo, the use of cotton had become
universal. When Hung-wu established the Ming dynasty (1368),

> an order was issued that in all private fields from five to ten *mou*
> in extent, half a *mou* each was to be planted with mulberry, hemp,
> and cotton; from ten *mou* and above, the quantity had to be
> doubled. For hemp, eight ounces were levied per *mou*; for cotton,
> four ounces per *mou*.[59]

Table 1.3 Quantity of cottons given to soldiers by the Chinese government, 1385–96

	Cotton cloth (pieces)	Raw cotton (kin)[a]
1385	1,239,900	283,300
1386	1,317,074	424,343
1387	1,159,585	65,600
1388	1,117,800	441,600
1389	1,345,000	560,000
1390	1,489,740	511,100
1396	2,889,900	1,415,200

[a] 1 kin = 0.6 kg

Source: Sadao Nishijima, *Chugoku Keizai-shi Kenkyu* (Studies in Chinese Economic History), Tokyo, 1966, 760.

Cotton cloth as well as raw cotton was an object of tax. The government needed such cloth for various purposes. It was exchanged for Mongolian horses, which were required for military purposes, and for salaries of officials. The use of cotton for military uniforms was the most important need of all, and it increased year by year,[60] as indicated in Table 1.3.

There were two centres of cotton cultivation and manufacture in Ming China (1368–1644). One centred on the provinces bordering the Yellow River such as Hopei, Shantung, Shansi and Shensi in the north, and the second was in the Yangtze delta, Chekiang, Fukien, Kwangtung and Szechwan in the south. These centres maintained their continuity down to the twentieth century.[61] By the Ming period local specialization and commerce had developed between the two regions. The north, in which the socioeconomic structure was backward and the available technology primitive, exported surplus raw cotton, beyond that required for cosmetic use and tax payments, while the south, which had higher levels of textile technology inherited from the traditional silk industry but which lacked adequate supplies of raw cotton, imported it from the north and more or less concentrated on manufacturing cotton goods. The Sung-Ciang prefecture in the Yangtze delta, situated between the northern and southern cotton regions, could take particular advantage of both regions; it prospered both by growing raw cotton and by technology.[62]

The Chinese cotton industry, which witnessed localization and the division of labour in the Ming period, did not, however, show any further development in the following period. According to Elvin:[63]

Land that was used to grow cotton was land that could be used to grow grain; and by the sixteenth and seventeenth centuries there was very little land available in China for any crop except foodgrains. Any expansion in the supply of raw cotton beyond bare parity with population growth depended on raising higher a per-acre agricultural productivity that was already the highest in the world.

Korea

There exists a record which shows that by the thirteenth century cotton cloth was being imported from China into Korea, but it was a luxury used by the upper class. Before the introduction of cotton into Korea took place, the clothing materials available to the Koreans were hemp, ramie and silk. It was not until 1364, when Mun Ikku-jum was sent as an envoy to China and brought back cotton seed, that cotton seed was first introduced to Korean soil.[64] The strong encouragement offered by the Korean government then made possible the rapid spread of cotton cultivation throughout South Korea within a few decades.[65] Kyongsang and Cholla became cotton-growing regions and remained so until the end of the Yi dynasty (1392–1910).[66]

Korea's resource endowment in precious metals was very poor, so cotton goods acquired such importance that they were used as money in the home markets by a decree of King Sejong (1418–50). Cotton cloth was one of the most important financial assets of the Korean government,[67] and large amounts were also used in the manufacture of uniforms for soldiers deployed on the northern border.[68]

One of the most important factors which influenced Korean cotton production in the fifteenth and sixteenth centuries was the demand for these cottons from overseas, particularly from Japan. Japan did not have an indigenous cotton industry, but it did have abundant precious metals. Naturally, trade between two countries developed as an exchange between Korean cotton cloth and Japanese precious metals. For example, in 1439 a Japanese trade mission of 1,300 members was sent to persuade the Korean government to export more cotton goods to Japan. Korea declined the request for financial reasons. Another envoy was sent in 1471. This time Japan was able to secure an increased supply of Korean cotton cloth in exchange for gold. In 1482, 4,532

Table 1.4 Korean exports of cotton cloth to Japan

Year	Pieces	Japanese importer*	Year	Pieces	Japanese importer*
1418	1,539		1481 Oct.	300	
1419	412		1482 Feb.	3,206	Sou
1420	2,280		1482 May	300	
1421	5,430		1483 Apr.	1,000	Sou
1422	–		1483 Oct.	1,100	
1423	2,640		1486	500,000	
1424	130		1488 Jan.	6,212	Sou
1450 May	998		1488	100,000	
1451 Mar.	2,394		1489 Sep.	1,000	
1453 Jun.	3,860	Doan	1489 Dec.	1,339	Miura
1464 Sep.	1,082		1489 Dec.	480	Taira
1467 Aug.	10,000		1490	10,754	Government
1468 Mar.	2,000		1490	9,294	Sou
1470 Aug.	500		1491 Feb.	10,906	Sou
1470	1,000	Ise	1492 Mar.	15,245	Sou
1471 Dec.	3,000		1494 Mar.	28,839	Government
1472 Jan.	100		1500	10,454	Sou
1474 Aug.	200		1525	85,000	Government
1474 Dec.	500		1528	21,500	Ouchi
1475	27,208		1529	60,000	Government
1476 Jan.	3,000	Sou	1538	8,000	Ouchi
1476	37,421		1542 Apr.	60,000	Government
1477 Jul.	400		1544	20,000	Shouni
1479 Jul.	200		1544	45,000	Government
1480 Jul.	400				

*Where the name is identified.
Source: Koji Ono, *Nihon Sangyo Hattatsu-shi no Kenkyu* (Studies in Japanese Industrial Development), Tokyo, 1941, 301–19; K. Sudō, 'Kōrai Makki yori Chōsen shoki ni itaru Orimonogyo no Hatten', *Shakai Keizai-shigaku*, 12 (1942): 39–45.

pieces of cotton cloth were exported to Japan. The volume of cotton cloth exports soon reached 500,000 pieces annually, an amount double the volume of the annual levy on cotton farmers in the form of taxes. The domestic demand for cotton cloth was such that Korea soon had to reduce its export value by half. In 1500 Japan proposed to exchange 110,000 *kan* of her copper for Korean cotton cloth (1 *kan* = 3.75 kg). Korea reversed its policy and accepted the copper in exchange for great quantities of cotton cloth, the bulk of which was provided at the expense of Korean cotton farmers.[69] A rough idea of the quantity of cotton cloth exported from Korea to Japan can be obtained from

Table 1.4. The figures in the table cover only those recorded by the government. The total quantity exported, including consignments sent without being recorded or by illicit traders, would undoubtedly exceed these figures.

Korean exports of cotton goods to Japan declined in the second half of the sixteenth century, as Japan began to increase her imports of these goods from China. Korean exports to Japan finally dried up in 1592 when the Japanese invaded Korea. The trade between the two countries was not resumed until 1609. This stoppage of trade damaged Korea more than Japan, because Japan had succeeded in transplanting cotton seeds by that time and had begun to manufacture cotton goods, whereas Korea could not obtain the necessary goods, such as precious metals and spices, which had previously been provided by Japan. Moreover, the export-orientated cotton textile industry of Korea suffered from a recession because of the abrupt stoppage.[70] After the treaty of 1609, strictly regulated trade was carried on between Korea and a Japanese *daimyo*,[71] on the basis that Japanese goods up to the equivalent value of 56,000 pieces of Korean cottons could be exchanged at the Korean port. This regulation lasted for about forty years. In 1651 the So family demanded rice instead of cotton in exchange for Japanese goods consisting mainly of silver, copper and spices, because the rapid development of the cotton industry in Japan had made the country self-sufficient in cottons to such a degree that the imported cotton cloth was no longer profitable. Korea acceded to the request by providing them with rice equivalent to 15,000 pieces of cloth, 26 per cent of the total. A few years later, the share of rice in the total value increased to 36 per cent. The remaining 64 per cent was paid in cotton cloth, but these cotton goods were illicitly exchanged by the Japanese traders for other goods such as ginseng and silk fabrics before they left the Korean port. In 1774 only 5,000 pieces of cotton cloth were brought back to Japan. By that time cotton cloth from Korea had virtually ceased to be used in Japan.[72] The further development of the cotton industry in Korea was impeded by the imposition of increasingly heavy tax burdens.[73]

Japan

An authentic history compiled in 841 stated that cotton seed was first brought into Japan by a Malay who came from Pasei (the north-eastern part of Sumatra) to Japan in 799 AD. Referring to this cotton, another authentic history, compiled in 892, described the method of cotton-growing and the geographical distribution of cotton in the country. But this cotton, which is believed to have been *G. arboreum* var. *indicum*, had become extinct by the Kamakura period (1192–1333).[74]

The new cotton seed was brought into Japan during the course of the sixteenth century from China via either Korea or Ryukyu (Okinawa). A number of contemporary records postulated that the introduction had taken place either between the 1490s and the 1510s, or in 1558, or in the period 1592–5. These different dates suggest that the cotton seed was probably brought to Japan from Korea or from Ryukyu on different occasions and its introduction attempted in different regions. But undoubtedly by the early sixteenth century there had been cotton cultivation and manufacturing in the Mikawa region, because a few contemporary records suggest that there were sales of Mikawa-made cotton in Nara from the 1510s onwards, and that Mikawa merchants who were under the protection of their local lord, Tokugawa, were trying to expand the markets for their textiles to Kyoto. Toomi and Suruga (the present Shizuoka prefecture) are also reported to have developed cotton textile production by the middle of the sixteenth century. In the 1570s Musashi (in the present Tokyo and Saitama prefecture) had local markets for cotton textiles. About the same time tax was collected in the form of cotton textiles at the town of Kofu (the capital of the present Yamanashi prefecture).[75]

The places mentioned above were all situated in the eastern part of Japan, between Nagoya and Tokyo. But cotton production throughout the Edo period (1600–1868) was consolidated in the western half of Japan – Osaka and the surrounding Kinai region and the coastal region of the Inland Sea. Production then moved westwards in the late sixteenth century. Cotton is reported in 1591 to have been grown in Yamato (in the present Nara prefecture). It seems to have spread from Yamato further westwards to Osaka. Osaka as a cotton region appears for the first time in a record of 1623; it states that a merchant group was organized to obtain *hoshika* (dried sardine or dried herring), used as a fertilizer for growing cotton. By this time cotton cultivation had been established. In 1644 this trade organization developed into a guild which monopolized the trade in *hoshika* brought from Chiba prefecture over a distance of 500 km. In 1658 another guild was formed to monopolize sales of raw cotton for export to northern Japan. *Nōgyōzensho* (Encyclopaedia of Agriculture) (1597) and *Hyakushōd-enki* (Record of Peasantry) (1580–2) both mentioned Kawachi, Izumi (Osaka), Harima, Setts (Hyogo prefecture), and Bingo (Hiroshima prefecture) as the main centres of cotton production in the late seventeenth century. Cotton products brought into Osaka in 1735 consisted of cotton cloth (74 per cent), cotton yarn (16 per cent) and ginned and raw cotton (10 per cent). The quantity of ginned cotton amounted to 50,000 *kan* (1 *kan* = 3.75 kg) and that of raw cotton 350,000 *kan.* These figures rose to an annual average of 2 million *kan* and 1.5 million *kan* respectively between 1804 and 1834. The cotton-growing area in the early nineteenth century was almost the same as in the early Meiji period.[76]

Concerning the quality of Japanese-made cotton cloth, Ono stated, 'what is certain is that the early home-made cotton fabrics would have been much thicker than we imagine; because the Japanese had hemp for summer clothing, cottons were initially employed for winter clothing; they were very thick'.[77]

The introduction of cotton into Japan placed her on the threshold of a new era in her industrial history, an era characterized by rising prosperity and productive energy. The rapid development of the Japanese cotton industry was one of the most important commercial achievements of the Tokugawa regime.[78] It is now an accepted view that the transition from an agrarian to a modern industrial society following the Meiji Restoration was the result of the industrial and commercial progress which was already in motion in pre-modern Japan and in which the cotton industry played a pioneering role. Japan in the sixteenth century was far behind China and Korea in cotton textile production, just as England lagged behind all other European countries. Both countries, though starting last in the race, but in quite different historical contexts, subsequently outstripped every other competitor in the West and the Far East respectively in the nineteenth century.

THE WESTWARD SPREAD OF COTTON

In comparison to the eastward spread of cotton, its westward movement can be described briefly.[79] The spread of Indian cotton to the West was triggered by the so-called Arab Agricultural Revolution[80] which took place during the period 700–1100. At the heart of the revolution was the introduction of many new crops into Arab territory. One of these crops was cotton, which spread across Egypt to North Africa, Spain, southern Italy and Sicily. The commercial contact between the East and the West as a consequence of the Crusades brought large quantities of cotton into Europe.

The dramatic expansion of European cotton imports was closely related to the growth of the handcraft cotton textile industry (mostly fustian, the mixed fabric with cotton weft and linen warp). But there were at least three factors which prevented the medieval cotton (fustian) industry from developing further. First, climatic conditions precluded the introduction of cotton cultivation into Europe except in the southern area. Second, constant wars, particularly the Thirty Years War, dealt a serious blow to the fustian industry. Third, the importation of exotic Indian textiles into Europe caused serious damage to the industry.

It was only after inexpensive high-quality Indian cotton textiles were brought to Europe from India that Europeans really became acquainted with pure cotton textiles. Europeans, who used to wear apparel made of woollen fabrics, were charmed by the beautiful thin cotton cloth from India, which people described as 'a web of woven air'. Cotton cloth, unlike woollen fabrics, could be washed easily and was very cheap.

It was treasured by the Europeans, and an enormous demand was generated. In 1708 Defoe could write that 'almost everything that used to be wool and silk, relating either to the dress of the women or the furniture of our houses, was supplied by the Indian trade'. European countries needed to counteract the mounting imports of thin cotton textiles from India.

In Britain, Parliament passed two Calico Acts, in 1700 and 1720, to ban Indian calicoes. These prohibition laws forced the East India Company to engage in the re-export business, which led to the establishment of markets for cotton textiles in the three continents bordering the Atlantic Ocean. In order to produce in Europe a 'substitute' for the thin Indian cotton textiles, fine yarn was necessary. The opportunity for producing this in Europe came when the New World varieties of cotton plant with their long, thin staple were discovered, as described earlier. Also, the mule spinning machine, capable of spinning fine yarn, was invented by Samuel Crompton in 1779. In this way, a link was established between the New World, which produced the raw material, Britain, which provided the technology, and the Atlantic rim (Europe, America and the African continent), which constituted the market.

The Atlantic markets for these cotton products were distinct from the cotton markets of East Asia. In the latter, short-staple cotton, coarse yarn and thick textiles were produced and consumed. Therefore, these two types of product did not compete for the same purchasers. It was the East Asian market for cotton goods, demanding qualities of goods distinct from those demanded by the West, that Japan supplied during the late nineteenth and twentieth centuries, when she became involved in the intra-Asian trade after the opening of her ports in 1859.

NOTES

1. *Encyclopaedia Britannica*, 9th edn, 1877, VI: 482; 11th edn, 1910, VII: 257.
2. C.P. Brooks, *Cotton Manufacturing*, London, 1888: 17.
3. *Encyclopaedia Britannica*, 11th ed, 1910, VII: 256.
4. G. Watt, *The Wild and Cultivated Cotton Plants of the World*, London, 1907.
5. He wrote supplementary articles to the work in 1926 and 1927, both entitled '*Gossypium*', which appeared in *Kew Bulletin*.
6. G.S. Zaitzev, 'A contribution to the classification of the genus *Gossypium* L.', *Bulletin of Applied Botany and Plant Breeding*, 18(1) (1928) (translated from *Trudy Po Prikladonoi Botnike*, Genetike I, Selekts II.
7. Ibid., 45–6.
8. In fact, as far as this point is concerned, as early as 1905, Professor Gammie found, through his field observations of Indian cottons, that 'all Indian cottons can be hybridised freely by artificial means, and the progeny, exhibiting an equal blending of the qualities and characters of their parents, do not fall off in fertility. Out of the numerous crosses made by me none between an American and Indian variety has survived with the solitary exception of one between *G. hirsutum* [and] *G. herbaceum*. Even in this instance doubts are now entertained whether the plant may not be of the nature of a sport' (G.A. Gammie, *The Indian Cottons*, Calcutta, 1905, 2).
9. 'Contribution to the Classification' 46–7.
10. Ibid., 55–64.
11. S.C. Harland, 'The general conception of the species', *Biological Review*, 11 (1936): 91–6.
12. R.A. Silow, 'The genetics of species development in the Old World cottons', *Journal of Genetics*, 46 (1944): 62–73; *G. herbaceum* was confined almost entirely to the drier and cooler season, while races of *G. arboreum* were more generally grown in the wetter, warmer *kharif* (monsoon) season. (J. B. Hutchinson, R.A. Silow and S.G. Stephens (eds) *The Evolution of Gossypium*, Oxford, 1947, 95.)
13. Sir Joseph Hutchinson, *The Application of Genetics to Cotton Improvement*, Cambridge, 1959, 17; for example, forms of *G. herbaceum* var. *wightianum* were found growing mixed with *G. arboreum* var. *bengalense* in western India, and with *G. arboreum* var. *indicum* in Madras. Similar mixtures of *G. herbaceum* var. *kuljianum* and *G. arboreum* var. *sinense* were reported from western China. In these mixed crops the two species maintain their integrity in spite of some crossing (Silow, 'Genetics of species development', 71).
14. Hutchinson, *Application of Genetics*, 17.
15. Sir Joseph Hutchinson, 'New evidence on the origin of the Old World cottons', *Heredity*, 8(2), (1954): 238. For example, genetic breakdown in F_2 and later generations was demonstrated in crosses between *G. herbaceum* var. *wightianum* and *G. arboreum* var. *indicum*, and between *G. herbaceum* var. *percicum* and *G. arboreum* var. *bengalense*. Moreover, attempts to produce agriculturally acceptable cottons from *G. herbaceum* var. *wightianum* × *G. arboreum* var. *indicum* crosses failed repeatedly.

16. Watt, *Wild and Cultivated Cotton Plants*, 322.
17. Hutchinson *et al.*, *The Evolution of Gossypium*, 82.
18. According to Zaitzev, 'with a few exceptions, all these places lie within the limits of the northern and southern isotherm of the coldest month showing 18°C (64.5°F), i.e., within the region that is considered to be the region of the tropical countries.' (Zaitzev, op. cit., 40).
19. Hutchinson *et al.*, *The Evolution of Gossypium*, 81.
20. Ibid., 88.
21. The development of annual types brought about a fundamental change in the whole physiology of the plant. They could be grown as an annual in areas where there was a long dry season or which were subject to frost. Even in the tropics where perennials could make satisfactory growth, a demand arose for annual forms in order to ensure the production of cotton of the best quality, to facilitate the way in which the plants were managed, and to keep insects and pests in check (*ibid.*, 82; *Encyclopaedia Britannica*, 11th edn, VII: 256). There can be little doubt that commercial pressures led to the establishment of annual cropping (J.B. Hutchinson, *Evolution Studies in World Crops*, Cambridge, 1974, 154.)
22. Hutchinson *et al.*, *The Evolution of Gossypium*, 84.
23. Hutchinson, 'New evidence ...', 235.
24. Hutchinson, *Application of Genetics*, 17.
25. Hutchinson, 'New evidence ...', 232–3.
26. Hutchinson, *Application of Genetics*, 12.
27. Hutchinson, *Evolution Studies in World Crops*, 90. It is also accepted that a form of one of the Old World cottons, the South African *G. herbaceum* var. *africanum* alone is an ancient truly wild plant, and is the modern representative of the wild ancestor of all diploid cottons (Hutchinson, 'New evidence ...', 229).
28. J.B. Hutchinson, 'Changing concepts in crop plant evolution', *Experimental Agriculture Review*, 13 (1971): 24.
29. Hutchinson, 'New evidence ...', 235.
30. J.B. Hutchinson, 'A note on some geographical races of Asiatic cottons', *Empire Cotton Growing Review*, 27(2), (1950): 125.
31. Ibid.
32. J.B. Hutchinson and R.L.M. Ghose, 'The composition of the cotton crops of central India and Rajputana', *Indian Journal of Agricultural Science*, 7 (1937): 24.
33. Marco Polo, *The Travels*, Harmondsworth: Penguin Books, 1958, 291.
34. J.B. Hutchinson, 'The distribution of *Gossypium* and the evolution of the commercial cottons', Indian Central Cotton Committee, *Papers Read and Summary of Proceedings, First Conference of Scientific Research Workers on Cotton in India*, Bombay, 1938, 359.
35. *Parliamentary Papers 1847*, XLII (439): 'Return of the Papers in the Possession of the East India Company, showing what Measures have been taken since 1836 to promote the Cultivation of Cotton in India, with the Particulars and Result of any Experiments which have been made by the said Company, with a view to introduce the Growth of American Cotton, or to encourage the Production of Native Cotton in India', with Plans, &c., no. 199, (Mr Price to Mr Secretary Halliday), p. 269.

36. Nazil Ahmad, 'Discussion', in Indian Central Cotton Committee, *First Conference*, 36.
37. Hutchinson, *Evolution Studies in World Crops*, 91. The development of the annual can be dated fairly well. Dr Hove collected in Gujerat in 1787 the annual G. *herbaceum wightanum*. Watt noted, 'Dr Hove's specimens are in the British Museum, and it has to be admitted that they could not be separated botanically from any corresponding set of more recent data' (Watt, *Wild and Cultivated Cotton Plants*). With the knowledge now available about the origin of the annual habit it may be postulated with some confidence that G. *herbaceum* var. *wightianum* was developed in western India following the introduction of annual, open-bolled forms of the species from Persia in the early eighteenth century (Hutchinson, *Application of Genetics*, 16).
38. Hutchinson and Govande calculated that the mean hair length in inches of northern *arboreum* was 0.77, while that of southern *arboreum* was 0.85, and that the highest standard warp count of the former was 15.5s, while the latter was 28s (J.B. Hutchinson and G.K. Govande, 'Cotton botany and the spinning value and hair properties of cotton lint', *Indian Journal of Agricultural Science*, 8 (1938): 35).
39. Ginning percentages higher than 28 were very rare in India in 1840, but the range of ginning percentages of the northern annual type was from 28 to 40 (Hutchinson, 'Distribution of *Gossypium*', 353); Hutchinson *et al.*, *The Evolution of Gossypium*, 94.
40. Hutchinson and Ghose, 'Composition of the cotton crops', 32.
41. The first shipment to China was made in 1704 by the East India Company. The amount exported rose continuously until it reached a peak level of about a half-million piculs in the 1830s (1 picul is approximately equal to 60.48 kg) (see Kang Chao, *The Development of Cotton Production in China*, Cambridge, Mass., 1977, 102–4).
42. *Parliamentary Papers 1847*, XLII (439), no. 205 (Mr Price to Mr Secretary Halliday), 275.
43. Hutchinson, *Evolution Studies in World Crops*, 92.
44. Hutchinson *et al.*, *The Evolution of Gossypium*, 95.
45. Sir Joseph Hutchinson, 'History and relationships of the world's cottons', *Endeavour*, 21 (1962), 7–8.
46. Hutchinson, 'Distribution of *Gossypium*', 353.
47. Hutchinson, *Evolution Studies in World Crops*, 92.
48. Hutchinson, 'History and relationships of the world's cottons', 8.
49. Silow, 'Genetics of species development', 68–9.
50. Hutchinson *et al.*, *The Evolution of Gossypium*, 94.
51. Hutchinson, *Application of Genetics*, 19.
52. Hutchinson, 'History and relationship of the world's cottons', 7.
53. Hutchinson, 'Note on some geographical races of Asiatic cottons', 125.
54. Kang Chao, *Development of Cotton Textile Production in China*, 4–10.
55. Marco Polo, *The Travels*, 232.
56. Paul Pelliot, *Notes on Marco Polo*, I, Paris, 1959, 499–507.
57. See Hutchinson, 'The Distribution of *Gossypium*', 354.
58. Kang Chao, *Development of Cotton Textile Production in China*, 11.
59. Pelliot, *Notes on Marco Polo*, 506.

60. S. Nishijima, *Chūgoku Keizai-shi Kenkyu* (Studies in Chinese Economic History), Tokyo, 1966, 760.
61. Shigeru Kato, *Shina Keizai-shi Kōshō* (Studies in Chinese Economic History), II, Tokyo, 1953, 711–12.
62. Nishijima, *Chūgoku Keizai-shi Kenkyu*, 732–50.
63. Mark Elvin, *The Pattern of the Chinese Past*, Stanford, Cal., 1973, 214–15. He also mentions other social factors which tended to inhibit technological innovations (ibid., 276–84).
64. Kichiyuki Sudō, 'Kōrai Makki yori Chōsen Shoki ni itaru Orimonogyo no Hatten' (Development of the textile industry from the late Koryo dynasty to the early Yi dynasty), *Shakai Keizai-shigaku*, 12 (1942): 5–8.
65. Ibid., 8–10.
66. Tohei, Sawamura, 'Li-cho kōki Momen no Chōshū-chiiki to Seisan-ritch' (Cotton-growing conditions of localities where tax on cottons was imposed in the Yi dynasty), *Keizai-shi Kenkyu*, no. 28 (1942): 50–1.
67. Sudo, 'Kōrai Makki yori Chōsen Shoki ni itaru Orimonogyo no Hatten', 24, 88.
68. Sung Jae Koh, *Stages of Industrial Development in Asia*, Philadelphia, 1966, 289.
69. Ibid., 290–1.
70. As the government had prohibited commerce with Japan in 1523, the trade was carried on by way of smuggling by the Chinese from Fukien. The cotton cloth from China flooded into Japan in the 1570s and exceeded that from Korea (Sung Jae Koh, *Stages of Industrial Development*, 293; Koji Ono, *Nihon Sangyo Hattatsu-shi no Kenkyu* (Studies in Japanese Industrial Development), Tokyo, 1941, 326–8).
71. The So family was the only *daimyo* allowed to trade with Korea by both Japanese and Korean governments.
72. T. Sawamura, 'Li-cho jidai Momen Yushutsu no Shumatsu' (The end of cotton textile exports in the Yi dynasty), *Keizaishi-Kenkyn*, no. 31 (1944), 1–20.
73. Sung Jae Koh, *Stages of Industrial Development*, 312–13.
74. Kentaro Shiba, 'Momen no Seisan-Bunpai ni kansuru Kyokutō-Kōtsū-Bunkashiteki Kōsatsu (1)' (A note on production and distribution of cottons in the commercial and cultural history of the Far East), *Kōtsūbunka*, no. 2 (1938): 138–9.
75. Kōji Ono, *Nihon Sangyo Hattatsu-shi no Kenkyo*, 345–9.
76. Toshio Furushima, *Nihon Hōken Nōgyōshi* (Agricultural History of Feudal Japan), Tokyo, 1941, 197–215; idem., *Kinsei Nihon Nōgyō no Kōzō* (structure of Pre-modern Japanese Agriculture), Tokyo, 1943, 273–9, 378; idem., *Kinsei Nōgyō Gijutsushi* (History of Agricultural Technology of Pre-modern Japan), Tokyo, 1953, 357–9, 538.
77. Ono, *Nihon Sangyo Hattatsu-shi no Kenkyo*, 356, 367.
78. See, for example, the discussion by William B. Hauser, *Economic Institutional Change in Tokugawa Japan*, Cambridge, 1974.
79. A full and detailed account is given in H. Kawakatsu, 'International competition in cotton goods', University of Oxford, unpublished D.Phil. thesis, 1984, 25–80.
80. A.M. Watson, 'The Arab agricultural revolution and its diffusion, 700–1100', *Journal of Economic History*, 34 (1974).

2

THE CERAMIC TRADE IN ASIA, 1602–82

Chuimei Ho

In the seventeenth century, the long-established international ceramic trade of the Far East and South-East Asia entered a fast-paced and changeable era. The elements involved – the suppliers, the merchants and the markets – were different from those of the fifteenth and sixteenth centuries. China had been the sole exporter of porcelain and stoneware for many decades before Japan became a supplier in the mid-seventeenth century. Western European trading corporations tried, but largely failed, to restrict indigenous mercantile activity, much of it in Chinese hands. Europe and the Americas became new markets for Asian ceramics. Some of these changes were no doubt part of the larger pattern of the new Asian–European commercial relationship but some were unique to the ceramic trade.

The subject of Far Eastern ceramic trade in the seventeenth century has been less extensively researched than that of more valuable trade goods such as textiles, copper and spices. Moreover, the subject has been more often in the hands of art historians and archaeologists – the author is one herself – than in those of economic historians. The few works on the seventeenth-century ceramic trade that have appeared thus far have been focused on particular types of traded vessels, such as Tianqi blue-and-white wares (Impey and Tregear, 1983) and martaban jars (Adhyatman and Abu Ridho, 1984). The subject is also discussed in several works that cover longer periods (Grove, 1990) and particular regions: the Philippines (Locsin and Locsin, 1967), Japan (TKCM, 1983), Malaysia (SEAS, 1985), America (Mudge, 1986), and South-East Asia in general (Guy, 1986).

The key work consulted for this study is Volker's (1954) monumental effort in translating and compiling all ceramic-related entries in the *Dagh Registers* of the Dutch East India Company or VOC (*Vereenigde Oost-indische Compagnie*), from the trading stations at

Hirado and Deshima in Japan and at Batavia in Indonesia, between 1602 and 1682. Based on Volker's research, the present chapter aims at tracing the development of the Far Eastern ceramic trade in the seventeenth century and at understanding this in relation to rises and falls of coastal merchant activity in China. Two other sources of data from Dutch records are used here in addition to Volker's: Nagazumi (1987) and Bronson (1990) list trade goods and quantities. Archaeological data are included for discussion when appropriate.

The VOC itself was a major player in the ceramic trade, and its intelligence network at that period was of excellent quality. However, the figures reported in the *Dagh Registers* represent only a part of the actual traded volume. In reality the quantity carried away from China would have been larger than the available figures indicate; the VOC had little information concerning the quantities arriving at Manila, Malacca, Siam or Tongking (North Vietnam), all major destinations for Chinese traders. Moreover, the volume carried to Europe would also have been higher since the VOC did not always succeed in keeping track of rival European traders or of private trading by its own employees.[1] Given the quality of the data available, the outline constructed below may be considered representative but not comprehensive.

THE THREE PHASES OF CERAMIC TRADE IN THE SEVENTEENTH CENTURY

Ceramic trade in Asia during the period 1602 to 1682 did not develop evenly, nor did it accelerate over time as did the trade in Far Eastern copper (Glamann, 1981, 175). The volume of ceramics surged in the first few decades but dropped by one-half in the middle of the seventeenth century. It picked up again only towards the 1680s (Table 2.3). Three broad phases can be discerned.

Phase I (1602–44) witnesses the beginning of the VOC involvement, and ends in the year when the Ming Dynasty was replaced by that of the Manchus. It is a period when China was the only supplier of ceramics to other parts of Asia. Her major markets were the South Seas and Japan. The phase also marks the beginning of regular import of Chinese ceramics into Europe and the Americas by European traders.

Phase II (1645–61) marks the period when China began to lose Japan as a market. Japan not only reduced its ceramic imports to one-fifth, but also began to export her own. The phase also coincides with the zenith of the Zhengs, the leaders of a Fujian Chinese merchant group which successfully challenged both the Manchus and the Dutch. The last year of the phase marks the end of the 'Chinese' period in ceramic export, as pointed out by Volker (1954, 109). The year also sees the VOC ousted from their Taiwan base by Coxinga, the head of the Zheng family. The Zhengs and the VOC had been brought face-to-face in their trading competition in South-East and East Asia; during this period the Zhengs appear to have gained the upper hand, forcing the VOC to turn elsewhere for new suppliers of ceramics.

Phase III (1662–82) sees the last struggle of the Zhengs before they were wiped out by the Manchus in 1683, a sharp decline in Chinese ceramic exports, and the establishment of the VOC base at Batavia in Java as the main hub for the international trade in Asian ceramics, with supplies coming from Japan, China, Tongking, Persia and Holland. Tongking appeared as a new and strong competitor, supplying over 40 per cent of recorded international sales of Asian ceramics.

Phase I (1602–44)

Compared with later phases, Phase I is the worst-recorded; political upheavals in China were least disturbing and the volume of overseas ceramic sales was greatest (Table 2.3, Appendices 2.1, 2.2). There are several characteristics of Phase I which are not repeated later on: China was the sole ceramic exporter in the region; several entrepôts in South-East Asia, among them Ayuthia and Patani in Siam as well as Batavia, were strategic entrepôts for the transhipment of Chinese goods; and an

Table 2.1 Average annual Chinese ceramic exports in the seventeenth century

Phase	Total pieces	Europe	Exports to South Seas	Japan
I (1602–44)	404,535 100%	65,970 16%	245,067 60%	93,498 23%
II (1645–61)	129,366 100%	41,292 31%	69,254 53%	18,820 14%
III (1662–82)	95,858 100%	5,384 5%	89,312 93%	1,162 1%
Total	629,759 100%	112,646 12%	403,633 63%	113,480 23%

Table 2.2 Average annual Japanese ceramic exports in the seventeenth century

Phase	Total pieces	Exports to	
		Europe	South Seas
II	101,960	9,102	92,858
(1659–61)	100%	8%	91%
III	95,828	8,988	86,840
(1662–82)	100%	9%	90%
Total	197,788	18,090	179,698
	100%	9%	90%

assortment of nationalities were active as ceramic traders: Chinese, Dutch, Portuguese, English, Siamese, Japanese (at Quinam in Vietnam), Golcondan (from southern India) and 'Moorish' (from western India and the Middle East).

From the standpoint of the Chinese, foreign markets for ceramics at the beginning of the seventeenth century could be divided into three main geographical units: Japan, the 'South Seas'[2] and Europe. The first two had purchased Chinese porcelain long before the seventeenth century, whereas the European buyers were new. The official closure of Japan in 1634 does not seem to have affected the China–Japan ceramic trade. Almost one-quarter of recorded Chinese exports went to Japan between 1634 and 1644 (Table 2.1, Appendix 2.3). Further, Japan

Table 2.3 Average annual ceramics traded in the South Seas in the seventeenth century

Phase	Total pieces	Made in					
		China	Japan	Tongking	Burma	Persia	Holland
I	405,581	404,535	–	–	46	–	–
(1602–44)	100%	99%					
II	237,286	129,366	101,960	–	60	5,900	Some
(1645–61)	100%	54%	42%			2%	
III	332,292	95,858	95,828	137,030	105	3,469	Some
(1662–82)	100%	28%	28%	41%		1%	
Total	974,160	629,759	197,788	137,030	211	9,369	Some
	100%	64%	20%	14%		0.9%	

absorbed products covering a full range of quality, as indicated by the range of costs (Table 2.4) as well as by archaeological finds.[3] The South Seas markets took more than half of the total volume of exports but this was mostly low-priced coarse wares, with some medium-quality wares going to India and the Middle East. Thus, the South Seas and Japan were the large and stable markets. Europe, in its infancy as a recipient of Far Eastern ceramics, absorbed only 16 per cent of the total recorded export volume (Table 2.1, Appendix 2.1). However, in terms of sale value the European markets are not to be dismissed as insignificant; the expensive high-quality wares exported to Europe accounted for up to 50 per cent of the total value of Chinese ceramic exports. A piece of fine ware imported to Holland cost about ten times as much as one of the coarse wares intended for the South Seas (Table 2.4).

China's prosperity in the ceramic trade started before the arrival of Europeans in Asian seas. The demand for ceramics in the South Seas and Japan was already substantial in the fifteenth and sixteenth centuries, as shown by archaeological data from Japan (Table 2.5), Thailand,[4] the Philippines and Indonesia. Siam and Vietnam were both ceramic producers at an earlier period, but both had dropped out of the export trade by the mid-sixteenth century.[5] China enjoyed an even greater volume of business after that.[6] Many export goods, including ceramics, travelled in Chinese ships based at coastal cities in Fujian and Guangdong provinces. By the 1630s, an increasing number of these ships were coming under the control of the Zheng family.

The demand for fine Chinese wares in Europe had begun in the late sixteenth century but only became significant in the seventeenth, with the arrival of Dutch and other northern European traders in Asian waters. This increase in demand must have encouraged the diversified growth of new ceramic centres in China. As the old and prestigious ceramic factories at Jingdezhen in Jiangxi came to commit more of their resources to fine ware production, often custom-made for European customers, new centres in Guangdong and Fujian were left to take care of making coarser wares for non-European markets. Factories at Yaoping in Guangdong (Yang, 1985) and at Dehua-Anxi in Fujian[7] (Ho, 1988) specialized in low quality blue-and-white wares,[8] suitable for South Seas demand. The Fujian centres were especially active during Phase I, since ships leaving for the South Seas mostly sailed from ports in the Amoy (Xiamen) area and Fuchou (Fuzhou); these are still the main outlets for present-day Fujian ceramics.

European traders were responsible for giving the ceramic trade a global status, with East Asian porcelains reaching all parts of Europe

Table 2.4 Average price per piece (Volker, 1954)

	Price of Chinese wares carried to	
Japan *florin/year*	South Seas *florin/year*	Europe *florin/year*
0.025/1635	0.030/1620	2.240/1608
6.000/1638	0.140/1618	0.800/1608
0.230/1639	0.070/1637	6.000/1610
0.065/1644	0.040/1645	0.175/1612
0.010/1645	0.020/1645	0.170/1614
0.040/1646	0.060/1637	0.320/1616
	0.060/1647	0.280/1616
		0.170/1624
		0.045/1629
		0.580/1631
		0.850/1635
		0.240/1635
		0.130/1635
		0.240/1636
		0.250/1639
		4.700/1639
		0.270/1639
		0.270/1643
		0.140/1643
		0.240/1646
		0.250/1647
		0.120/1681
		0.600/1681
	Price of Japanese wares carried to	
	South Seas	Europe
	0.075/1669	0.210/1660
	1.400/1669	0.170/1662
		0.500/1663
		0.290/1663
		2.850/1663
		5.000/1663
		5.700/1663
		4.000/1663
		8.500/1663
		7.000/1663
		1.000/1665
		0.440/1665
		1.850/1681

Table 2.5 Ceramics from archaeological sites in Japan

Site	Total pieces	Chinese	Japanese
1. *c.*1615	2,919 (100%)	784 (26%)	2,129 (72%)
2. 1600–40	52 (100%)	28 (53%)	21 (40%)
3. 1644–*c.*64	1,117 (100%)	116 (10%)	1,001 (89%)
1644	48 (100%)	6 (12.4%)	42 (87%)
1600–44	1,553 (100%)	261 (16.8%)	1,292 (83%)

Notes
1 = Sakai Kangou Toshi site, Layer V (Morimura, 1984)
2 = Sumiyagura site (Wada, 1989)
3 = Toda River Bed site (Murakami, 1986)

and the Americas as well. The popularity of those porcelains stimulated the development of imitative industries in Europe. By the end of Phase II, glazed blue-and-white earthenware made in Delft had begun to be exported to Asia.

Phase II: 1645–61

The volume of recorded ceramic trade during Phase II was low, the average annual exports from China and Japan amounting to only one-half of exports during Phase I from China alone (Table 2.3). China was now only supplying half of the international demand for Far Eastern ceramics. Japan became an exporter of porcelain in 1658, thus ending the long-standing Chinese monopoly (Table 2.3). The entry of Japan was initiated by Chinese merchants under the Zheng family and then much encouraged by the VOC because of a decline in ceramic exports from China. At the end of the phase, martaban jars, very large storage vessels many of which were made in Burma, also began to appear as regularly traded items (Appendix 2.7).

China as an exporter

The decline of Chinese supply in Phase II has usually been seen as an effect of the devastation of kiln centres by the fighting that occurred during the conquest of China by the Manchus and their establishment of the new Qing dynasty. However, it seems possible that the decline in exports was not entirely due to decreased activity in the manufacturing sector. As is argued below, Chinese exporters, then completely controlled by the anti-Manchu Zhengs, may have preferred to go slow in promoting ceramic sales abroad when faced with declining foreign markets.

There is a need to distinguish between the drop in ceramic production and the decrease in exports. While it is logical to assume that export trade must have been affected sporadically by the conflicts between first the Manchus and the Ming government, and then between the Manchus and the Fujian-based Ming loyalists led by the Zhengs, there is no proof that ceramic production within China was badly hit. The great kiln centre of Jingdezhen seems to have continued making porcelain with few interruptions, as shown by the number of dated vessels known from the transitional period between Ming and Qing (Appendix 2.8). The fact that Jingdezhen was already being patronized by the Manchu court a few years after the conquest suggests that the infrastructure for production was still sound.[9] If the kilns had suffered from setbacks during the change of government, they appear to have recovered very quickly.

Between 1645 and 1658 the Zheng family led by Coxinga had almost full control of overseas trade – something no other Chinese traders had ever achieved. The Zhengs were almost the only traders carrying ceramics from China to Japan, the South Seas and the Dutch trading stations at which porcelains were transhipped for Europe. In spite of the Zhengs' privileged position, however, they seem not to have capitalized on the situation. Indeed, their interest in selling ceramics appears to have dropped: the volume carried by them was much less than in the previous phase. The reasons for their lack of enthusiasm are not entirely clear but must have included the fact that in the 1650s Japan ceased being a major market for imported ceramics.

There is no doubt that Coxinga's traders continued to be able to acquire fine and medium-quality wares from Jingdezhen in spite of Manchu interference.[10] The question is, was it worth taking the risk to bring the wares from the interior of China? The overall market for fine wares did not look good: Japan, now a ceramic producing country herself, had cut her imports by 80 per cent (Table 2.1, Appendix 2.3). Demand in Europe for Far Eastern wares had also declined (Tables 2.1 and 2.2). Facing a waning market for fine and medium-grade porcelain, the Zhengs would have been justified in de-emphasizing this sector of their business.

During Phase II, the average annual Chinese export of coarse wares to the South Seas was reduced to less than 30 per cent of export levels in the previous phase (Table 2.1). However, there is no reason to assume that demand in the South Seas, which had represented a stable market for several centuries, was falling off. There is also no reason to think that supply was a problem. The Zheng merchants would have had no trouble in obtaining low-quality ceramics from the nearby Dehua, Anxi or Tongan kilns, which are just 30 km from Amoy and were well within Coxinga's area of control. Yet the fact is that not enough coarse wares were reaching the South Seas. Why was Coxinga not interested in selling home products from Fujian? The answer perhaps is that the profit yield from coarse ceramics was too low to be attractive at a time when voyages were risky, due to the danger of Dutch interception, and when large trading profits were needed to maintain Coxinga's ships and troops in their struggle against the Manchus.[11]

Japan as an exporter

In spite of the loss of the Japanese market for fine and medium-quality wares, there was still some demand west of the Malay Peninsula, especially in Europe. The shortage of Chinese wares of this kind was soon relieved by exports from Japan. Since the beginning of the seventeenth century, Japan had begun to produce porcelain. In 1658 the first cargo of Japanese export wares made its debut, carried by Chinese traders from Japan to Amoy.[12] The VOC followed suit in 1659 (Appendix 2.4). From then on, both the Chinese and the Dutch regularly brought Japanese ceramics from Nagasaki to South-East Asia, whence many were reshipped to Europe and the Persian Gulf.

Although Japan was active as an exporter only for the last three years of Phase II, she sold almost as much porcelain as China did in the nine years of Phase II for which records are available (Table 2.3). The rapid rise in Japanese export volume became even more significant during the two subsequent decades in Phase III, when Nagasaki supplied the bulk of the high-quality wares exported by the VOC to Europe. China did not regain her position as the leading exporter of fine porcelain until the late 1680s.

The Zhengs vs. the VOC

Phase II witnesses the competition of two major warlike trading powers in the South Seas: the VOC based at Batavia in Java and the Zhengs on the Fujian coast. If the success of the former is considered to be the result of a strikingly new institutional structure characterized by flexibility, good planning and massive capitalization (Steensgaard,

1973, 412), it is interesting that the latter should have competed so effect-ively. Arguably, the Zheng organization had some of the same traits as the VOC.

In the case of the ceramic trade the Zhengs demonstrated their flexi-bility by adopting a new line of sales in order to keep a foothold in the failing Japanese market. When the development of the Japanese domestic ceramic industry left little room for imported Chinese porcelain, Coxinga's merchants began to import fancy teapots for elite users,[13] antique ceramics for collectors, and pigments (probably cobalt) for porcelain manufacture (Appendix 2.3).

The turning of the Zhengs towards Japan for the supply of fine and medium-quality wares also reflects their ability to implement a planned trading policy. Instead of depending only on Chinese sources, which were becoming risky at the time, the Zhengs began to develop Japan as an alternative supplier for foreign luxury markets. It was the Zhengs who first hit on the idea of marketing Japanese wares abroad in 1658: the VOC reacted fast enough to do the same thing the following year.

The Zhengs were capable of using trading policies for political ends. A notable example is the economic sanctions imposed by Coxinga against the VOC between 1655 and 1661, in order to advance his claim to Dutch-occupied Taiwan.[14] The shortage of Chinese ceramics and silk during those years was often noted by VOC officials; Coxinga's conquest of Taiwan in 1661 was due to the weakened economic condition of his opponents as well as to his ability to field an army and navy of exceptional quality.

In general, Chinese commerce before Coxinga had been character-ized by the 'free enterprise of individual merchants or small family groups' (Furber, 1976, 331), although certain of these groups attained substantial power.[15] However, they tended to lack co-ordination and foresight in long-term investment, and were often defenceless against government abuses. The situation changed with the rise of Coxinga. His strength in the ceramic trade at this period lies not only in his access to Chinese goods but also in his good navy and weaponry,[16] and his excellent connections in Japan and South-East Asia. He disposed of sufficient capital and military power to make a serious bid for control of the East Asian sea lanes, his only source of finance for his attempt to restore the fallen Ming dynasty.

The Zhengs' networks of commercial and political intelligence must have been at least as effective as those of either of his main enemies, the Manchus and the Dutch.[17] Coxinga was well-connected enough in South-East Asia to be able to command expatriate Chinese merchants, many of them Fujianese,[18] to co-operate with his military and commercial campaigns,[19] and his being half Japanese put him in a favourable position when dealing with Japan.

Phase III: 1662–82

The overall trade in ceramics seems to have fared better in Phase III than in the previous phase, with a rise of almost 50 per cent in average annual volume, even though this was still behind that of Phase I (Table 2.3). The increase came partly from Japan and China, but the major contributor to the increase was Tongking, which accounted for 41 per cent of the coarse wares arriving at South Seas ports (Appendix 2.5). Other suppliers such as Burma[20] exported martaban jars in small quantities and at high prices[21] (Appendix 2.7). Moreover, non-Asian ceramics from Persia and Holland also began to circulate in the South Seas (Appendix 2.6; Table 2.3). It is true that these were basically for European residents in Asia, but a small number are known to have passed into the hands of local elites, as noted in the Deshima Register of 1678 (Volker, 1954, 165).

Japan was completely closed to ceramic imports after 1668.[22] Even the sale of pigment for ceramic manufacture was much reduced in volume (Appendix 2.3). The European market was slackening as well (Appendix 2.1), possibly due to wars between the European powers (Volker, 1954, 1974). Thus the small rise in trade during this phase must have been mostly for the South Seas market, where a traditional pattern of demand persisted.

Throughout the 21 years of Phase III (1662–82), the focus of Chinese ceramic exports shifted back and forth between Canton–Macao in Guangdong and the Amoy area in Fujian. Between 1661 and 1676 the Guangdong ports were doing well. From 1676 to 1680, the bulk of ceramic exports came from Fujian, but after 1680 Canton again was the chief exporter (Table 2.6). These shifts of focus between the two exporting regions coincided with shifts in the fortunes of the Zhengs. Until 1676, the Zhengs were closely confined to Taiwan by the Manchu forces:[23] as a consequence, no Fujian boats brought Chinese ceramics to Batavia. Between 1676 and 1680, the Zhengs managed to re-establish themselves in Amoy[24] and immediately resumed sending ships carrying Fujianese cargoes to the South Seas.[25] VOC sources show that more than 680,000 pieces of porcelain reached South-East Asia during this five-year period, carried in junks from the Amoy area.[26] The fast comeback of Fujian ceramics in South Seas markets reflects the

Table 2.6 Ceramic exports from Guangdong, Fujian and Kyushu, 1662–82

Period	Guangdong	Fujian	Unspecified China port	Kyushu
1662–76	265,630	–	132,300	325,343
1677–80	315,144	680,679	92,200	198,703
1680–2	204,460	–	6,532	163,906

Note: Only those shipments with a definite port of origin are included in this table.
Figures are extracted from Appendices 2.2–2.4. See also Table 2.3

resourcefulness not only of the Zheng traders but of the Fujianese potters as well.

With Canton and Macao playing a more active role in export, the monopoly on sea trade enjoyed by the Zhengs during Phase II was gone.[27] The ceramics shipped from Canton and Macao must have been made locally at Yaoping in north-eastern Guangdong province, which was probably the third-largest centre for blue-and-white porcelain in China, after Jingdezhen in Jiangxi and Minnan in Fujian.[28] The designs and shapes of the coarse blue-and-white wares made at Yaoping are very similar to those made at Fujian kilns, arguing strongly that the two kiln centres shared a common market.[29]

The competition between the Zhengs and the VOC continued through the early 1680s, with the former allying themselves with the English and the latter with the Manchus. Neither the English nor the VOC obtained many ceramics directly from their allies. During the second phase there was a close contest in ceramic business between the Zhengs and the VOC, whilst the third phase sees the decline of the Zhengs as competitors. The Zhengs were frequently checked by the VOC, in Fujian and abroad.[30]

Various other traders – Macao Portuguese, English, independent Dutch 'Burghers', Siamese and Cantonese – appear to have been more active in carrying ceramics during this phase than in the previous one, probably replacing the less vigorous Zhengs in the South China Sea. Their supply came from Canton, and sometimes directly from Japan as well.[31] With the more active participation of these traders, transhipment from South-East Asian ports became active again. Substantial volumes of ceramics arrived at Batavia from Malacca, Bantam and Siam. The VOC at this time seems to have been happy to play a transhipper's role rather than attempting to carry porcelains directly from their countries of origin.

MARKETS FOR CERAMIC EXPORTS DURING THE SEVENTEENTH CENTURY

The seventeenth century is not a typical period in the history of ceramic trade in the South Seas; there were new suppliers, traders and markets. But perhaps no period is typical in that sense since the South Seas markets in general, and markets for ceramics in particular, have always to be understood in terms of regional political and commercial changes.

Certain seventeenth-century Chinese trading reactions appear to conform with events that had occurred earlier. There were periods in the past when China had lost her monopoly position as a supplier of porcelains,[32] but she had always bounced back when political conditions became favourable again. In the case of the seventeenth century, she dropped drastically from supplying almost all the export market demand to less than one-third (Table 2.3), but she picked up again towards the end of the third phase, and indeed by the early eighteenth century was once again the largest exporter of all grades of ceramics. As a supplier China repeatedly demonstrated her flexibility and toughness in holding on to her markets in the South Seas and, later, in Europe. In ordinary times she showed herself able to sell cheaply in large quantities, an ability which – as Dutch traders often complained – Japanese potters of that period had not yet acquired.

Japan demonstrated remarkable economic flexibility in capturing almost half of the recorded ceramic sales upon entering the competition during Phase II. Japan's success was repeated by Tongking in Phase III. Why Tongking was temporarily able to outdo both China and Japan is an interesting issue for further study.

Most of the early seventeenth-century Chinese merchants were organized as regionally based clan-orientated groups, just as they were in earlier and later times. However, the Zhengs of the mid-seventeenth century managed to transform a family business into an enterprise that in many respects resembled the contemporary East India Companies of Europe, with an international viewpoint, very large financial resources, major military power, and well-co-ordinated commercial strategies. The Zheng organization was perhaps the only Asian counterpart of the VOC, capable of competing on a level footing with that corporation in Eastern seas. However, the Zhengs' system was still built around a family and one remarkable individual within that family; the death of

Coxinga in 1662 precipitated the fall of the Zheng 'dynasty' and the disintegration of the organization. The ensuing vacuum, ironically, was filled by regionally based groups, mostly from Guangdong, of the traditional clan-orientated type.

Before and after the Coxinga period, regions within China competed with one another in trade. The rivalry extended to manufacturers, who must have had close working relations with local traders. Hence at markets in the South Seas, the Fujian-based merchants promoted Minnan wares, whereas the Canton–Macao traders sold mostly Canton-made ceramics. The export of wares from these two regions appears to be complementary in time: whenever the Amoy area was more active, Canton was less active, and vice versa.

THE ROLE OF EUROPEAN TRADERS

What would have happened to the ceramic trade in the South Seas if there had been no European traders in the seventeenth century? Perhaps the business would have never been so well-recorded, but otherwise the overall market development in the South Seas would have been pretty much the same, a viewpoint advocated by historians such as Furber (1976, 333–5). As noted previously, the demand for common wares in the South Seas had been persistent ever since the fourteenth century. The volume of porcelain consumed in Asia during the seventeenth century was stable enough not to be altered by the inclusion of traders of a new ethnic origin.

Hence the coming of the Western traders broadened the market for Asian ceramics but did not alter its basic pattern. China, which had occupied the leading position as ceramic exporter for many centuries, was seriously challenged by Japanese manufacturers in the middle of the seventeenth century, an activity promoted by the VOC. However, it was not because of the VOC but because of the political situation that China temporarily lost her overseas markets.

The appearance of Japanese competition perhaps should not be credited entirely to the VOC either. It was only a matter of time before Japanese wares began to be exported, since Japan had been making its own porcelain for over half a century. Besides, it was the Zheng fleet that first sailed away with a shipment of Japanese ceramics to the South Seas in 1658, before the VOC showed any interest in marketing Japanese wares.

While the overall ceramic market in Asia was not greatly altered by the participation of Westerners, the Western traders did open up a new market in Europe for Asian ceramics. The average annual Chinese export to this new market came to only 16 per cent of total exports during Phase I, and total exports were of course only a tiny fraction of the volume of ceramics made for the vast home market in China. Similarly, most of Japan's overseas shipments of ceramics went to the South Seas; on average, less than 10 per cent of annual exports went to Europe throughout Phases II and III. But the appearance of a new and wealthy market for fine-quality wares did make a difference to some kiln areas, and this encouraged the growth of further specialization among producers.

The international ceramic trade from Asia into Europe eventually stimulated ceramic manufacturing in Europe. It took the potters in England and Holland about a century to master the production of glazed wares that more or less resembled those of the Far East, and European ceramics began to be exported to Asia shortly after that. But Western ceramics, unlike other industrial products such as textiles, iron and paper which eventually suffocated Asian industries, never did supplant Eastern ceramics in Asian markets. Ceramics are one of the few commodities which have always maintained a heavier traffic from East to West. Price and quality might have favoured the sales of Far Eastern porcelain, but the flexibility of oriental potters to custom-make for a new market must also be part of the reason for their continuing success (Kamazawa, 1984). Even today, Chinese, Japanese and Thai dinner-sets are often sold in London and New York, while European rice bowls are not at all common in Hong Kong.

APPENDICES

Appendix 2.1 Chinese ceramic exports to Europe[a]

Year	Carrier/from	Quantity (pieces)
Phase I (1602–44)		
1602	*San Jago*	4,200
1604	*Catharina*	100,000
1603	*J.V. Spilbergen*	some
1608	*Gouda* (Patani)	15
	Bantam	278
1610	*R.L. Pijlen*	9,227
1612	*W.V. Amsterdam*	25
	Vlissingen	38,641
1614	*Gelderland*	69,057
	Der Veer	440
1616	*Rotterdam*	36,033
	Mauritius	23,023
	Dolphyn	7,679
	Hart	3,730
1622	*Gouda*	25,300
	L.V. Jacatr	6,363
1623	*Mauritius*	63,931
	Walcheren	10,845
1624	*Tertholen*	10,175
1625	*Hollandia*	9,790
1626	*Schiedam* (Chincheuw)	12,814
1627	*Hollandia* }	3,210
	F. Hendrick }	31,011
	W.V. Delft (Chincheuw)	9,440
1628	*P. Willem*, etc.	15,200
1629	*W.V. Delft*	5,320
1634	*Middleburgh*	25,345
1635	*Catherine* (English)	7,000
1636	6 fleets	259,380
1637	*Wesel*, etc.	210,219
1638	*Zutphen*, etc.	88,840
1639	*Ackersloot*, etc. }	
	Breda, etc. }	366,269
1640	*M. Medicis*	7,438
	Amsterdam, etc.	75,997
1642–3	10 fleets	47,056
Total (24 years)		1,583,291

Minimum average exports: 65,970

Phase II (1645–61)

1647	*Haerlem, Oliphantg*	123,337
1654[b]	Canton viceroy	440
1658	*Batavia* fr. Ulisses	100
Total (3 years)		123,877

Annual average exports: 41,292

Phase III (1662–82)

1680	*Ternate*	1,635
1681	*Africa*	4,000
	Hollandse Tuyn	5,133
Total (2 years)		10,768

Annual average exports: 5,384

Total exports 1602–81: 1,717,936

Notes

[a] Only shipments with bills of lading or invoices for Europe are included here. The cargoes were not taken direct from China. Hence figures for Chinese exports to the South Seas (Appendix 2.2) may include shipments intended for Europe

[b] Records for 1649–52 are missing

Appendix 2.2 Chinese ceramic exports to the South Seas

Year	Carrier/from	Arrived at	Quantity (pieces)	Annual total
Phase I (1602–44)				
1632	*Seeburgh* etc.	Batavia	4,890	4,890
1633	*Blyde Bootschap*	Batavia	14,100	14,100
1634	*Bredamme* (Formosa)	Batavia	6,263	
	Oudewater (Formosa)	Batavia	24,720	
	junk	Batavia	108,171	
				139,154
1635	*Texel* (Formosa)	Batavia	10,400	
	Gallias (Formosa)	Batavia	39,780	
	Noordwych (Formosa)	Batavia	94,866	
	Swaen (Formosa)	Batavia	71,572	
				216,618
1636	junk	Formosa	some	
	Texel, Bommel (Formosa)	Batavia	90,356	90,356
1637	*d'Keyserin* (Formosa)	Batavia	24,190	
	Amsterdam (Formosa)	Batavia	112,755	
	Teyouan (Formosa)	Batavia	160,000	
	Petten	Batavia	5,958	
	VOC (Formosa)	Siam	41,240	
	Groll (Formosa)	Quinam	29,575	
	junk	Batavia	161,419	
	J.M. Joseph (Macao)	Malacca	42,544	
	8 junks (Amoy)	Batavia	100,000	
	Amoy junk	Batavia	80,000	
	Fuchou junk	Batavia	66,000	
	Fuchou junk	Batavia	46,110	
	Amoy junk	Batavia	58,000	
	3 Amoy junks	Batavia	10,600	
	junk	Batavia	15,800	
	Amoy junk	Batavia	3,900	
	3 Fuchou junks	Batavia	171,770	
				1,129,861
1638	*Oostcappel* (Formosa)	Batavia	32,000	
	Hollandia (Formosa)	Batavia	12,467	
	Amoy & Fuchou junks	Batavia	272,900	
	Petten (Formosa)	Batavia	42,335	
				359,702
1639	*Rijp* (Formosa)	Batavia	66,673	
	Otter (Formosa)	Batavia	116,391	
	Petten (Formosa)	Batavia	71,781	
1640	*V.D. Grafft* (Formosa)	Batavia	107,799	
	Middleburgh (Formosa)	Batavia	48,861	
	Castricum (Formosa)	Batavia	104,061	

Appendix 2.2 (continued)

Year	Carrier/from	Arrived at	Quantity (pieces)	Annual total
				260,721
1641	VOC junk	Batavia	14,400	14,400
1642	*Lillo* (Formosa)	Batavia	129,036	129,036
1643	Formosa junk	Batavia	18,205	
	Salamander (Formosa)	Batavia	91,556	
	Formosa junk	Batavia	26,000	
	Formosa junk	Batavia	19,500	
	Formosa junk	Batavia	27,000	
				182,261
1644	Portuguese (Macao)	Batavia	1,600	
	West Vrieslandt	Formosa	28,950	
	Batavia	Formosa	6,890	
	6 junks (Formosa)	Batavia	3,595	
	Haerlem (Formosa)	Batavia	146,564	
	Saayer (Formosa)	Batavia	202,332	
				389,931
Total (13 years)				3,185,875

Minimum average annual exports: 245,067

Phase II (1645–61)

Year	Carrier/from	Arrived at	Quantity (pieces)	Annual total
1645	*Hasewindt* (Formosa)	Batavia	400	
	Castricum (Formosa)	Batavia	38,101	
	Zutphen (Formosa)	Batavia	74,949	
	junks off Manila	captured	55,960	
	Batavia	Batavia	25,163	
				194,573
1646	*K.V. Polen* (Formosa)	Batavia	21,606	
	junks	Batavia	200,000	
	Meerman (Formosa)	Batavia	36,200	
				257,806
1650	junks	Formosa	8,684	
	Formosa junk	Batavia	5,420	
				14,104
1651	20 junks (Amoy, Man)	Formosa	27,805	
	Formosa junk	Manila	14,600	
	Amoy junk	Formosa	15,000	
				57,405
1654	5th junk (Formosa)	Batavia	1,260	
	2 junks	Formosa	9,200	
	5 junks	Formosa	3,810	
	Breda	Batavia	15,349	
				29,619

Appendix 2.2 (continued)

Year	Carrier/from	Arrived at	Quantity (pieces)	Annual total
1655	junk	Formosa	26,110	
	Angelier (Deshima)	Batavia	3,209	
				29,319
1657	Amoy junk	Batavia	7,000	
	Ulisses (Deshima)	Batavia	100	
	Junks?	Batavia	2,500	
				9,600
1659	junks? (Quinam)	Malacca	13,050	13,050
1661	junk from China	Johore	many	
	junk via Quinam	Batavia	6,212	
	junk via Patani	Batavia	1,300	
	junk via Johore	Batavia	1,000	
	junk via Patani	Batavia	2,500	
	junk via Siam	Batavia	600	
	junk via Quinam	Batavia	1,500	
	Portuguese (Macassar)	Batavia	4,700	
				17,812

Total (9 years)   623,288

Minimum annual average exports: 69,254

Phase III (1662–82)

Year	Carrier/from	Arrived at	Quantity (pieces)	Annual total
1663	junks via Quinam	Batavia	5,100	5,100
1664	junks	Batavia	10,400	
	Japanese via Quinam	Batavia	9,500	
	Junk via Cambodia	Batavia	950	
				20,850
1665	Portuguese Macao	Batavia?	15,220	15,220
1666	China junk	Batavia	1,100	1,100
1667	Portu. Macao (Malacca)	Batavia	2,800	
	Gulden Tyger–VOC Fuzhou	Batavia	500	
				3,300
1669	China junk	Batavia	52,400	52,400
1670	Portuguese Macao	Batavia?	15,940	
	Canton junk	Batavia	1,700	
	N.S. *Casbrotas* (Portug)	Batavia	12,340	
	Canton junk	Batavia	620	
				30,600
1671	Portuguese Macao	Batavia	150	
	Portuguese Macao	Batavia	61,000	

Appendix 2.2 (continued)

Year	Carrier/from	Arrived at	Quantity (pieces)	Annual total
	N.S.N. *St Anthonio* (Macao)	Batavia	3,000	
				64,150
1672	Portuguese Macao	Batavia	6,300	
	China coast	Batavia	3,350	
	Pauw (Macao)	Batavia	1,200	
	N.S. *de Rosario* (Portug)	Batavia	3,300	
	St Joris (Eng) Kedah	Surat	20,000	
	Haren secunde (Acheen)	Surat	some	
	Surat Marchiand (Siam)	Surat	29,000	
				63,150
1673	Macao (3 Burg)	Batavia	1,440[a]	
	Macao (3 Burg)	Batavia	700	
	Macao (Chinese)	Batavia	20,610[b]	
	Macao (1 Chinese)	Batavia	940[c]	
	Macao (6 Burg)	Batavia	20,000	
	Canton (2 Chinese)	Batavia	12,300	
				55,990
1674	Canton (2 Chinese)	Batavia	20,710	
	Macao (1 Chinese)	Batavia	some	
	Macao (6 Burg)	Batavia	10,100	
				30,810
1675	Macao (3 Burg)	Batavia	54,860	
	Macao (1 Bantam)	Batavia	some	
	China (2 Chinese)	Batavia	400	
				55,260
1676	Macao (Portuguese)	Bantam	some	
	Amoy (1 Chinese)	Batavia	some	
	Taiwan (1 English)	Batavia	some	
	Chinese junk	Tongking	5,400[*d]	5,400
1677	Amoy (1 Chinese)	Batavia	some	
	Taiwan (1 English)	Batavia	some	
	Macao (2 Chinese)	Batavia	270	
	Macao (1 Chinese)	Batavia	4,231	
	Chincheuw (2 Chinese)	Batavia	186,910	
	Chincheuw (1 Chinese)	Batavia	34,829	
	Macao (1 Chinese)	Batavia	118	
	Macao (1 Chinese)	Batavia	400	
				226,758
1678	Macao (Portuguese)	Batavia	some	
	Macao (Chinese)	Batavia	63,547	
	Amoy (2 Chinese)	Batavia	144,116	

Appendix 2.2 (continued)

Year	Carrier/from	Arrived at	Quantity (pieces)	Annual total
	Quemoy (1 Chinese)	Batavia	20,370	
	Canton (1 Chinese)	Batavia	4,800	
				232,833
1679	Canton (1 Chinese)	Batavia	6,200	
	Chincheuw (3 Chin)	Batavia	290,814	
	Macao (1 Chinese)	Batavia	18,490	
				315,504
1680	Macao (1 Chinese)	Batavia	65,000	
	Macao (1 Portuguese)	Batavia	some	
	Macao (1 English)	Batavia	some	
	Canton (1 Chinese)	Batavia	32,908	
	Macao (1 Chinese)	Batavia	44,130	
	Chincheuw (1 Chin)	Batavia	3,640	
	Canton (1 Chinese)	Batavia	25,900	
	Chinese via Cambodia	Malacca	1,800*	
	Macao	Malacca	49,150*	
	Tongking (1 junk)	Malacca	85,000*	
				307,528
1681	Canton (1 Chinese)	Batavia	21,000	
	Canton (1 Chinese)	Batavia	some	
	Macao (Portuguese)	Batavia	69,880	
	Fuzhou (1 VOC)	Batavia	6,000	
	Canton (1 Chinese)	Batavia	22,390	
				119,270
1682	China (1 VOC:Brantgans)	Batavia	532	
	Canton (3 Chinese)	Batavia	37,940	
	Macao (1 Chinese)	Batavia	38,650	
	Macao (Prot: S. Antonio)	Bantam	14,600*	
				91,722
Total (19 years)				1,696,945

Average annual exports: 89,312

Notes
Barrel = 200 pieces; parcel = 20 pieces; bundle = 10 pieces;
case/chest/nest/tubs//basket/valet = 100 pieces; wicker hamper = 30 pieces; package = 200 pieces; corgel = 20 pieces
[a] From 1673 the figures presented here come from Bronson's list (1990)
[b] Volker (1954, 212) gives a total of 55,990 pieces carried away from Macao in this year by Dutch freeman vessels and Chinese junks. The figure 20,610 is obtained by subtracting from the Volker total
[c] The unit used is vat, assuming this to be similar to bale here.
[d] Between 1673 and 1682 entries marked * come from Volker (1954)

Appendix 2.3 Chinese ceramics and ceramic pigment exports to Japan

Year	Carrier/from	General ceramics (pieces)	Teapots (pieces)	Pigment for ceramics (kg)
Phase I (1602–44)				
1634	Formosa	6,058	–	–
1635	*Groll* etc.	135,905	–	–
1636	Portuguese	–	18	–
	Formosa	336	–	–
1637	6 Portuguese	101	–	–
	Formosa	39,075	–	–
	Junks	750,000	–	–
1638	2 Portuguese	3,235	–	–
1639	93 junks	1,577	–	–
1640	Junks	260	–	–
1641	Junks	24,400	2,122	
1642	Junks	54,357[a]	1,379	
1643	Nanking junk	2,200	–	–
1644	Junks	6,478	1,682	–
Total		1,023,282	5,201	

Grand total (11 years): 1,028,483
Average annual exports: 93,498

Year	Carrier/from	General ceramics (pieces)	Teapots (pieces)	Pigment for ceramics (kg)
Phase II (1645–61)				
1645	Junks	229,040	433	–
1646	Junks	70,000	487	–
1647	Fuchou	–	1	–
1648	Junks	–	35	–
1649	Junks	10,400	174	–
1650	Junks	1,108	39	10,381
1651	Junks	207	–	812
1652	Junks	1,100	–	312
1653	Junks	5,670	22	1,012
1654	Junks	–	38	1,746
1655	Junks	–	–	384
1656	Junks	–	–	562
1657	Junks	–	–	284
1658	Junks	–	3	837
1659	Junks	–	–	562
	Hilversum	900?	–	–
1660	Junks		289	714
1661	Junks	–	–	256
Total		318,425	1,521	17,862

Grand total – ceramics (17 years): 319,946
Average annual exports: 18,820

Appendix 2.3 (continued)

Year	Carrier/from	General ceramics (pieces)	Teapots (pieces)	Pigment for ceramics (kg)
Phase III (1662–82)				
1662	Junks	–	–	818
1663	Junks	10,000	–	156
1664	Junks	20	800	1,887
1665	Junks	–	800	1,260
1666	Junks	–	2	218
1668	Junks	–	–	762
1680	Junks	–	–	934
1681–2		–	–	1,058
1682–3		–	–	656
Total		10,020	1,602	7,749

Grand total – ceramics (10 years): 11,622
Average annual exports: 1,162

Note
[a] Here 5,000 taels-worth of porcelain was listed (Volker, 1954, 123). Assuming that 2.5 florins = 1 tael, and that an average fine porcelain piece in Japan cost 0.23 florin (Volker, 1954, 121), then 5,000 taels could buy 54,357 pieces

Appendix 2.4 Japanese ceramic exports to the South Seas

Year	Carrier/from	Arrived at	Quantity (pieces) Europe	South Seas
Phase II (1645–61)				
1659	VOC	Mocha		21,567
	Vogelsanck	Batavia		20,000[a]
1660	*Vogelsanck*	Holland	5,656	
	Oyevaer	Malacca		57,150
	Veenenburg, VOC	Holland	12,432	
	6 Dutch (Deshima)	Malacca		57,173
1661	*Vollenhove* (Deshima)	Batavia		13,612
	Anjelier & *Oyevaer*	Holland	9,218	
	Junk	Siam		65,000
	VOC (Deshima)	Batavia		25,383
	Junk via Quinam	Batavia		7,000
	Buyenskercke, etc.	Batavia		38,995
Total (3 years)			27,306	305,880

Average annual exports to Europe: 9,102
Average annual exports to South Seas: 92,858

Year	Carrier/from	Arrived at	Europe	South Seas
Phase III (1662–82)				
1662	Siam junk	Siam		some
1663	*'t R. Hardt* & *Nieuwpoort*	Holland	48,000	
	Kennemerlandt	Holland	9,992	
	Veenenburg	Batavia		51,839
	Rynlandt	Holland	8,519	
	Siam junk	Siam		some
1664	VOC	Ceylon		2,000
	Alphen & *Sparendam*	Batavia		45,752
	Amerongen	Batavia		22,930
	Chinese junk	Amoy		some
	Siam junk	Siam		24,550
	Spreeuw	Tongking		some
	Chinese junk	Batavia		83,090
	Chinese junk	Batavia		30,900
1665	*Cogge*	Holland	29,467	
	Walcheren etc.	Holland	16,285	
	Nieuwenhoven	Holland	19,229	
	Junk?	Batavia	2,821	
1666	Chinese junk	Taiwan		some
	Junk	Batavia		2,300
1667	*Hilveersum* (Deshima)	Batavia		1,000
	4 VOC (Deshima)	Malacca		2,482
	Overveen	Tongking		some
	2 junks	Batavia		49,000

Appendix 2.4 (continued)

Year	Carrier/from	Arrived at	Quantity (pieces) Europe	South Seas
1668	Buyenskercke	Batavia		9,500[b]
	8 VOC	Holland	4,611	
	Eendracht	Tongking		146
	Hilversum	Batavia		1,780
	Junks	Batavia		78,400
1669	Eendracht	Batavia		600
	Chinese junk	Batavia		87,700
	Chinese junk	Batavia		27,750
1670	Chinese junk	Taiwan		some
	Bedyckte Schermer	Batavia		9,180
	Junks?	Batavia		57,700
1671	Junk	Quinam		some
	Junk	Siam		some
	Junk	Taiwan		some
	Pauw	Batavia		20,976
	Chinese junk	Batavia		60,200
1672	Chinese junks	Batavia		34,900
	Buren	Batavia		1,853
	Beemster	Batavia		13,255
	Stermeer	Batavia		1,515
1673	4 Chinese junks	Batavia		540,000*
	1 Chinese junk	Batavia		11,600*
	1 Chinese junk	Batavia		some*
	Laaren	Holland	8,500[c]	
	Buren	Batavia		806
	Laaren	Batavia		10,692
1674	B.V. Leyden	Holland	797	
	H. Tuyn	Holland	1,084	
	N. Middelburgh	Holland	567	
	Willem Hendrick	Holland	297	
	Buren	Holland	279	
	Beemster	Holland	171	
	Spanbroeck	Holland	633	
	't Hoff van Breda	Holland	1,062	
	Hasenbergh	Batavia		51,545
	1 Chinese junk	Batavia		26,400*
	2 Chinese junks	Bantam		some*
1675	Goylandt	Batavia		6,007
	Ternate	Holland	1,496	
	2 Chinese junks	Batavia		46,500*
1676	't Huys ter Spyck	Batavia		37,527
	Formosa junk	Tongking		96,600
	Eagle (English)	Bantam		some

Appendix 2.4 (continued)

Year	Carrier/from	Arrived at	Quantity (pieces)	
			Europe	South Seas
1677	*Janskercke*	Batavia		4,013
	Chinese junk	Batavia		21,000
1678	*Bloemendael*	Holland	8,960	
	2 Chinese junks	Batavia		52,600*
1679	*Voorsightigheyt*	Batavia ⎱		
	Merwede	Batavia ⎰		5,150
	junk	Batavia		61,800
1680	*'t Huys te Merwe*	Holland	6,342	
	Ternate	Holland	5,898	
	1 Chinese junk	Batavia		54,140
1681	*Vrije Zee*	Holland	3,715	
	Java	Holland	1,050	
	VOC fleet	Batavia		5,813
	Chinese junk	Tongking		4,500
	Chinese junk	Tongking		2,635
	Chinese junk	Batavia		94,180
	Hellevoetsluys	Batavia		33,694
1682	Chinese junks	Taiwan		5,050
	Chinese junk	Batavia		1,500
	Goudesteyn	Batavia		21,534
Total (20 years)			179,775	1,916,584

Average annual exports to Europe:[d] 8,988
Average annual exports to South Seas: 86,840

Notes
[a] The entry is 40 cases. Here each case is arbitrarily estimated at 500 pieces per case
[b] Volker (1954, 209) states it was 905 bundles, but on p. 157 it was 905 packages
[c] Volker (1954, 159) does not specify a quantity here but notes that the order from Holland asks for 6,000 florins-worth of porcelain. At 0.7 florin/piece (in 1671) this would come to 8,500 pieces
[d] The volume going into the South Seas would have included the volume going onward to Europe
* Entries from Bronson (1990)

Appendix 2.5 Tongking ware exports to the South Seas

Year	Carrier/from	Arrived at	Quantity (pieces)
Phase III (1662–82)			
1663	Tongking junk	Batavia	10,000
1666	Tongking	Batavia	60,000
1667	Tongking (VOC)	Batavia	30,000
1668	Tongking	Batavia	40,000
1669	*Overveen* (VOC)	Batavia	381,200
	Pitoor (VOC)	Batavia	177,240
	Chinese junk	Batavia	70,000
1670	Tongking junk	Batavia	95,000
1670	*Pitoor*	Batavia	214,160
1670	*Cabel jauw*	Batavia	89,000
1672	Tongking junk	Batavia	5,000
1672	Batavia	Aracan	some
1675	Tongking	Batavia	30,000
1678	Tongking	Batavia	100,740
1680	Tongking	Malacca	85,000
1681	Tongking	Batavia	120,000

Total (11 years): 1,507,340
Average annual exports: 137,030

Appendix 2.6 Persian ware exports to the South Seas

Year	Carrier/from	Arrived at	Quantity (pieces)
Phase II (1645–61)			
1654		Batavia	some
1655		Batavia	some
1656	Tortelduyv	Batavia	some
1659	Weesp	Batavia	some
1661	Phoenix	Batavia	5,900

Total (1 year): 5,900
Minimum average annual exports: 5,900

Year	Carrier/from	Arrived at	Quantity (pieces)
Phase III (1662–82)			
1663	Brouwershaven	Batavia	4,646
1668	Muysenbergh	Batavia	2,268
1669	Pauw	Batavia	4,823
1670–72	Vliegh	Batavia	6,638
	Pouleron	Batavia	1,700
1675	Cattenburgh	Batavia	1,700
	Flaman	Batavia	1,960
1676	Hasenbergh	Batavia	1,900
1677	Silversteyn	Batavia	3,921
1680	China	Batavia	622
1681	N. Middelburgh	Batavia	4,556
1682	Macassar	Batavia	6,900

Total (12 years): 41,634
Average annual exports: 3,469

Appendix 2.7 Martaban jars traded in the South Seas

Year	Carrier/from	Arrived at	Quantity (pieces)
Phase I (1602–44)			
1610	Bantam	Amboina	1 (opium)
1610	Bantam	N. Moluccas	2 (opium)
1636	Pulicat	Batavia	83
1637	Portuguese vessel	?	some with oil
1643	Pulicat	Batavia	54 with oil

Total (3 years): 140
Minimum average annual exports: 46

Phase II (1645–61)			
1645	Pulicat	Batavia	72
1646	Pulicat	Batavia	79
1646	Pulicat	Batavia	48
1647	Pulicat	Batavia	12
	Pulicat (Lillo)	Batavia	8
1655	Aracan	Batavia	6
1659	?	Batavia	70
1660	Siriang	Masulipatum	65
1661	*Moondaes* (Tenasserim)	Surat	65

Total (7 years): 425
Average annual exports: 60

Phase III (1662–82)			
1663	*Zuylen* (Pegu)	Masulipatam	12
1665	Coromandel	Batavia	6
1668	Coromandel? (VOC)	Batavia	32
1669	Coromandel	Batavia	30
1670	Coromandel	Batavia	40
1675	Siriang	Pulicat	251
1677	Pegu	Batavia	223
1679	Pegu	Batavia	198
1680	Toulogbauw?	Batavia	159

Total (9 years): 951
Average annual exports: 105

Appendix 2.8 Jingdezhen porcelain with datable inscriptions after 1644

Year	Inscription abstract
1646	The year of Bingxu, Shunzhi (Art Institute of Chicago, no. 1964. 671)
1648	Made for Baihua Studio
	Written by Xinshang Studio
1651	Supervised by Jiangxi Official
1654	Long live the Emperor, dedicated by Zhang
1655	Made in the year of Yiwei
	Sponsored by Huang, a native of Anhui, the year of yiwei, Shunzhi
1657	Sponsored by Y. Chen, the year of Dingyou, Shunzhi
1658	Sponsored by Wang, a Jiangxi official
	Sponsored by Z. Cheng, a native of Jiangxi, in the 15th year of Shunzhi
1659	Sponsored by Dai, a native of Nanchang (Jiangxi), in the 16th year of Shunzhi
1660	Sponsored by Zhang and his wife, in the 17th year of Shunzhi
	Sponsored by R. Chen, in the Gengzi year of Shunzhi
1661	Sponsored by J. Cheng, in the 18th year of Shunzhi
1662	Sponsored by Gui, a native of Shanxi, in the first year of Kangxi
1663	Sponsored by Fan
1666	The year of Bingwu, Great Qing (Yu, 1982, 138)
1667	The year of Dingwei, Great Qing (Yu, 1982, 138)
	Made in the year of Dingwei, Kangxi
1668	The year of Moushen, Great Qing (Yu, 1982, 138)
1671	Sponsored by the Chen Family, in the Xinhai year of Kangxi
	Made in the Xinhai year of Kangxi
	Made for the Zhonghe Tang, in the Xinhai year of Kangxi (Tong, 1984, 69)
1672	Made for Zhonghe Tang, in the Renzi year of Kangxi
1673	Written in the year of Guichou
1675	Written in the year of Youmou
1679	Written in the year of Jiwei by a fisherman
1683	Made for the Yinju Caotang, in the 22nd year of Kangxi

Note: All items before 1662 from Geng (1984, 14); after 1662 from Geng (1984, 65), unless otherwise stated

NOTES

1. For instance, the hundreds of pieces of porcelain recovered from the wreck of the *Witte Leeuw*, sunk in 1613 near St Helena, were not included in the cargo list at all (van der Pijl-Ketel, 1982, 18–19).

2. For the South Seas (Nanhai) here I include the markets of South-East Asia, India, the Middle East and Africa. The main entrepôts were always in South-East Asia, from which ceramics and other goods were transhipped to more distant places.

3. For instance, the sites at Sakai Kangou Toshi reveal a wide range of quality of wares from China, as well as from Vietnam and Japan (Morimura, 1984).

4. In Thailand two important entrepôts built up since the thirteenth and fourteenth centuries were Nakorn Sri Thammarat in the south and Ratchaburi in the central part of the country (Gumperayarnnont, 1985). Ayuthia may have begun to import Chinese ceramics in the late fourteenth century. Excavated shipwrecks of the thirteenth to sixteenth centuries in the Gulf of Siam also testify to the fact that large volumes of ceramics were carried from China to South-East Asia (FAD, 1988).

5. A number of reasons have been offered for the collapse of the Sri Satchanalai kilns in Thailand: some suggest that a severe flood caused the end of production sometime in the sixteenth century (Hein, 1986); others see the Burmese invasions of the mid-sixteenth century and the sacking of the Siamese capital in 1569 as the main cause. Whatever the reason, a lack of demand was not one of them. Prior to the seventeenth century, Siamese and Vietnamese wares had already built up substantial markets in Japan (Tuzuki, 1989), the Philippines (Fox, 1959), Indonesia (Harkantiningsih, 1985), and the Middle East (i.e., at Julfar; Hansman, 1985, 42–3).

6. The lifting of the sea ban in 1567 by the Ming government, relaxing controls on coastal Chinese merchants, must have helped to accelerate the trade.

7. Archaeological evidence shows that these blue-and-white kilns probably started operation in the sixteenth century and survived through the nineteenth century.

8. This type of porcelain, with blue designs on a white background, was the type most commonly traded in Asia and Europe; it was also made for export in Japan and Vietnam at some periods. Monochrome and polychrome wares were traded too, but in much smaller quantities.

9. According to records, the Manchu court started to commission wares from the Jingdezhen kilns in 1651, and the official kilns were established there in 1654 (Sayer, 1951, 11).

10. For instance, in 1655 they were still active in bringing out fine ceramics from Wenzhou to Fujian. That particular cargo was intercepted by the Manchus and thus described in contemporary records (Nan, 1982, 205).

11. It is estimated that the Zhengs could make a 200 per cent average profit in trading with Japan but only 100 per cent in trading with South-East Asia where their buying power was lower (Han, 1982, 153–4). The Zheng strategy was to sell silk, textiles and hides in Japan which they got from China and South-East Asia. Then from Japan they carried back copper which sold

well in Manila, Siam, and Vietnam, receiving spices and hides in return (ibid., 140).

12. The wares were not intended for the Chinese home market; they were shipped onward to South-East Asia.

13. These are likely to be the well-known teapots made at Yixing in Jiangsu province. The fashion of tea-making in Yixing clay teapots caught on widely among connoisseurs of tea in Japan and China. The equivalent Japanese teapots did not appear for at least another century.

14. In 1655 (Dutch documents suggest 1657; Volker, 1954, 59) Coxinga forbade Chinese trading junks to sail for Formosa. The boycott lasted for about two years and was resumed again in 1660 (Han, 1982, 144).

15. Coxinga's father, Zheng Zhilong, is a typical example. He rose rapidly as a great merchant and pirate in the Nanhai trade but later became an official of the Ming government.

16. By 1655, Coxinga commanded some 2,000 warships and well over 100,000 troops, making extensive use of European weaponry (Parker, 1988, 112).

17. On the Zheng network of business espionage, composed mostly of family members and clansmen, see Nan (1982: 196–7).

18. For instance, a 1664 Siam–Dutch peace treaty forbade King Narai to use any Chinese for long-distance sailing, as a means of restricting Siam from trading with Japan. Narai attempted to renegotiate the terms of the treaty in the following year, asking if it would be acceptable for him to use Chinese as long as they were not Coxinga's men (na Pombejra, 1984, 302–4). Patani and Nakorn Sri Thammarat both had strong Chinese communities of Fujianese origin (Skinner, 1957, 7–8).

19. In 1661 he asked junks in South-East Asia to sail to Amoy in order to supply provisions for battles (Cao, 1982, 359). Some of these junks must have been part of his own organization, but some were obviously of Siamese origin.

20. The provenance of these large storage jars may be Pegu in Burma (Adhyatman and Abu Ridho, 1984, 48–9), but south-western China is also a possible source.

21. The price in 1645 was 5 florins piece and 24.25 florins piece in 1647 (Volker, 1954, 202–3). These prices are many times higher than those of Japanese and Chinese wares (Table 2.4).

22. The gradual decline and eventual closure are reflected in archaeological data as well as in trading figures (Tables 2.1, 2.3, 2.5).

23. An alliance between the VOC and the Manchus was apparently effective in cornering the Zhengs. The VOC were given the green light to attack at sight any junks along the Fujian coast. This the VOC did, extending their commerce destruction to waters near Nagasaki in Japan. On land few settlements in coastal Fujian escaped forced evacuation by the Manchus (Wills, 1974, 29–100).

24. With the death of Coxinga in 1662, the Zhengs' trading empire began to decline. Coxinga's son, Zheng Jing, managed to keep it going for almost twenty years but with increasing difficulty (Jin, 1982).

25. A Fujian junk captain arriving at Japan at the end of 1674 reported that he was asked by the Zhengs to spread the news that the sea ban imposed at

Fuzhou forbidding traders to visit that city was not to be observed any more (Lai, 1982, 284).

26. In 1675 Amoy was receiving English ships as well as those from Bantam, Siam and Annam (ibid.).

27. Some Cantonese merchants still seem to have been under the Zhengs, especially those near Dongguan, but they had to negotiate with the more powerful groups based in Canton (Wills, 1974, 157).

28. The Yaoping kiln complex has been investigated on two occasions (He *et al.*, 1982; Yang, 1985). It was already in operation in the sixteenth century and seems to have remained active until the nineteenth century.

29. Fujian had a second line of production, the well known *blanc de chine* ware (Donnelly, 1969). But the market for this was largely confined to China; only a small number of pieces were exported as curios.

30. The VOC's attacks on Zheng shipping along the Fujian coast met with little resistance (see e.g. Wills, 1974, 71). The VOC's blockade in Siam succeeded in stopping the Zhengs' participation in the King's trade (Na Pombejra, 1984, 304–6). It was only in Japan that the VOC was forbidden to attack ships sailing to or from Nagasaki (Nagazumi, 1987, 9; Wills, 1974, 35).

31. In addition to the usual Chinese and the VOC carriers, a number of Siamese ships sailed to Japan during this period: one Patani ship in 1675 and several from Ayuthia between 1679 and 1682 (Viraphol, 1977, 259, 264). Most of the crews of these ships are believed to have been Chinese.

32. The same thing happened in the fifteenth and sixteenth centuries: when the supply of Chinese export wares failed, Siamese and Vietnamese kilns moved in to fill the gap. At the site of Calatagan in the Philippines, for instance, 13 to 22 per cent of the imported ceramics present came not from China but from Siam and Vietnam (Fox, 1959, 361).

REFERENCES

Adhyatman, S. and Abu Ridho (1984) *Martavans in Indonesia*, Jakarta.

Bronson, Bennet (1990) 'Export porcelain in economic perspective: the Asian ceramic trade in the 17th century', in C.M. Ho (ed.) *Ancient Ceramic Kiln Technology in Asia*, Centre of Asian Studies, University of Hong Kong, 126–51.

Cao, Yonghe (1982) 'A study of Zheng Chenggong from Dutch documents' in *A Collection of Papers on Zheng Chenggong in Taiwan* [Taiwan Zheng Chenggong Yanjiu Lunwenxun], ed. Xiamen University, Fujian, 352–73.

Donnelly, P.J. (1969) *Blanc de Chine: The Porcelain of Tehua in Fukien*, London.

FAD (Fine Arts Department, Thailand) (1988) *Underwater Archaeology in Thailand*, Bangkok.

Fox, Robert (1959) *The Calatagan Excavations: Two Fifteenth Century Burial Sites in Batangas, Philippines*, Manila.

Furber, Holden (1976) *Rival Empires of Trade in the Orient, 1600–1800*, Minneapolis.

Geng, Baochang (1984) *Identification of Ming and Qing Ceramics: Qing Volume* [Ming Qing Ciqi Jianding], Taipei.

Glamann, Kristof (1981) *Dutch–Asiatic Trade, 1620–1740*, The Hague.

Grove, Migs (1990) *Seventeenth Century Chinese Porcelain from the Butler Family Collection*, Alexandria.

Gumperayarnnont, Malinee (1985) 'Chinese ceramics from Mae Klong river', *SPAFA SEAMEO Project in Archaeology and Fine Arts – Technical Workshop in Ceramics (T-W4)*, Bangkok, 65–71.

Guy, John (1986) *Oriental Trade Ceramics in South-East Asia, Ninth to Sixteenth Centuries*, Singapore.

Han, Zhenhua (1982) 'Zheng Chenggong's overseas trade between 1650–1662', in *A Collection of Papers on Zheng Chenggong* [Zheng Chenggong yanjiu lunwenxun], ed. Xiamen University, Fujian, 136–87.

Hansman, John (1985) *Julfar, An Arabian Port: Its Settlement and Far Eastern Ceramic Trade from the 14th to the 18th Centuries*, London.

Harkantiningsih, Naniek (1985) 'Thai Ceramics from archaeological sites in Indonesia', *SPAFA SEAMEO Project in Archaeology and Fine Arts – Technical Workshop on Ceramics (T-W4)*, Bangkok, 169–82.

He, J.S., Peng, R.C. and Qiu, L.C. (1982) 'Blue-and-white kilns at Jiucun, Yaoping', *A Collection of Chinese Kiln Reports from Surveys and Excavations* [Zhongguo gudai yaozhi diaocha fajue baogaoji], Beijing.

Hein, Donald (1986) Personal communications, Thai Ceramics Archaeological project, Bangkok.

Ho, Chuimei (1988) *Minnan Blue and White Wares: An Archaeological Survey of Kiln Sites of the 16th–19th Centuries in Southern Fujian, China*, Oxford.

—— (1991) 'Ceramics found at Southern Thailand: Ko Kho Khao and Laem Pho', *Trade Ceramic Studies*, (Fukuoka), no. 11, 53–80.

Impey, O. and Tregear, M. (1983) 'An investigation into the origin, provenance and nature of Tianqi porcelain', *Trade Ceramics Studies*, (Fukuoka), no. 3, 103–18.

Jin, Chengqian (1982) 'Zheng Jing yu Ming Zheng', in *A Collection of Papers on Zheng Chenggong in Taiwan* [Taiwan Zheng Chenggong Yanjiu Lunwenxun], ed. Xiamen Univesity, Fujian, 317–32.

Kamazawa, Yo (1984) 'Ceramic exchange between the East and West in the 17th–18th Century', in *The Inter-influence of Ceramic Art in East and West*, Idemitsu Museum, Tokyo, 110–20.

Lai, Yongxiang (1982) 'Comments on trade between the Zhengs and the British', in *A Collection of Papers on Zheng Chenggong in Taiwan* [Taiwan Zheng Chenggong Yanjiu Lunwenxun], ed. Xiamen University, Fujian, 271–92.

Locsin, Leandro and Locsin, Cecilia (1967) *Oriental Ceramics Discovered in the Philippines*, Rutland.

Morimura, Kenichi (1984) 'On the porcelains recently excavated in Sakai-Kangou-toshi: the kinds, distribution and functional use', *Trade Ceramics Studies*, (Fukuoka), no. 4, 41–9.

Mudge, Jean McClure (1986) *Chinese Export Porcelain in North America*, New York.

Murakami, Isamu (1986) 'Ceramics found with the date "Kanei 21" (AD 1644) found from Toda river bed site '81 IP-SB020', *Trade Ceramics Studies* (Fukuoka), no. 6, 61–6.

Na Pombejra, Dhiravat (1984) 'Political History of Siam, 1629–1688', unpublished Ph.D. thesis, University of London.

Nagazumi, Yoko (1987) *Quantity of Imports and Exports, 1637–1833* [Tosen yushuchunuhin shulyo yikan], Shobusha, Tokyo.

Nan, Qi (1982) 'A study on the five merchants of the Zhengs', in *Taiwan Zheng Chenggong Yanjiu Lunwenji* [A Collection of Papers on Zheng Chenggong], ed. Xiamen University, Fujian, 194–208.

Parker, Geoffrey (1988) *The Military Revolution, Military Innovation and the Rise of the West, 1500–1800*, Cambridge.

Sayer, Geoffrey (1951) *Ching-te-chen Taolu: A Translation with Notes and Introduction*, London.

SEAS (South-East Asian Ceramic Society, West Malaysia Chapter) (1985) 'A Ceramic Legacy of Asia's Maritime Trade: Song Dynasty Guangdong Wares and other 11th to 19th Century Trade Ceramics found on Tioman Island, Malaysia*, Selangor.

Skinner, G.W. (1957) *Chinese History in Thailand: An Analytical History*, Ithaca, N.Y.

Steensgaard, Niels (1973) *The Asian Trade Revolution of the Seventeenth Century*, Chicago and London.

TKCM (Kyushu Ceramic Museum) (1983) *Seventeenth Century Jingdezhen and Imari*, Kyushu.

Tong, Yihua (1984) *A Collection of Signatures and Inscriptions on Ceramics* [Zhongguo lidai taodi kuanshi huiji], Hong Kong.

Tuzuki, Shinichirou (1989) 'The Swankhaloke with four handles excavated from the Sakai Kangou Toshi site during the 15th and 16th century', *Trade Ceramics Studies* (Fukuoka), no. 9, 123–33.

van der Pijl-Ketel, C.L. (1982) *The Ceramic Load of the Witte Leeuw 1613*, Amsterdam.

Viraphol, Sarasin (1977) *Tribute and Profit: Sino-Siamese Trade, 1652–1853*, Cambridge, Mass.

Volker, T. (1954) *Porcelain and the Dutch East India Company, 1602–1682*, Leiden.

Wada, Yosifumi (1989) 'Chinese ceramics excavated from the site of Hitoyoshi Castle, Sumiyagura, Kumamoto Prefecture', *Trade Ceramics Studies* (Fukuoka), no. 9, 107–22.

Wills, John (1974) *Pepper, Guns and Parleys: The Dutch East India Company and China, 1662–1681*, Cambridge, Mass.

Yang, Shaoxiang (1985) 'A preliminary study of Guangdong blue-and-white wares', *Journal of Oriental Studies* (Hong Kong), no. 23(2): 156–67.

Yu, Gang (1982) 'Investigation on the two remains of ancient kilns in Jingdezhen', *Zhongguo Taoci* (Jingdezhen), no. 7: 136–40.

3

CHINA AND THE MANILA GALLEONS

*Dennis O. Flynn and Arturo Giraldez**

INTRODUCTION

Beginning in the 1570s, silver initiated significant and continuous trade at the global level. Conservative official estimates indicate that Latin America alone produced about 150,000 tons of silver between 1500 and 1800 (Barrett, 1990, 237), perhaps exceeding 80 per cent of the entire world's production over that time span (Cross, 1983, 397). And virtually all of it engaged in intercontinental trade. Explanation for the spectacular dominance of silver in the early-modern world economy requires analysis of both the demand and the supply sides of that industry. On the demand side, China was by far the most significant end-market customer. China's paper-money system suffered a crisis in the fourteenth century and had virtually collapsed by the middle of the fifteenth century; silver imports provided a stable substitute for fiduciary money. Thus, a partial explanation for significant demand for silver in China dates to the fifteenth century when silver helped satisfy

*Research for this paper was funded in part by a 1993 Eberhardt Summer Research Fellowship; University of the Pacific's School of International Studies funded its subsequent presentation at the World History Association meeting in Honolulu in 1993. Helpful encouragement and/or criticisms of earlier drafts deserve acknowledgement, especially those of William S. Atwell, Jerry Bentley, Maxine Berg, Jan Black, Edmund Burke III, David A. Chappell, K.N. Chaudhuri, Han-sheng Chuan, Christopher Connery, Jan Devries, John H. Elliott, Marc Flandreau, James H. Flynn, Jack A. Goldstone, Takeshi Hamashita, Frank H.H. King, A.J.H. Latham, Brian Moloughney, Walter A. McDougall, John R. McNeill, William A. McNeill, Martin Needler, Geoffrey Parker, Kenneth Robinson, Michael Shoemaker, David Smith, David J. St Clair, and John J. Tepaske. Thanks also to Richard Sutch and Gavin Wright, who organized a presentation at the December 1993 Stanford–Berkeley Economic History Seminar, and to other participants who were kind enough to feed us first, then discuss and argue vigorously late into the evening. All stimulated our thinking, but the authors alone are liable for the arguments advanced in this essay.

the void created by worthless paper money. China's multi-century appetite for silver did not stem, however, solely from the monetary sector; rather, it grew from a mix of fiscal (government revenues and taxation), monetary (medium of exchange) and private-sector developments. The private sector favoured silver and increasingly taxes became payable in that medium. This trend spread to the government sector, culminating with the Ming dynasty's 'single-lash-of-the-whip' tax system, which consolidated numerous Chinese taxes and specified payment in silver in the middle of the sixteenth century.[1]

On the supply side of the equation, silver originated mostly from Peru and Mexico in the West, and Japan (especially in the late sixteenth and early seventeenth centuries) in the East. Supplies were controlled by the Spanish Emperor and the Shogun. Both indirectly sold to China. Political hostilities precluded direct official trade of Japanese silver into the Chinese market by merchants of either country, although private Chinese merchants did call on Nagasaki.[2] That role fell to European and other Asian intermediaries in the Sino-Japanese silver trade.

Europeans were also middlemen in the silver trade between Spanish America and China. New World silver traversed the Atlantic and passed through Europe – following countless trade routes via the Baltic, the Levant and the Cape – and eventually on to a Chinese destination. Attman's (1986, 78) 'minimum estimates' of bullion flows through Europe and on to Asia are 2–3 million rix-dollars in 1550, 4.4 million in 1600, 6 million around 1650, and 8.5 million by 1700 (one rix-dollar = approximately one peso). The Pacific Ocean furnished an alternative, the direct trade route from America to China. Silver-laden Manila galleons sailed out of Acapulco to the Philippines, where the cargo was transferred to junks for shipment to China.

The contention of this essay is twofold. First, the amount of silver flowing to China via the Manila galleons was far larger than is generally recognized; sometimes it may have equalled the volume of silver passing to China via Europe. These Acapulco–Manila galleons seem to have carried as much silver to Asia as the Portuguese *Estado do India* and the Dutch and English East India Companies combined. Second, the demand for silver in China implies immense repercussions in terms of Western history: there would have been neither the same type of 'price revolution' in Europe and China[3] nor a Spanish Empire[4] in the absence of the transformation of Chinese society to a silver base in the early modern period.

THE ROLE OF CHINA

Use of paper money was widespread in China from at least the eleventh century. The state sought to fix the value of paper money to coins, but such efforts were futile because the paper was inconvertible. As a result, a promissory note with a nominal value of one *liang* of silver in 1375 (= one thousand copper coins) fell to less than one-thousandth of a *liang* (= less than one copper coin) by the year 1445: 'So although the notes remained in circulation until about 1573 the issues had to be suspended in 1450 and afterwards were seldom resumed' (Gernet, 1982, 415). Atwell (1977, 4; 1982, 79, 83) has correctly pointed to China's transition to silver-based money as a significant source of demand for silver.

It is noteworthy that the Ming never did mint silver coins after the collapse of their paper-money system. Copper cash was used for normal day-to-day purchases. Increased use of silver ingots for larger transactions evolved in the merchant community early in the fifteenth century, especially in commercial regions such as Kwangtung and the lower Yangtse. Demand in these regions alone must have been significant considering that Nanking contained over one million inhabitants and Peking around 660,000 in the late Ming period (Rodzinski, 1979, 201). Payments in silver emerged in a somewhat disorderly way:

> In the clumsy circulation of pure lump silver, the unit of account (the ounce or tael) varied from place to place and also as between trades and between agencies of government. Twenty different silver tael units of account might be in common use in one city at one time, requiring a different 'currency' for each commodity, like salt or cotton cloth, and for payments going to certain other places. Each ingot had to be weighed and also assayed for its purity.
>
> (Fairbank, 1992, 135)

At first forbidden by the Ming, this trend towards silver gained momentum in the second half of the fifteenth century. The emergence of local silver production within China and the clandestine trade with Japan (the main source of the white metal) resulted from this conversion to silver in the private sector, which ultimately had a profound effect on the Ming fiscal structure.

The Ming tax structure was highly decentralized. Taxes themselves came to be collected in silver, not because it was 'planned but merely resorted to out of necessity in the failure of all other currencies' (Fairbank, 1992, 135). Taxation in silver grew in popularity in the second half of the fifteenth century:

> The following items were paid in silver: tribute from the provinces from 1465 onwards, the taxes of the salt producers from 1475, and the taxes exempting craftsmen from their periods of compulsory labour in 1485. From 1486–1500 onwards it was also agreed that the peasantry could be exempted from certain corvees by the payment of taxes in silver.
>
> (Gernet, 1982, 415–16)

This evolution of the fiscal structure continued into the sixteenth century and was systematized in the 1570s under the name of the 'single-whip method', which unified numerous taxes and specified that virtually all duties and taxes were to be paid in silver.

Tribute payments also converted to silver. The Chinese monarchy considered itself the world's true centre of civilization and, as such, exacted tribute from neighbouring vassal states:

> To sum up, the entire tribute and interregional trade zone had its own structural rules which exercised a systematic control through silver circulation and with the Chinese tribute at the center. This system, encompassing East and Southeast Asia was articulated with neighboring trade zones like those of India, the Islamic region and Europe.
>
> (Hamashita, 1988, 18)

The payment of tribute in silver implied that the major trading routes of Asia were heavily impacted by the flow of bullion toward Peking. In the case of Korean tribute, for example, Tashiro (1989) has shown that Japanese silver exports via Tsushima and Korea matched month-for-month the schedule of tribute payments from Korea to Imperial China.

To reiterate the main points, the gradual conversion of Imperial China to a 'silver zone' was initiated by merchants when the fiduciary money system collapsed. Local and regional taxes came to be paid in silver. Imperial tribute became payable in silver too, but not by Ming design. On the contrary, the dynasty attempted to thwart the pro-trade and pro-silver forces of trade and industry.[5] Mercantilistic regulation of the tribute-trade system did indeed stifle private trade, but this policy alienated merchants who sided with the Manchus in overthrowing the Ming dynasty in the mid-1600s. According to Hamashita, it was the private-sector challenge to the traditional mercantilistic tribute-trade monopoly which nudged a reluctant China into the silver camp. The Ch'ing dynasty, successor to the Ming, also had to accommodate the rise of the merchant class:

'Modernization' in Asia was generated as a negative reaction to the all-inclusive superior–subordinate relations of the traditional tribute system. Mercantilist control over tribute by the Ch'ing dynasty led overseas Chinese merchants to oppose the trade policy and expand their own private trade. As a result, the Ch'ing dynasty was in turn compelled to shift from the role of monopolistic trader-merchant to that of tax collector [in silver].

(Hamashita, 1988, 23)

According to this interpretation, China began to modernize when the central government was forced to reduce its role as monopoly trader in favour of collecting taxes from the private sector.

The important point for our purposes is to establish that China's demand for silver was vast and growing over time. China contained over a quarter of the world's population (around 160 million by 1644, according to Fairbank, 1992, 128) and was the centre of the largest tribute-trade system in the world. When such a large percentage of the world economy is committed to purchase of a specific commodity that is high in value and transportable among continents, the impact on that industry is bound to be global. The early-modern silver industry was no exception.

It was the conversion of China's economic structure to silver that caused its value to soar above that of any other location in the world. Relative bimetallic ratios are perhaps the clearest indicator of silver's high valuation in China.

From 1592 to the early 17th century gold was exchanged for silver in Canton at the rate of 1:5.5 to 1:7, while in Spain the exchange rate was 1:12.5 to 1:14, thus indicating that the value of silver was twice as high in China as in Spain.

(Chuan, 1969, 2)

Divergent bimetallic ratios imply that one could theoretically use an ounce of gold to buy, say, eleven ounces of silver in Amsterdam, transport the silver to China and exchange the eleven ounces there for about two ounces of gold. The two ounces of gold could be brought back to Europe and exchanged for twenty-two ounces of silver, which could again be transported back to China where its value was double again. This process of 'arbitrage' would continue until China's silver stock rose sufficiently to lower its value there to that prevailing in the rest of the world. What we are describing here is a Ricardian-type mechanism for the transfer of silver, previously explained in detail in Chaudhuri's (1978) classic account.[6] By the same process, sufficient gold was simultaneously exported to Europe and America to lower its value there to that of the rest of the world. The same arbitrage mechanism which attracted silver from the West, of course, attracted silver from other Asian countries. In the 1590s the bimetallic ratio was about 10:1 in Japan and 9:1 in Moghul India, significantly higher than in China, which 'was the basic reason why China remained for so long the suction-pump (bomba-aspirante) which absorbed silver from all over the world' (Boxer, 1970, 461). The arbitrage mechanism for attracting silver to the Chinese 'suction-pump' explains part of the story. What we are suggesting is that institutional changes in the private sector within China, along with fiscal and monetary developments, are what created the arbitrage potential itself.

Did reality conform to the arbitrage-theory prediction that the profit motive would eventually integrate world markets in terms of price? The answer is yes. By 1640 bimetallic ratios around the world had converged (Yamamura and Kamiki, 1983, 352). Silver's high valuation in China caused the white metal influx from production sources around the world (mostly Spanish America and Japan) because it was profitable to satisfy China's vast demand. The relocation of the product from low-value to high-value areas roughly equalized its price everywhere; silver became more abundant in the scarce area and more scarce in the abundant areas. The arbitrage-dominated phase of the silver trade had ended around the middle of the seventeenth century.

If simple arbitrage explains the flow of silver to China up to about 1640, then what mechanism explains the continued flow of thousands of tons of silver to China *after* that date, when arbitrage profits had diminished? The answer is that arbitrage represents only one avenue of business profit. Normal, non-arbitrage profits are commonplace today and always have been. Products are often sent to expanding market areas, not because they offer higher prices, but because they offer more buyers at the same price. Products have always gravitated to growing areas, places where imported items share roughly the same prices they command in low-growth areas. Businesses often extend into new markets, in other words, even though per-unit profit may be normal. Turning back to early-modern China, there is evidence of an expanding market in the later Ming period:

Within China, large-scale production of ceramics, silk, and cotton cloth accompanied the spread of trade in salt and cereals, the growth of cities, and of a more affluent merchant class engaged in interregional trade. The flow of silver into China was only one factor in this growth. A number of historians point to late Ming achievements in literature, art, and urban life as harbingers of a dynamic renewal in society and culture as well as in the economy.

(Fairbank, 1992, 141–2)

Silver continued to gravitate to the Chinese market in the second half of the seventeenth century, therefore, not because silver was more valuable there than elsewhere, but because there was a huge number of buyers at a relatively stable world price.[7]

In sum, it seems clear to us that one cannot understand the global nature of the silver trade in early-modern times – that is to say, the birth of the world economy – without reserving a central place for China. Silver simply flowed to the area offering the best price. When its price there subsided to the world price, extensive and growing demand assured the continued importation of silver into China; there just were no longer such unusual profits per unit of product.

THE MANILA GALLEONS

On the production side, Peru and Japan dominated the silver market in the late sixteenth and early seventeenth centuries. Japanese production fell off after the 1630s, although the drop may have been less pronounced than once thought (Goldstone, 1991, 373). Peruvian output fell in the second half of the seventeenth century too, but the decline was gradual and the combination of Peruvian and Mexican output was larger in the seventeenth century than it had been in the sixteenth (Barrett, 1990, 242–3). The preponderance of scholarship has focused on the Atlantic–European leg of American silver's journey to the Far East. Little attention has been paid to the Pacific route to China via the Manila galleons.

The American side of the Pacific experienced a momentous innovation in the 1570s. The previously booming mines of Potosi were experiencing financial crisis by this time, when implementation of the mercury-amalgam method for extracting silver reduced production costs suddenly and dramatically.[8] Potosi became the most prolific silver producer the world has ever known. Despite an altitude of nearly three miles (15,000 feet) and transportation of two-and-a-half months by pack animal from Lima, the population of Potosi surged to equal or exceed that of London or Paris by the early seventeenth century. It may have been world history's most spectacular boom town. Profits were gigantic because the cost of producing silver had fallen suddenly, while its world price declined only gradually.[9] In other words, at the same time that the complex of forces culminating in the 'single whip' caused silver's value to rise on the Asian mainland, the cost of producing it in the New World fell dramatically. Extensive demand explains the high value of silver in China, while low-cost supply explains its low value in America. The potential for extended arbitrage profits had never been greater.

Spain was arguably the most powerful force in Europe at the beginning of the seventeenth century. And it was a Spanish product that was sent from Europe to Asia – American silver – but ironically the Portuguese, the Dutch and the English controlled the Europe–Asia trade. Spaniards were excluded. Spain was also excluded from the lucrative inter-Asian trade, at times an even greater source of enrichment for European rivals. The only avenue available for Spanish participation in Asian trade was via Mexico, over the Pacific Ocean.

The most important product imported into Mexico from the Philippines was silk, a portion of which was re-exported to Europe. Mexican merchants preferred direct trade with Asian silk suppliers rather than operating through Spanish intermediaries; transportation was cheaper, they could avoid taxes, and the Crown could not confiscate Pacific silver, as was done inside Spain (Yuste Lopez, 1984, 41). During the initial years of commercial relations between America and Manila there was no official control. A highly profitable business was organized amongst Manila, Mexico and Peru, taking advantage of cheap luxury prices for Oriental goods (from the American perspective) and cheap New World silver (from the Chinese perspective). Fleets of Peruvian ships, the '*peruleros*', joined the Mexican galleons in search of oriental products. A letter from a Spanish official in Lima to Philip II in 1594 explains the motivation for this frenzied activity: 'A man can clothe his wife in Chinese silks for two hundred reales, whereas he could not provide her clothing of Spanish silks with two hundred pesos' (quoted in Borah, 1954, 122). An eight-to-one price differential is no doubt an exaggeration (a ratio of three-to-one is more common in the literature), but any sizeable price disparity was not about to go unnoticed; the Pacific commercial network seriously disrupted the Atlantic monopoly of the *Casa de Contratacion* because silk was supplied much cheaper. Merchant complaints in Seville persuaded Philip II to issue a series of decrees to control the Pacific trade. In 1591 commercial relations between Peru, Guatemala, Panama and the Philippines were forbidden. In 1593 a limit of 300,000 pesos on merchandise from Manila and 600,000 pesos from Acapulco was imposed. The trade between Peru and Mexico was interrupted by a 1631 order; the order was repeated in 1634. Profits were formidable, however, and illicit relations between the two viceroyalties continued with the port of Realejo serving as the trading port (Yuste Lopez, 1984, 30). The Pacific trade provided such lucrative profits that every conceivable means of corruption and smuggling was invoked to evade Crown control.

The Crown also attempted to interdict the silk–silver trade in Asia. In 1633, after the King had issued a decree forbidding trade between Macao and Manila, Spanish galleons used any pretext to visit Macao to buy silks and 'a single galleon usually brought about half a million silver dollars for this contraband' (Boxer, 1948, 136). This amount of silver in a single ship – equal to conservative estimates of an entire year's exports out of Acapulco (to be discussed in the next section) – hints at a vigorous commercial relationship between merchants in Mexico and Manila. The secretary of Portuguese India observed in 1634–5 that the trade between Macao and Manila was permanent (Magalhaes Godinho, 1984, 1: 133).

Entrepreneurs overlooked no avenue by which to profit in transporting silver to China, including via the direct Pacific route. Spain maintained legal control over the best ports on either side of the Pacific: 'Manila had probably the best harbor in the Far East, as excellent a western terminus of the navigation as Acapulco was the eastern' (Schurz, 1959, 29). The problem was that the great distance precluded actual Crown control over the Pacific trade. Smuggling and corruption ran rampant. Spanish merchants had trouble competing via the Atlantic, but attempts at prohibiting competition in the Pacific were futile and prodigious quantities of silk flowed eastward out of Manila. In exchange, thousands of tons of silver were shipped westward out of Acapulco and into the Asian marketplace in the seventeenth century.

QUANTITIES OF SILVER

Atlantic trade has been studied extensively, yet controversy persists concerning estimates of the amount of silver flowing to (and through) Europe during the early-modern period. Pacific trade has mostly been ignored by historians, on the other hand, so it is not surprising that reliable estimates of quantities of silver flowing to (and through) the Philippines during the sixteenth and seventeenth centuries do not exist. Many authors recognize that the Manila trade was significant, especially in the late sixteenth and early seventeenth centuries. A large portion of the trade was contraband, however, which explains measurement difficulties. John J. TePaske (1983, 437) has surveyed this literature and concludes that the contraband trade was substantial: 'That the Philippines siphoned off large sums of silver from the New World cannot be denied, but measuring that flow is virtually impossible.' Official records by definition exclude contraband, so how is one to estimate the size of the overall Philippines trade?

TePaske's figures, taken from Earl J. Hamilton's work, are divided into two categories. First is the '*situado*', a subsidy sent in silver by Mexican authorities to support the Manila administration. *Situado* payments averaged 200,000 pesos annually overall, although in the first half of the seventeenth century the Philippines received a quarter of all bullion shipped out of New Spain 'and during the 1640s, perhaps in response to the Dutch threat in the islands, over 40% of Mexican surplus income' flowed to Manila as *situado* payments (TePaske, 1983, 434). Also based on Hamilton's work, TePaske estimates private remittances alone to the Philippines at 316,693 pesos annually (8,095 kg) between 1591 and 1660. In a recent survey of the literature, Ward Barrett (1990, 249) uses TePaske's tables and figures from Humboldt's *Political Essays* to generate a higher estimate of private remittances to Manila, 463,281 pesos (11.86 tons) annually between 1581 and 1700. Basically, TePaske estimates overall (both the *situado* and private) remittances at about 517,000 pesos per year while Barrett elevates the total to about 660,000 pesos per year. Barrett does point out a glaring discrepancy, however, between production figures in Spanish America (based on figures from Humboldt, Soetbeer, Merril and Ridgeway) and Morineau's upwardly revised shipments to Europe. Production exceeded exports over the Atlantic by 40,000 tons, which converts to 5.5 million pesos (135 tons) per year. Barret reasons that the 5.5 millions must have either remained in America or gone to the Philippines (Barrett, 1990, 236). We have previously discussed the powerful institutional magnet in Asia, attracting silver from all parts of the globe. No comparable silver magnet existed in America, on the other hand, so China-via-Manila is the likely candidate for the receipt of millions of pesos annually. Keep in mind that 5.5 million pesos per year to Manila is roughly ten times greater than the conservative estimates of TePaske and Barrett.

Is it possible that over 5 million pesos per year traversed the Pacific? Supporting evidence does exist for such lofty figures around the turn of the century. In 1602 the Cabildo of Mexico City claimed that 5 million pesos (127.8 tons) annually went to Manila and that an astonishing 12 million pesos (306.7 tons) was shipped in the single year of 1597 (Borah, 1954, 123). It is important to remember that these figures have not been confirmed by other sources and that the Cabildo of Mexico City may have exaggerated for political reasons. In any case, most authors seem to have accepted as fact that the large shipments of the early period declined dramatically as the seventeenth century progressed. This assumption appeared plausible for a couple of reasons: first, people used to think that New World production declined dramatically during the seventeenth century and, second, the Pacific trade suffered disruptions because of war with the Dutch.[10] This line of thought seemed to be confirmed by Pierre Chaunu, based on his study of the '*almojarifazgo*' taxes, who identified three phases in the Manila trade: (a) continuous increase until 1616–20; (b) a high plateau with slight decline after 1620; and (c) a precipitous fall after 1640 (Chaunu, 1960, 250). His estimates were consistent with the old idea that there was a general decline in the production of silver mines in Peru and Mexico (Chaunu, 1951, 460).

American production did not, of course, decline throughout the 1600s. It mostly grew; and when decline did come late in the seventeenth century, it was far more gradual than had been customarily reported in the literature. The work of Morineau and others has taught us that silver flows over the Atlantic grew over the seventeenth century (taken as a whole). It seems logical to consider the possibility that the Pacific trade may have grown as well – rather than shrinking – during the seventeenth century. Not all Western scholars accept the conservative TePaske–Barrett estimates of 515,000–600,000 pesos per annum. According to Cross (1983, 412), an average of 2–3 million pesos (53,000–79,000 kg pure silver) was sent *with official sanction* from Peru to Mexico between 1580 and 1610. According to Borah (1954, 88, 123), inclusion of the contraband trade at that time raises the total to more than 100,000 kg annually (i.e., more than 4 million pesos). There was no reason to ship silver from Peru to Mexico, other than to forward it on to Asia via the Manila galleons, so there seems to be indirect evidence of millions of pesos in silver annually over the Pacific in the seventeenth century.

Research from the Asian side of the Pacific support the contention that the Manila trade may not have declined over the seventeenth century. Han-Sheng Chuan, using documents collected by Blair and Robertson (1903–9), provides figures which indicate that the quantities of silver crossing the Pacific did not decline. Chuan quotes letters and reports sent by friars and Spanish officers to the central government in Madrid. His estimates are shown in Table 3.1 (Chuan, 1969, 79). Chuan's figures are somewhat higher than those of Schurz, who stated: 'There can also be little doubt that the average for the more prosperous periods was about 2,000,000 pesos or even more were quite possible, though not common.' Schurz recognized that during the war with the Dutch, and when there were other adverse circumstances, the silver cargo could have fallen under 1 million pesos (Schur, 1959, 190). Chuan's numbers do not indicate a secular decline in shipments of silver to the Philippines; rather, there is a steady yearly average of around 2 million pesos throughout the century. The absence of a downturn in Chuan's work is consistent with other trends and indicators of the Manila trade.

The city of Manila was an entrepôt with no purpose other than the silver–silk trade. If the trade experienced secular decline, then why did the city contain 42,000 inhabitants in the middle of the seventeenth century (Wolf, 1982, 153), approximately the same population as Barcelona, Valladolid, Danzig, Vienna, Marseille and other major trading centres with broader-based economies at the dawn of that century (de Vries, 1984, Appendix 1; Mols, 1977, 42–3)? Of Manila's 42,000 people, around 30,000 were Chinese and 12,000 Spaniards (Schurz, 1959, 81). The trade must have been huge, because there were only 6,000 Portuguese male nationals who went out to the *Estado da India*, by comparison, and only 10,000 Portuguese male nationals over-

Table 3.1 Quantities of silver crossing the Pacific

Year	Amount (pesos)	Amount (metric tons)
1598	1,000,000	25.56
1601	2,000,000	51.12
1602	2,000,000	51.12
1604	2,500,000	63.90
1620	3,000,000	76.68
1633	2,000,000	51.12
1688	2,000,000	51.12
1698	2,000,000	51.12
1699	2,070,000	52.50

seas in the entire world (Boxer, 1969, 19–20). No doubt more than half the Spaniards in Manila were males, so they must have at least equalled their Portuguese counterparts in Asia in the seventeenth century. But the Spaniards were concentrated in Manila and there were two-and-a-half times as many Chinese in Manila as Spaniards! Considering the strict dependence between the galleons and the prosperity of the city, it must have been the periodic arrival of silver during the seventeenth century that sustained the community, partly supplied by Philippine natives but mainly by Chinese merchants. Fernand Braudel situates the Philippines in a global perspective: 'The centre of gravity of this huge super-world-economy became stabilized in the East Indies, with their busy ports of Bantam, Atjeh, Malacca and – much later – Batavia and Manila.' And he continues: 'We are gradually becoming more and more clearly aware of "a network of maritime traffic comparable in volume and variety to that of the Mediterranean or of the northern and Atlantic coast of Europe"' (Braudel, 1986, 3: 486–7).

Chuan's claim that an annual flow of more than 2 million pesos in silver persisted through the seventeenth century seems reasonable. If anything, future research will render these numbers overly conservative. It may be helpful to digress momentarily to gain perspective by comparing the magnitude of the annual Pacific trade (i.e., +51.12 tons of silver) with that flowing simultaneously to Asia out of Europe at that time. According to Steensgaard (1974, 87), Portuguese exports 'for the projected pepper purchase at the end of the 16th century lay at 150–200,000 cruzados', which converts to a maximum of 8.47 metric tons of silver per year. According to Gaastra (1983, 451), during the second half of the seventeenth century the Dutch East India Company sent 1.6 million florins to the Orient; Morineau's (1974, 773) calculation is 50 per cent higher, at 2.4 million florins, which is equivalent to 24.93 tons of silver. The English East India Company sent a total of 702,852 kg of silver to Asia between 1660 and 1700, an average of 17.57 tons per year (Chaudhuri, 1978, 177). If we add the figures for Portugal in the early period to those reported for the Dutch and British East India Companies combined for the later period, the total is just over 50 tons of silver per year. This is approximately the same as the amount Chuan estimates for the Manila trade throughout the seventeenth century (2 million pesos or 51.12 tons). While the average quantity of silver passing on to Asia via all of Europe was probably at least triple this Manila estimate (Attman, 1986, 78), the Pacific trade may have been equal to the Europe–Asia trade of the Portuguese and English and Dutch East India Companies combined.

SUMMARY AND CONCLUSIONS

Silver's migration in the early-modern period constituted the genesis of intercontinental trade at the global level. The cause of this phenomenon on the supply side is obvious: extraordinarily rich mines were discovered in Japan and Spanish America and new technologies for extraction of the metal were implemented. Production costs dropped and the boom was on. There would be no boom without customers, however, and the biggest collective buyer of all was giant China, whose paper money system fell apart in the fifteenth century. First, the merchant sector converted to silver, followed by local tax jurisdictions. Eventually, the Ming acquiesced to silver's dominance; this was acknowledged in the form of the single-whip tax system implemented in the second half of the sixteenth century. The white metal had 'conquered' the world's largest economy.

China's shift to a silver base affected not just domestic affairs, but its entire Asian tributary economy, one which coexisted symbiotically with commercial trade relations. Private trade and tribute activity were so intertwined, in fact, that it was sometimes difficult to distinguish between them:

> [The Ming tribute] system was often, in effect, only an outward form for very considerable foreign trade. In many cases foreign merchants, especially those from Central Asia, presented themselves as the bearers of fictitious tribute from imaginary states solely for the purpose of conducting trade.
>
> (Rodzinski, 1979, 197)

For our purposes, the important point is that the entire Chinese tribute-trade system evolved into the silver camp:

> The tribute trade zone [of East and South-East Asia] formed an integrated 'silver zone' in which silver was used as the medium of trade settlement. The key to the functioning of the tribute trade as a system was the huge 'demand' for commodities outside of China and the difference between prices inside and outside of China.... On the whole, this tribute trade system took on the attributes of a silver circulating zone with multilateral channels of trade settlement in which silver was used as medium.
>
> (Hamashita, 1988, 17)

So Asian demand for silver encompassed more than China's quarter of the world; perhaps one-third or one-half of the world's economy had converted to a silver system. East Asia experienced technological advance, population growth and urbanization during this period, all of which augmented the demand for silver. Small wonder that silver migrated to East Asia in such massive quantities.

Silver poured into the mainland through all important trade routes. China's primary source in the late sixteenth and early seventeenth centuries was Japan, which shipped as much as 200 tons per year at times, but fell off in the second half of the seventeenth century.[11] Attman's conservative figures indicate that the flow of silver through Europe into Asia averaged at least 150 tons annually in the seventeenth century. Chuan says that an average of over 50 tons per year traversed the Pacific via the Manila galleons; and his numbers may be low.

The economic and political impact of this silver trade around the globe was immense. The worldwide 'price revolution' would not have occurred in the absence of the Chinese factor.[12] Silver affected all corners of the globe, but none more so than Japan or Spain, the two countries controlling silver-mine production. Under the circumstances outlined above – high initial value relative to low production costs – the mines produced prodigious profits. American profits financed the Spanish Empire; when the inevitable evaporation of mining profits occurred, Spain faded as the dominant power in Europe (Flynn, 1982). Japanese mining profits helped finance consolidation of that country under the Tokugawa shogunate. This was instrumental in Japan's withdrawal from China's tributary system; market-orientated reforms were implemented, followed by centuries of *Pax Tokugawa* (Flynn, 1991). Imperial Spain used mining profits to attack the emerging capitalistic powers in north-west Europe. Tokugawa Japan used her mining profits to establish capitalism in Asia. It is hard to see how either of these developments could have occurred in the absence of Chinese demand for silver. Elimination of the world's largest customer would have devastated profits at points of production.

William Atwell (1977; 1982; 1986) has for years emphasized the importance of New World silver on commercial and political developments inside China. Jack Goldstone (1991, 371) now challenges Atwell's interpretation, insisting that domestic and *inter*-Asian influences – rather than those from Europe – explain structural changes inside of Ming and Qing China. Goldstone's (1991, 371–5) criticism of conventional monetary explanations of the impact of Western silver on China is cogent, yet his views are compatible with the microeconomic and monetary argument of this essay.[13] Our argument complements those of both Atwell and Goldstone by emphasizing that, during silver's era on the global centre-stage, developments inside Asia impacted the West even more profoundly than any reciprocal Western influence on Asia. Just as both blades of a scissors are required, silver's demand side (China) and its supply side (New World and Japan) must be placed in global perspective. The silver trade affected the entire world. Scholars should continue to debate the impact of the West on Asia, but it is also time to consider the profound impact of China on the West.

Wallerstein (1974) and other advocates of 'world-systems' thinking would have us believe that the early-modern economy was not yet global. There are purported to have been several 'world systems', connected only superficially via inconsequential 'luxury' trade. Our analysis contrasts sharply with this image. Integration of the world economy embraced all continents for the first time, beginning with global silver trade in the sixteenth century. That trade played an integral role in worldwide price inflation, the rise and fall of Spain, the emergence of Japan, the birth of the Pacific Rim economy, and a host of other structural developments.

That intercontinental trade mainly involved luxury goods is a truism. Given the state of transportation technology, how else could expensive voyages be financed but by shipping high-value, non-perishable goods?[14] The same principle holds for long-distance trade today; falling transportation costs keep bringing ever-lower-priced goods into the fold. In general, trade from the late sixteenth century to today is best viewed as a technological and economic continuum. Early-modern silver trade around the globe represented the birth of the 'world economy'. Much of what passes for isolated, local history was in fact determined by forces which can only be understood in the context of world history.

NOTES

1. See Liang (1970). A more detailed account can be found in Huang (1974).
2. Tashiro (1982, 288–92) explains that Chinese and Dutch merchants dealt directly with the Bakufu in the seventeenth century, rather than through normal foreign relations: from 'the Chinese point of view, the Nagasaki trade was an exercise in smuggling' (288).
3. It is frequently stated that China did not experience price inflation, a 'price revolution' similar to that in Europe and elsewhere (see, for example, Kellenbenz, 1981, 325). This conclusion seems correct only when measuring prices in terms of a bronze unit-of-account money. When Chinese rice prices are converted into 'silver-content prices', as is the custom in European historiography, Chinese prices exhibit an inflationary

trend like that in Europe and elsewhere. See Cartier (1981) and Goldstone (1991, 359–60) for full details.

4. See Flynn (1982) and Flynn (1984).
5. The Ming had good reason to resist China's conversion to a silver-based economy, according to Goldstone, because land taxes were 'fossilized' (i.e. fixed) in terms of payments in silver, while imperial expenses (in terms of silver) mushroomed. Inflation-adjusted taxes fell at the central-government level, in other words, leading ultimately to the overthrow of the Ming in 1644: 'The outcome was a political crisis rooted in fiscal bankruptcy. The crisis was not due to over-taxation relative to the available resources of the society. In fact, the government's share of national wealth diminished. Rather, the crisis was due to an overall under-taxation as inflexible land-tax systems failed to capture growing output and tax evasion became increasingly common among influential elites' (Goldstone, 1991, 374–5).
6. See Flynn (1986) for an unconventional microeconomic theory in support of Chaudhuri's argument with Kristof Glamann.
7. In terms of theory, Flynn (1986) explains the arbitrage portion of the West-to-East flow of silver via demand and supply analysis. For a more complete discussion of 'non-arbitrage world trade' in silver, including a graphical depiction of the process, see Flynn (1991, 343–7).
8. According to Cross (1983, 402), registered output in Potosi fell from 68,759 kg of silver in 1565 to 28,633 in 1572. There was a radical transformation of the area in 1573 with implementation of the mercury-amalgam process.
9. See Doherty and Flynn (1989) for an explanation of the cause of this gradual decline in the value of silver.
10. The argument that war with the Dutch disrupted trade in Asia cannot be applied after 1647; Spain settled with the Dutch then and silver shipments resumed (Glamann, 1981, 52).
11. See Innes (1980), esp. ch. 6.
12. See Doherty and Flynn (1989) for an explanation of the production-point-of-view interpretation of the price revolution.
13. Goldstone's (1991) criticism of monetary explanations for price inflation in China is twofold: (a) Western silver comprised an insignificant fraction of China's silver stock; and (b) there was a 'chronology problem', in that periods of silver imports did not match at all with Chinese price trends. For a discussion of why such silver and price trends are consistent with our (unconventional) microeconomic view of silver, see Doherty and Flynn (1989); Flynn (1986); and Flynn (1991).
14. While it is generally true that long-distance trade involved high-value goods, lower-value goods were sometimes shipped great distances too. Japanese copper, for example, rivalled Swedish copper in seventeenth-century Europe (Glamann, 1981, 174).

REFERENCES

Attman, Artur (1986) *American Bullion in the European World Trade, 1600–1800*, Uppsala: Almqvist & Wicksell Tryckeri.

Atwell, William S. (1977) 'Notes on silver, foreign trade, and the late Ming economy', *Ch'ing-shih wen-t'i*, 3: 1–33.

—— (1982) 'International bullion flows and the Chinese economy *circa* 1530–1650', *Past and Present*, no. 95: 68–90.

—— (1986) 'Some observations on the 'seventeenth-century crisis' in China and Japan', *Journal of Asian Studies*, 45(2): 223–44.

Barrett, Ward (1990) 'World bullion flows, 1450–1800', in James D. Tracy (ed.) 'The Rise of Merchant Empires: Long-distance Trade in the Early Modern World, 1350–1750, Cambridge: Cambridge University Press, 224–54.

Blair, E.H. and Robertson, J.A. (1903–9) *The Philippine Islands*, 55 vols, Cleveland, Ohio: Arthur H. Clarke.

Borah, W. (1954) *Early Colonial Trade and Navigation between Mexico and Peru*, Berkeley and Los Angeles, Cal.: University of California Press.

Boxer, Charles R. (1948) *Fidalgos in the Far East*, The Hague: Martinus Nijhoff.

—— (1969) *Four Centuries of Portuguese Expansion*, Berkeley and Los Angeles.

—— (1970) 'Plata es sangre: sidelights on the drain of Spanish-American silver in the Far East, 1550–1700', *Philippine Studies*, 18: 457–78.

Braudel, Fernand (1981–6), *Civilization and Capitalism, 15th to 18th centuries*, 3 vols, New York: Harper & Row.

Cartier, Michel (1981) 'Les importations de metaux monetaires en Chine: essai sur la conjuncture chinoise', *Annales E.S.C.*, 36: 454–66.

Chaudhuri, K.N. (1978) *The Trading World of Asia and the English East India Company, 1660–1760*, Cambridge: Cambridge University Press.

Chaunu, Pierre (1951), 'Le Galion de Manille: grandeur et decadence d'une route de la soie', *Annales*, 4: 447–62.

—— (1960) *Les Philippines et le Pacifique des Iberiques (XVIe, XVIIe, XVIIIe, siècles)*, Paris: SEVPEN.

Chuan, Han-Sheng (1969) 'The inflow of American silver into China from the late Ming to the mid-Ch'ing Period', *Journal of the Institute of Chinese Studies of the Chinese University of Hong Kong*, 2: 61–75.

Cross, Harry E. (1983) 'South American bullion production and export, 1550–1750', in J.F. Richards (ed.), *Precious Metals in the Later Medieval and Early Modern Worlds*, Durham, N.C.: Carolina Academic Press, 397–424.

de Vries, Jan (1984) *European Urbanisation 1500–1800*, Cambridge, Mass.: Harvard University Press.

Doherty, Kerry W. and Flynn, D.O. (1989), 'A microeconomic quantity theory of money and the price revolution', in E. van Cauwenberghe (ed.) *Precious Metals, Coinage and the Changing Structures in Latin America, Europe and Asia*, Leuven: KUL Press.

Fairbank, John K. (1992) *China: A New History*, Cambridge, Mass.: Harvard University Press.

Flynn, Dennis O. (1982), 'Fiscal crisis and the decline of Spain (Castile)', *Journal of Economic History*, 42: 139–47.

—— (1984) 'El desarrollo del primer capitalismo a pesar de los metales preciosos del Nuevo Mundo: una interpretación anti-Wallerstein de la España Imperial', *Revista de Historia Economica*, 2: 29–57.

—— (1986) 'The microeconomics of silver and East–West trade in the early modern period', in W. Fischer, R.W. McInnis and J. Schneider (eds) *The Emergence of a World Economy, 1500–1914*, Stuttgart: Franz Steiner Verlag Wiesbaden, 37–60.

—— (1991) 'Comparing the Tokugawa shogunate with Hapsburg Spain: two silver-based empires in a global setting', in J. Tracy (ed.) *The Political Economy of Merchant Empires*, Cambridge: Cambridge University Press.

Gaastra, F.S. (1983) 'The exports of precious metals from Europe to Asia by the Dutch East India Company, 1602–1795', in J.F. Richards (ed.) *Precious Metals in the Later Medieval and Early Modern Worlds*, Durham, N.C.: Carolina Academic Press, 447–76.

Gernet, Jacques (1982) *A History of Chinese Civilization*, Cambridge: Cambridge University Press.

Glamann, Kristof (1981) *Dutch–Asiatic Trade, 1620–1740*, 2nd edn., The Hague: Martinus Nijhoff.

Goldstone, Jack (1991) *Revolution and Rebellion in the Early Modern World*, Berkeley, Cal.: University of California Press.

Hamashita, Takeshi (1988) *The Tribute System and Modern Asia*, Memoirs of the Research Department of the Toyo Bunko, no. 46, Tokyo.

Huang, Ray (1974) *Taxation and Governmental Finance in Sixteenth-century Ming China*, Cambridge: Cambridge University Press.

Innes, Robert LeRoy (1980) *The Door Ajar: Japan's Foreign Trade in the Seventeenth Century*, Ph.D. dissertation, University of Michigan.

Kellenbenz, Hermann (1981) 'Final remarks: production and trade of gold, silver, copper, and lead from 1450 to 1750', in H. Kellenbenz (ed.) *Precious Metals in the Age of Expansion*, Stuttgart: Klett-Cotta, 307–61.

Liang, Fang-chung (1970) *The Single-whip Method of Taxation in China*, Cambridge, Mass.: Harvard University Press.

Magalhaes Godinho, V. (1984) *Os Descobrimentos e a Economía Mundial*, 2nd edn, 4 vols, Lisbon: Eitorial Presença.

Mols, Roger (1977) 'Population in Europe, 1500–1700', in C.M. Cipolla (ed.) *The Fontana Economic History of Europe*, vol. 2: *The Sixteenth and Seventeenth Centuries*, Glasgow: Collins, 15–82.

Morineau, Michel (1974) 'Quelques remarques sur l'abondance monetaire aux Provinces-Unies', *Annals E.S.C.*, 29(5): 767–76.

Rodzinski, Witold (1979) *A History of China*, Oxford: Pergamon Press.

Schurz, Lyle W. (1959) *The Manila Galleon*, New York: E.P. Dutton.

Steensgaard, Niels (1974) *The Asian Trade Revolution of the Seventeenth Century: The East India Companies and the Decline of the Caravan Trade*, Chicago, Ill.: University of Chicago Press.

Tashiro, Kazui (1982) 'Foreign relations during the Edo period: Sakoku reexamined', *Journal of Japanese Studies*, 8(2): 283–306.

—— (1989) 'Exports of Japan's silver to China via Korea and changes in the Tokugawa monetary system during the 17th and 18th centuries', in E. van Cauwenberghe (ed.) *Precious Metals, Coinage and the Changes of Monetary Structures in Latin America, Europe and Asia (Late Middle Ages–Early Modern Times)*, Leuven: KUL Press, 99–116.

TePaske, John J. (1983) 'New World silver, Castile and the Philippines, 1590–1800', in J.F. Richards (ed.) *Precious Metals in the Later Medieval and Early*

Modern Worlds, Durham, N.C.: Carolina Academic Press, 425–46.

Wallerstein, Immanuel (1974) *The Modern World-system: Capitalist Agriculture and the Origins of the European World-economy in the Sixteenth Century*, New York: Academic Press.

Wolfe, Eric (1982) *Europe and the People Without History*, Berkeley and Los Angeles, Cal., and London: University of California Press.

Yamamura, Kozo and Kamiki, Tetsuo (1983) 'Silver mines and Sung coins: a monetary history of medieval and modern Japan in international perspective', in J.F. Richards (ed.) *Precious Metals in the Later Medieval and Early Modern Worlds*, Durham, N.C.: Carolina Academic Press, 329–62.

Yuste López, C. (1984) *El Comercio de la Nueva España con Filipinas, 1590–1785*, Mexico: INAN.

4

THE TRIBUTE TRADE SYSTEM AND MODERN ASIA

Takeshi Hamashita

INTRODUCTION

It has long been the practice to analyse modern Asia from the viewpoint of nations and international relationships. Through this bipartite framework, much historiographical labour has been expended examining the degree of so-called 'nation-building' and the acceptance of 'international' law in the respective Asian countries. This approach has also been understood to reveal the degree of 'modernization' of Asian countries.

After much controversy concerning the adaptability of this Western-orientated modernization model to Asia, however, it has also been argued that 'areas' or 'regions' – an intermediate category between the nation and the world generally – should be analysed in their full historical meaning. In fact, the region ΄is an historical reality which encompasses a variety of social ties not adequately dealt with under the nation–international framework.

In studies of economic history, the regional economies which mediate national and international economies should indeed be given much more weight. At the same time, those carrying out regional studies should avoid limiting themselves to local matters which constitute only a part of the overall picture.[1]

Using the regional studies approach, it is necessary to reconstruct the whole historical process of modern Asia. That is, the history of modern Asia needs to be clarified, not in terms of the 'stages of development' of the Western modernization model, but in terms of the complex of interrelationships within the region itself, in the light of Asian self-conceptions.

Generally speaking, Asian history is the history of a unified system characterized by internal tribute or tribute-trade relations, with China at the centre. This tribute system is the premise of the 'modern' Asia which has emerged in the Asia region and is reflected in several aspects of contemporary Asian history.[2]

STRUCTURE OF THE TRIBUTE SYSTEM

Looked at from one point of view, the tribute 'system' was a relationship between two countries, China and the tribute-paying country, with tribute and imperial 'gifts' as the medium, and the Chinese capital as the 'centre'. Modifying this perspective, however, is the fact that the 'system' did not function in this single dimension only, but involved several other lesser or satellite tribute relationships not directly concerning China, and forming a considerably more complex system of reciprocal relations. The tribute system in reality embraced both inclusive and competitive relations extending in a web over a large area. The case of the Liu-ch'iu or Ryūkyus, for example, shows China and Japan in a competitive relationship, because the Liu-ch'iu kings sent missions to both Peking and Yedo during the Ch'ing period.

In the case of Korea, too, we find that, while it was most certainly a tributary of China, it also sent missions to Japan. And Vietnam required tribute missions from Laos. Thus all these countries maintained satellite tribute relations with each other and constituted links in a continuous chain.[3]

The other fundamental feature of the system that must be kept sight of is its basis in commercial transactions. The tribute system in fact paralleled, or was in symbiosis with, a network of commercial trade relations. For example, trade between Siam, Japan and southern China had long been maintained on the basis of profits from the tribute missions, even when much of the non-tribute trade was scarcely remunerative. In the eighteenth century, when the rice trade from Siam to Kuang-tung and Hsia-men became unprofitable, the traders shifted their emphasis to Liu-ch'iu and Nagasaki in Japan, thus maintaining and even strengthening the general multilateral trade relationship.[4] The story of the commercial penetration of Chinese merchants into South-East Asia and the emigration of 'overseas Chinese' is historically intertwined with the building of this trade network. Commercial expansion and the tribute-trade network developed together. Trade relations in East and South-East Asia expanded as tribute relations expanded.[5]

It should also be noted that this tribute trade functioned as an intermediate trade between European countries and the countries of East Asia. In the records of trade from Holland and Portugal to China in

(a) The Chinese world order

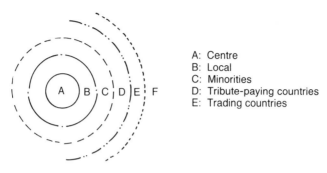

A: Centre
B: Local
C: Minorities
D: Tribute-paying countries
E: Trading countries

(b) Tribute relation   (c) Satellite–tribute relation

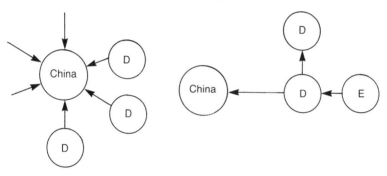

(d) Tribute-trade system

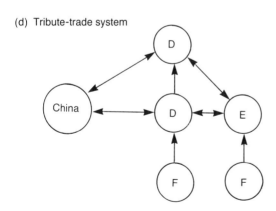

Figure 4.1 Structure of the tribute-trade system

93

the K'ang Hsi period, we find listed several cotton textile items made in Europe, as well as woollens. European cotton textiles can also be found on lists of tribute articles from Sulu to China in the fifth year of Yung-Ch'eng; for example, there is at least one article from Europe, and Western shirting and great Holland wool appear in the records of tribute from Siam in the eighth year of Yung-Ch'eng (1730).[6] These examples show that the tribute system played an intermediary role in trade. Tribute relationships in fact constituted a network of tribute trade of a multilateral type, absorbing commodities from outside the network.

These aspects of the tribute trade as a system were accentuated with the transition from Ming to Ch'ing (sixteenth to seventeenth centuries). The developments may be summarized as follows:

1   The ideal of Sinocentric unity was expanded and consolidated, with Korea, Japan, and Vietnam being particularly strongly affected.
2   Tribute trade was expanded through the participation of European countries.
3   Private trade expanded along with the tribute trade, and trade-related institutions such as trade settlement and tax collection were simultaneously elaborated.

As for the Sinocentric international order, Sinocentrism stimulated the emergence of nationalism among China's tributary countries. Vietnam, for example, began to require tribute from Laos, and Korea insisted on the continuation of orthodox Sinocentrism under the Ch'ing dynasty, which was initially seen as a 'barbarian' dynasty by Korea. And Vietnam criticized China when forced to change its national name from Nan-yue to Yue-nan merely because a Nan-yue kingdom had previously existed in ancient China. These phenomena demonstrate how tributary countries began to take on national identities *vis-à-vis* China, based on their own understandings of Sinocentrism.[7] Thus the ideal of Sinocentrism was not solely a preoccupation of China but was substantially shared throughout the tribute zone. Nationalism was born in Asia from within the tribute system and through common ideals of tribute relationships. Satellite tribute zones surrounding the Chinese-dominated core had an historical existence of their own which continued down to their own modernization. These transformations are shown schematically in Figures 4.1 (a)–(d).

A much closer investigation of the contents of the tribute trade will be necessary in order to shed light on the internal sources of motive energy of these networks and to flesh out a picture of how they worked as an historical system. For the moment, we may classify aspects of the tribute trade in a three-fold manner:

1 the two-way relationship between formal tribute articles carried by tribute embassies, and 'gifts' from China;
2 licensed trade in the Peking Assembly Hall by the limited group of merchants allowed to accompany tribute embassies – the amount of commodities traded also being limited;
3 frontier trade between merchants along China's land frontiers and in specified Chinese ports.

The forms and frequency of tribute missions varied according to the degree of intimacy between the various tribute countries and China. The treatment of tribute missions by China also differed.

(a) The frequency of tribute from the 'native' tribes and districts was stipulated variously as once a year, once every two years or once every three years. Their tribute missions were allowed to open markets in the Assembly Hall in Peking, which fell under the jurisdiction of the Board of Ceremonies, and their major tribute articles were horses and gold and silver vessels. In return, the Chinese side 'gave' 100 taels of paper currency per horse. As recompense for simply demonstrating submission by way of tribute, the Chinese side granted 100 taels of paper currency and three bolts of satin to third- and fourth-rank officials, and 80 taels of paper currency and three bolts of satin to fifth-rank officials.[8] These rewards for tribute submission were comparatively large.

(b) In the early Ming dynasty, the Yung-lê Emperor carried out a 'pacification' policy in the north-east or Manchurian area. Later, Nü-chih groups in the area accepted Ch'ing control, were organized into a 'Pacification Guard' and established tribute relations with the Ch'ing dynasty. This type of tribute relation was virtually compulsory, similar to the tax payments of other subjects. Tribute articles consisted mainly of horses and fur products. The return 'gifts' of the Ch'ing court were divided into two groups. The first group of gifts was for the embassy proper; the institutional code of the Ch'ing stipulated that the governor of the Nü-chih was to receive four bolts of satin plus two bolts of silk commuted into paper currency, and the guards a fixed number of bolts of various grades of silk, some of it also commuted into currency.[9] The other group of gifts was really recompense for items brought in tribute; again, a fixed number of bolts of silk, some of it commuted into paper currency, was stipulated for each tribute horse, and one bolt of silk was to be given for each four pieces of fur products. Thus, 'gifts' from the

Ch'ing court were mainly of silk, though a certain part of this was replaced by paper currency. Besides these gifts, trade transactions in the mandated markets both in Peking and Fu-shun also served to increase exchange with the north-east.

(c) Korea maintained the closest relationship of all the tributaries with China. Tribute missions from Korea to the Ming court were initiated in the second year of Hong-wu, when the King of Korea sent an embassy reporting his enthronement and asked China to recognize his status. After the Yung-lê period, Korea paid tribute every year, sending gold and silver utensils, white cotton textiles, various hemp textiles, white paper and ginseng, as well as stud horses as stipulated in the Ming code. The prescribed gifts from China included books and musical instruments as requested by the embassy up to a certain number, and gifts to members of the embassy and to the King of Korea amounting to 100 taels of silver, four bolts of cotton textiles and twelve bolts of hemp textiles.[10]

After a brief pause in tribute missions during the period of chaos at the end of the Ming dynasty, the Yi dynasty in Korea started paying tribute again in 1636 and reopened the market at Yi-chou on the border between Korea and China. The first tribute articles to the Ch'ing consisted of 100 taels of gold, 1,000 taels of silver, paper, furs and skins, cotton textiles, medicine (ginseng), rice and other items – twenty-eight categories altogether. It should be noted that the appearance of such items as gold and silver among the tribute coincided with the expanded circulation of silver in China and that silver served alongside silk and brocade as a medium of exchange.[11]

In the tribute transactions here described, the relationship between tribute goods and 'gifts' was substantially one of selling and purchasing. In fact, it is quite legitimate to view tribute exchange as a commercial transaction. Even the Chinese court, then, acted as a party to business transactions. The mode of payment was often Chinese currency, whether paper money or silver. Seen from an economic perspective, tribute was managed as an exchange between seller and buyer, with the 'price' of commodities fixed. Indeed, 'price' standards were determined, albeit loosely, by market prices in Peking.[12] Given the nature of this transaction, it can be shown that the foundation for the whole complex tribute-trade formation was determined by the price structure of China and that the tribute-trade zone formed an integrated 'silver zone' in which silver was used as the medium of trade settlement. The key to the functioning of the tribute trade as a system was the huge 'demand' for commodities outside China and the difference between prices inside and outside China.

The actual working of the system was often a cause for complaint from both the tribute countries and Chinese merchants, because the stipulated 'prices' of tribute commodities often fell below actual market prices. And when China paid in paper currency, the profits accruing from tribute articles were pushed down by debasement, thereby reducing the funds the embassies had to buy Chinese goods. Despite these problems, the private – formal – trade which accompanied tribute embassies expanded, increasing silver circulation and leading to the absorption of silver from both Europe and the Americas. On the whole, this tribute trade system took on the attributes of a silver circulating zone with multilateral channels of trade settlement in which silver was used as a medium.[13]

To sum up, the entire tribute and interregional trade zone had its own structural rules which exercised a systematic control through silver circulation and with the Chinese tribute trade at the centre. This system, encompassing East and South-East Asia was articulated with neighbouring trade zones such as India, the Islamic region and Europe. This is illustrated by the following sections on the tribute trade and country trade, based on original sources.

CHINESE JUNKS AND TRIBUTE TRADE

Of all foreigners, the Chinese are the most numerous in the archipelago. Their junks never fail to bring a large supply of emigrants, and the European trading ships frequently do the same – as many as 450 have been known to sail in a single ship. Many of these return to their own country, 'and the first intention of every emigrant is probably to do so; but circumstances detain a number of them in the islands who, intermarrying with the natives of the country, generate a race inferior in energy and spirit to the original settlers, but speaking the language, wearing the garb, professing the religion, and affecting the manners of the parent country. The Chinese settlers may be described as at once enterprising, keen, laborious, luxurious, sensual, debauched, and pusillanimous. They are most generally engaged in trade, in which they are equally speculative, expert, and judicious. Their superior intelligence and activity have placed in their hands the management of the public revenue, in almost every country of the archipelago, whether ruled by natives or Europeans; and of the traffic of the archipelago with the surrounding foreign states, almost the whole is conducted by them. The principal part of these settlers are in Java, Borneo, Singapore and Penang; but a few scattered families are to be found in every island where the people are in any manner civilized.'[14]

The countries in the four quarters of the world, which send embassies to the emperor of China and pay tribute are Corea, Liúchiú, Laos, Cochinchina, Siam, Sulu, Holland, Burmah, and those of the western ocean; all the other countries have only intercourse and commerce. The periods for all tributary countries to send their tribute, the way for tribute-bearers to travel, and the number composing each embassy is fixed.

Whenever any tribute-bearers arrive, the local officers on the frontier must immediately report the same to the emperor; if the emperor does not permit the embassy to proceed, the said officers (on the frontier) must forward to his majesty the memorial which they have brought from their own government, and report the articles of their tribute; if the emperor permits the embassy to proceed, the said officers must fix its numbers, the ceremonies of their audience, grant them gifts according to the fixed rules, provide for them what is necessary.[15]

If a man would travel from one place to another, he must take two passes with him, the one from the governor, the other from the eunuch or lieutenant. The governor's pass permits him to set out on his journey and takes notice of the name of the traveller, and those also of his company, the age and family of the one and the other; for every body in China, whether a native, or an Arab, or any other foreigner, is obliged to declare all he knows of himself, nor can he possibly be excused the so doing. The eunuch's or lieutenant's pass specifies the quantities of money, or goods, which the traveller and those with him, take along with them.[16]

When merchants enter China by sea, the Chinese seize on their cargo, and convey it to ware-houses; and so put a stop to their business for six months, till the last Merchantman be arrived. Then they take three in ten, or thirty per cent. of each commodity, and return the rest to the merchant. If the Emperor wants any particular thing, his officers have a right to take it preferably to any other person whatsoever; and paying for it to the utmost penny it is valued at, they despatch this business immediately, and without the least injustice.[17]

CHINESE JUNK AND COUNTRY TRADE

The principal part of the junk trade is carried on by the four contiguous provinces of Canton, Fukien, Che-keang, and Kiannan. No foreign trade is permitted with the Island of Formosa; and I have no means of describing the extent of the traffic which may be conducted between China, Corea, and the Luchew Islands. The following are the countries with which China carries on a trade in junks: viz. Japan, the Philippines, the Sooloo Islands, the Celebes, the Moluccas, Borneo, Java, Sumatra, Singapore, Rhio, the east coast of the Malayan Peninsula, Siam, Cohin China, Cambodia, and Tonquin. The ports of China, at which this trade is conducted, are Canton, Tchao-tcheou, Nomhong, Hoei-tcheon, Su-heng, Kongmoon, Changlim, and Hainan, in the province of Canton; Amoy and Chinchew in the province of Fokien; Ningpo and Siang-hai [Shanghai], in the province of Tchekian; and Southceon, in the province of Kiannan. The following may be looked upon as an approximation to the number of junks carrying on trade with different places already enumerated; viz.

	Junks.		Junks.
Japan, 10 junks, two voyages,	20	East Coast of Malay Peninsula,	6
Philippine Islands,	13	Siam,	
Sooloo Islands,	4	Cochin China,	20
Celebes,	2	Cambodia,	9
Borneo,	13	Tonquin,	20
Java,	7	Total,	222
Sumatra,	10		
Singapore,	8		
Rhio,	1		

This statement does not include a great number of small junks belonging to the Island of Hainan, which carry on trade with Tonquin, Cochin China, Cambodia, Siam, and Singapore. Those for Siam amount yearly to about 50, and for the Cochin Chinese dominions, to about 43; these alone would bring the total number of vessels carrying on a direct trade between China and foreign countries to 307. The trade with Japan is confined to the port of Ningpo, in Chekiang, and expressly limited to 10 vessels; but as

			Taels.	Dollars
IMPORTS—COMPANY'S.				
Broad Cloth,	6,652 bales,	687,914 yards, ...	704,743	
Long Ells,	7,525 ditto,	150,186 pieces, ...	765,799	
Camblets,	450 ditto,	4,500 ditto, ...	61,176	
British Cotton				
Piece-Goods,	1,220 ditto,	30,500 ditto, ...	127,260	
Ditto Cotton				
Twist	1,000 ditto,	1,800 peculs, ...	66,090	
Ditto Stuffs, Union Satinets, & Chintzes, (experimental,) ...			4,806	
Ditto Iron,	1,202 tons,	20,202 peculs,	23,273	
Lead,	1,110 ditto,	18,655 ditto, ...	57,830	
			1,810,977	
Cotton, Beng. 23,824 bales,	53,719 peculs, taels 628,507			
Ditto, Bom. 21,978 ditto, 62,528 ditto,		697,972	1,326,479	
Ebony,	823 logs	141 ditto,	54	
			3,137,510	4,357,653

IMPORTS—ON PRIVATE ACCOUNT.

Cotton, Beng.	43,751 peculs, at 11t. 7m. p. pc.	511,887		
Ditto, Mad.	4,229 ditto, at 12t. 7m.	53,708		
Ditto, Bom.	278,413 ditto, at 10t. 6m.	2,951,178		
			3,516,773	4,884,407
Opium, P. & B. 7,511 chts. at 639 drs. p.ch. drs.		4,799,529	Drs.	
Ditto, M. & D. 10,102½ chts. at 675 do. p.ch. do.		6,819,187		
17,613½ chests			11,618,716	
Sandal Wood,	3,680 peculs,	at 11¼, drs per pecul, ...	41,400	
Pepper,	23,122 ditto,	8¼, ...	190,757	
Ratans,	13,052 ditto,	3, ...	39,156	
Betel-nut,	57,025 ditto,	2½, ...	142,562	
Putchuck,	2,105 ditto,	13½, ...	28,417	
Olibanum,	4,444 ditto,	4, ...	17,776	
Ebony,	2,634 ditto,	3, ...	7,902	
Broad Cloth,	9,574 pieces,	28 drs. per piece, ...	268,072	
Long Ells,	9,600 ditto,	10½, ...	100,800	
Worleys,	639 ditto,	12, ...	7,668	
Camblets,	571 ditto,	23½, ...	13,418	
Cotton Piece-				
Goods,	45,422 ditto,	4¾, ...	215,754	
Printed Ditto,		value	82,443	
Cotton Twist,	1,344 peculs,	40, ...	53,760	
Cochineal,	42 ditto,	340, ...	14,280	
Lead,	3,893 ditto,	4, ...	15,572	
Steel,	1,486 ditto,	4¾, ...	7,058	
Iron,	9,735 ditto,	2.70, ...	26,285	
Tin,	5,762 ditto,	16, ...	92,192	
Smalts,	325 ditto,	77, ...	25,025	
Watches, Clocks, value 50,713, Glass-ware, val. 12,508,			63,221	
Coral Beads,	18,480	Amber, value 5000 ...	23,480	
Skins,	18,069 in No.	value	17,306	
Pearls, Cornelians, and Diamonds,		...	289,287	
Ivory & Elephants' Teeth, 84 peculs, 74 drs. per pecul ...			6,216	
Fish Maws,	1,472 ditto,	56, ...	82,432	
Sharks' Fins,	5,348 ditto,	25, ...	133,700	
Birds' Nests,	630 catties,	21 drs. per catty, ...	13,230	
Cow Bezoar,	400 ditto,	22, ...	8,800	
Camphor,				
Baroos,	426 ditto,	24, ...	10,224	
Cloves,	610 peculs,	25 drs. per pecul, ...	15,250	
Nutmegs,	19 ditto,	84, ...	1,596	
Saltpetre,	6,044 ditto,	9, ...	54,396	
Rice,	258,822 ditto,	2.60, ...	412,937	
Sundries,		value	73,145	
Dollars,		ditto	20,500	14,234,733
		Total, Dollars,		23,476,793

		Taels.	Dollars
EXPORTS—COMPANY'S.			
TEA, for particulars, see page 112,		...5,122,014	
North American investment, (supercargo's			
commission included,)	taels, 366,356		
Cape and St. Helena stores,	... 20,345		
Stores to Bengal, Madras, and Bombay,	... 12,328		
		399,029	
Bullion, (shipment included,)	155,030	111,622	
Port Charges on 24 ships,	drs. ... 89,920		
Unloading charges, Canton Factory			
expences, &c.	101,612		
		191,532	
		5,824,197	8,089,163

EXPORTS—ON PRIVATE ACCOUNT.

		Taels	Dollars
TEA, for particulars, see page 113,	...	752,102	1,044,586
Raw Silk, Nankeen, 8,061 pls. at 332 p. pc., drs. 2,676,252			
Ditto, Canton, 1,418 do. at 276 p.pc., ... 391,368	Dollars.		
Do. Do. 5th sort, 441 do. at 67 p.pc., ... 29,547			
	3,097,166		
Nankeen Cloth, 30,600 ps. at 74 p. 100 ps. ...	22,644		
Silk Piece-Goods, value	332,844		
Sugar Candy, 10,734 pls. at 11 p. pc., ...	118,074		
Soft Sugar, 17,705 do. at 8¼ p. pc., ...	146,066		
Cassia Lignea, 17,607 do. at 8¼ p.pc., ...	145,258		
Tortoise shell and scraps, value	7,822		
Mother o'Pearl Shells, 2,049 do. at 16¼, ...	34,321		
Vermilion, 3,576 bxs. at 34 p. box. ...	121,584		
Camphor, 2,430 pls. at 22 p. pc.	53,460		
Alum, 10,213 do. at 2 p. pc., ...	20,426		
Rhubarb, 434 do. at 58 p. pc., ...	25,172		
Aniseed Oil, 20 do. at 165 p. pc., ...	3,300		
China-Root, Galingal,			
Gamboge, and Musk, value	33,457		
Floor and Table Mats, 28,691, ditto	13,055		
Bamboos and Whangees, ditto	14,389		
Pearls, False Pearls, and Glass Beads, ditto	26,291		
China Ware, ditto	13,525		
Paper, Kittisols, Lacquered Ware, Fire Works, ditto	106,543		
Brass Leaf, 81 bxs. at 46 p. box. ...	3,726		
Cotton Piece-Goods, 1,250 ps. at 6 p. piece, ...	7,500		
Cotton Twist, 201 pls. at 42 p. pc., ...	8,442		
Cochineal, 202 do. at 218 p. pc., ...	44,036		
South American Copper, 10,907 peculs, at 20 per pecul, ...	218,140		
Sundries, viz. Gold, Silver, Ivory, and Tortoise-			
shell Ware, Sweetmeats, Pictures, &c. ...	115,694		
Silver Bullion, (Sycee, South American Silver,			
and Dollars,)	6,062,790		
Gold, ...	513,795		
		11,309,521	
Disbursements on 20 regular ships, at 12,000 dollars each, 4			
chartered ships, at 4,000 dollars, 20 country ships, at 8,000			
dollars, 16 rice ships, at Whampoa, at 3,000 dollars, and 44			
ships at Lintin, at 1,500 dollars, ...	530,000		
Balance,	2,503,523		
Total, Dollars,	23,476,793		

Figure 4.2 Statement of the British trade at the Port of Canton for the year
ending 31 March 1834

Source: John Phipps, *A Practical Treatise on the China and Eastern Trade*, Calcutta,
1835, 182–3.

the distance from Nagasaki is a voyage of no more than four days, it is performed twice a year. With the exception of this branch of trade, the foreign intercourse of the two provinces of Chekian and Kiannan, which are famous for the production of raw silk, teas, and nankeens, is confined to the Philippine Islands, Tonquin, Cochin China, Cambodia, and Siam, and none of this class of vessels, that I am aware of, have ever found their way to the western parts of the Indian Archipelago. The number of these trading with Siam is 24, all of considerable size; those trading with the Cochin Chinese dominions, 16, also of considerable size; and those trading with the Philippines, 5; making in all 45, of which the average burden does not fall short of 17,000 tons.[18]

A junk of about 350 or 400 tons carries from eighty to one hundred seamen; a number sufficient to man at least five European vessels of the same tonnage.

The number of passengers arrived, by the whole of the junks this season, amount to about two thousand; very few of whom have remained on the island. For several days after their arrival, the sampan pucats and prahos, which trade to Rhio, Malacca, Penang, &c., were literally crowded with these emigrants, proceeding to various neighbouring ports, with the view of getting employment in the Pepper, Coffee, and Gambier Plantations, and in the Tin Mines, &c. Great numbers have gone down to Java, to the Sugar and Coffee Plantations; and many to Borneo and other parts, to collect gold dust. Without the enterprising spirit of these industrious emigrants, the trade of Singapore, which we believe, will amount to upwards of seven millions of dollars for the last year, would be comparatively trifling. – Singapore Chronicle, April 23rd, 1829.

In 1829–30, nine Chinese junks imported, viz. from Canton 1; Tew Chew, 2; Shanghai, 2; Amoy, 4. The whole burthen being 47,000 peculs, or about 3,000 tons.

The cargoes of those from Canton, Tew Chew, and Siang-hai, consist principally of Earthen-ware, Nankeens, Tiles, Silk Camblets, Umbrellas, a little Tobacco, and Dried Fruits. Those of the Amoy junks are composed of nearly the same articles, together with a considerable quantity of Raw Silk; of which article the other junks bring very little. The cargoes of these vessels are said to be worth, from 20,000 to 40,000 Spanish Dollars each.

Nankeens and Earthen-ware compose the most valuable parts

of their cargoes, and the demand here, for both these articles this year, is exceedingly limited; so much so, that many of the junk people, having been unable to dispose of more than one-fourth of their Nankeens in this market, have been obliged to charter one or two Siamese topes, and to send the principal part of their investments to the coast of Java. They have also sent considerable quantities of their Earthen-ware by the native craft, on freight, to Malacca and Penang; there being no possibility of disposing of the whole here. They all complain very much of the depressed state of this market for their goods; and many of them say, they will not be able to return next year, as they are sure to sustain very heavy losses this season.

Their return cargoes consist of Birds' Nests, Camphor, Bich de Mar, Sandal Wood, Ebony, Tortoise-shell, Ratans, Fins, Tripang, Opium, and a few pieces of European Woollens, and Cotton Piece Goods. None of the junks take more than from 600 to 800 Dollars' worth of British manufactures. It was generally supposed that there would be a considerable demand among them this year for the article of Cotton Yarn, in consequence of the increasing consumption of that article in China: but we know it to be a fact, that they have not yet made any inquiry for it; and that they have expressed their determination not to purchase a single pecul. These people have been in the habit of disposing of from 200,000 to 300,000 Dollars' worth of China produce here, annually, for the last 10 years; and we do not believe they ever took, more than from 5,000 to 7,000 Dollars' worth of British manufactures in any one year, and very frequently not so much. This simple fact will afford the manufacturers of England some idea of the extent of the field which they imagine will be opened to their goods in China, on the expected abolition of the Company's charter.[19]

Table 4.1 Abstract statement of the aggregate amount of British trade, including bullion,[a] with China ('000 dollars)

		East India Company's	Private	Total Company's & Private
1827–8	Imports	4,519	15,845	20,364
	Exports	8,765	10,157	18,922
	Total imports and exports	13,284	26,002	39,286
	Balance	4,246[b]	5,688[c]	1,442
1829–30	Imports	4,484	18,447	22,931
	Exports	7,848	13,409	21,257
	Total imports and exports	12,332	31,856	44,188
	Balance	3,364	5,038	1,674
1830–1	Imports	4,514	16,215	20,729
	Exports	9,936	10,456	20,392
	Total imports and exports	14,450	26,671	41,121
	Balance	5,422	5,759	337
1831–2	Imports	3,688	16,848	20,536
	Exports	9,214	8,553	17,767
	Total imports and exports	12,902	25,401	38,303
	Balance	5,526	8,295	2,769
1833–4	Imports	4,358	19,119	23,477
	Exports	8,089	12,884	20,973
	Total imports and exports	12,447	32,003	44,450
	Balance	3,731	6,235	2,504
Average of 5 years' imports and exports		13,083	28,387	41,470

Notes
[a] The Company imported no bullion, and the private trade only 126,700 dollars, into China, during this period
[b] By bills drawn by the Company's supercargoes at Canton, principally upon the Bengal government, for dollars paid into the treasury there; being part proceeds chiefly of opium and cotton of private merchants of India; and the rest, comparatively inconsiderable, by bills upon the Court of Directors
[c] Remitted to India chiefly by the foregoing mode

Source: John Phipps, *A Practical Treatise on the China and Eastern Trade*, Calcutta, 1835, 184.

Table 4.2 Account of the annual value of the trade between the subjects of Great Britain and China, from 1814–15 to 1826–7, both inclusive, distinguishing the trade of the East India Company from that of individuals (£'000)

Years	Value of exports and imports between India and China		Total	Value of imports and exports between England and China on account of the Company	Total value of British trade with China	Value of trade of individuals with China	Value of trade of the Company with China
	On account of individuals	On account of the Company					
1814–15	2,574	222	2,796	2,956	5,751	2,574	3,177
1815–16	2,379	356	2,735	4,286	7,021	2,379	4,642
1816–17	3,034	230	3,264	2,962	6,226	3,034	3,192
1817–18	3,328	710	4,038	2,183	6,221	3,328	2,893
1818–19	3,516	365	3,881	2,065	5,946	3,516	2,430
1819–20	2,190	335	2,525	3,092	5,617	2,190	3,427
1820–21	3,328	603	3,931	2,936	6,867	3,328	3,539
1821–22	3,011	470	3,481	2,700	6,181	3,011	3,170
1822–23	3,048	189	3,237	2,643	5,880	3,048	2,832
1823–24	2,735	721	3,456	2,815	6,271	2,735	3,536
1824–25	2,832	327	3,159	2,600	5,759	2,832	2,927
1825–26	3,944	291	4,235	2,687	6,922	3,944	2,979
1826–27	3,764	362	4,126	3,177	7,304	3,764	3,539

Source: As Table 4.1, 185.

NOTES

1. This chapter has grown out of the author's fundamental interest in the internal ties of the Asian area in the modern period. See also Takeshi Hamashita, 'Tribute and emigration: China's foreign relations and Japan', in T. Umesao and M. Matsubara (eds) *Control Systems and Culture*, Osaka: National Museum of Ethnology, 1989.

2. Although discussions of the world economic system stress the importance of the role of nations in the Western world, the Asian tribute system will be described here as a complex of areas. See John W. Meyer, 'World policy and the authority of the nation-state', in Albert Bergeson (ed.) *Studies of the Modern World System*, New York: Academic Press, 1980.

3. Kaneyoshi Uehara, *Sakoku to Han Boeki* (The Closing-up Policy and [*Liu-ch'iu-Satsuma*] Provincial Trade), Okinawa: Yaeyama Publishing Co., 1981; Fusataka Nakamura, *Nissen Kankeishi no Kenkyu* (Research into the History of Japan–Korea Relations), Tokyo: Yoshikawa Kobunkan, 1969; Ryōji Takeda, 'Gencho shoki no shin to no kankei, 1802–1870', in Tatsuro Yamamoto (ed.) *Betonamu-Chugoku Kankeishi* (History of Sino-Vietnam Relations), Tokyo: Yamakawa Publishing Co., 1975.

4. Sarasin Viraphol, *Tribute and Profit: Sino-Siamese Trade, 1652–1853*, Cambridge, Mass.: Harvard University Press, 1977, ch. 4; Harukatsu Hayashi and Nobuatsu Hayashi (eds) *Kai hentai* (Conditions Accompanying the Change from the Ming to the Barbarian Ch'ing), 3 vols, 1958–9 edition.

5. Hisanori Wada, 'Tōnan Ajia ni okeru shoki kakyō shakai', *Toyo Gakuho*, 42-1 (1959); H. Wada, 'Jūgo-seiki no Jawa ni okeru Chugoku-jin no tsū-shō katsudo', in *Ronshu Kindai Chugoku Kenkyu* (Chronicles of Batavia), Tokyo: Yamakawa Publishing Co., 1981.

6. *Ch'in-ting Ta-ch'ing Hui-tien Shih-li* (Regulations and Laws of Ch'ing Dynasty), vol. 503 (Ch'ao-kung Kung-wu), Peking: Commercial Press, 1908.

7. Pak Chi-won, *Yeol ha ilqi*, p. 5; Ryōji Takeda, 'Gencho shoki no shin to no kankei'; *Batabia-jō nisshi*, vols. 1–2, Tokyo: Japan–Dutch Society, 1937; Chang Tsun-wu, *Ch'ing-Han Tsung-fang Mao-i, 1637–1894*, Taipei: Academia Sinica, 1978; Yoshiharu Tsuboi, *L'Empire Vietnamien: face à la France et à la Chine, 1847–1885*, Paris: L'Harmattan, 1986.

8. *Ming Hui-tien* (Regulations of the Ming Empire), vol. 113 (Kei-tz'ŭ), Peking, 1587.

9. Hisao Ejima, 'Min-dai Jochoku chōkō bōeki no gaikan', *Shien*, 77.

10. *Ming Hui-tien*, vol. III (Kei-tz'ŭ).

11. *Ch'in-ting Ta-ch'ing Hui-tien shih-li*, vol. 503 (Ch'ao-Kung).

12. Shigeo Sakuma, 'Mindai no gaikoku bōeki-kohaku boeki no suii-', in *Wada Hakushi Kanreki Kinen Toyo-shi Ronshu* (Transformation of Tribute Trade in the Ming Period), Tokyo: Kodonsha, 1951.

13. Takeshi Hamashita, 'Kindai Ajia bōekiken ni okeru ginryū-tsū – Ajia keizaishi-zō ni kansuru ichi-kōsō', *Shakai Keizai Shigaku*, 51-1 (1985–4).

14. *The Chinese Repository*, Canton, 1834, II: 396–7.

15. Ibid., XIV: 153–4.

16. Ibid., I: 11–12.

17. Ibid., I: 11.
18. John Phipps, *A Practical Treatise on the China and Eastern Trade*, Calcutta, 1835, 202–3.
19. Ibid., 282–3.

5

BONDED WAREHOUSES AND THE INDENT SYSTEM, 1886–95

A study of the political power of British merchants in the Asian trade

Eiichi Motono

Since the epoch-making issue of *Shakai Keizaishigaku* in 1985,[1] Asian trade has been a popular topic of modern Asian economic history in Japan. Historians are now aware that Asian trade was as important for Japanese capitalism as trade with Western countries. Not only was it important for Japanese capitalism but it was also vital to the Chinese economy of the period. The popularity of the theme is mainly due to the fact that Japanese historians have defined the limit of the Western presence in China and Japan. British mercantile houses and colonial banks, which had previously been thought overwhelmingly powerful, were not able to dominate in either country. By the end of the 1860s their economic activity was confined to the foreign settlements in the treaty ports.[2] Even the British navy, which was thought to have a powerful influence on the two countries, was eliminated during the 1860s and 1870s.[3] As a result of these new findings, Japanese historians have shifted their interest from trade with the West to that with Asian countries. In order to analyse the development and influence of Asian trade upon the Chinese and Japanese economies, they have concentrated on four topics: the circulation of men, goods and capital among Asian countries,[4] and the economic strength of overseas Chinese merchants in Japan.[5]

However, this change in academic trend has created a new problem for Japanese historians. They have emphasized the importance of Asian trade and the strength of Chinese merchants so much that they in turn now underestimate the influence of Western mercantile enterprises. This is an inevitable outcome of the new viewpoint. They now take for granted that Asian trade was the socioeconomic background of Japanese capitalism and consequently overlook the fact that trade in other Asian countries was to some degree influenced by Western mercantile enterprise. The influence of Western mercantile enterprise can be seen in changes to the trade system and its regulation. Since these changes made a serious impact upon the profits of sellers and buyers, they were, as today, an important issue in politics and diplomacy. Japanese historians have not fully recognized the importance of the problem; so to emphasize the importance of the topic, this chapter deals with a change in the trade system and its rules and the impact of these changes upon trade in China; other chapters in this volume deal with the circulation of men, goods and capital in Asian trade.

In the case of late nineteenth-century China, one cannot forget the commercial activities of Western mercantile enterprises. Although they were contained within the foreign settlements by the local authorities from the 1860s, they had sufficient political power to alter the rules of trade with China. Weak though they were, they could still afford to oppose the Chinese authorities, and eventually they succeeded in rebuilding their influence on the Chinese economy after the oppression of the Boxer uprising. How did they achieve their intention of changing the trade rules and the system?[6]

As a case study this chapter deals with a series of disputes between British merchants and the Chinese authorities on the eve of the Sino-Japanese War. The cause of the trouble was the attempt by British merchants to secure profit from the British cotton trade. The decline in the British cotton cloth trade was thought to be due to the fall in the silver exchange rate and competition with native industry. But this was merely the background. The decline of the British cotton cloth trade in fact became inevitable when British trading companies failed to hold down the price rises caused by the fall in the silver exchange rate.[7] At first they intended to avoid the increase in prices by establishing a bonded warehouse system, but eventually they ended up introducing the Indent System in 1892. How their efforts brought about this result has not been fully studied because the introduction of the two systems has been regarded as a minor episode in the autonomy movement[8] or an insignificant change which followed the development of the Shanghai financial market.[9] However, the introduction of the two seemingly unrelated systems can be regarded as a typical example of the conflict between Western mercantile enterprises and the Chinese authorities, especially the Chinese Merchants' Steamships Navigation & Company (hereafter CMSNC).[10]

THE CRISIS OF THE BRITISH COTTON CLOTH TRADE

The 1880s was a turning point for China's foreign trade. Former major articles of trade, such as tea, silk, Indian opium and British cotton cloth, started to decline or came to a standstill during this decade. This crisis had an impact upon the old commercial conflict between Chinese merchants' guilds and government officials, on the one hand, and British trading companies, colonial banks and diplomats, on the other. Since the 1860s they had been struggling with each other for mastery of the Chinese inland market. At first, their main conflicts were concerned with sales and financial systems.[11] But from the 1880s, the crisis forced the parties to concentrate on the *likin* tax, and the reform of the production system and infrastructure. In the case of the British cotton cloth trade, the basic reason for the commercial battle was the fall in the silver exchange rate. As previous studies have revealed, the demand for British cotton cloth was not large in China. While thick durable cloth, made from short-staple native raw cotton was the most popular among the common people in China, the British cotton industry in contrast supplied thin, flimsy cloth made from long-staple American or Egyptian raw cotton.[12] So imported British cotton cloth was sold only in large cities or in the northern districts where native cotton was cultivated less. The limited demand for British cotton cloth was further diminished by the increase of the Indian cotton yarn trade after the 1880s. Since China and India were both silver-standard countries, trade between them was free from the exchange loss due to the fall in silver. The demand for Indian yarn from Chinese peasants, who produced handloom cloth, grew rapidly.[13]

Despite these unfavourable conditions, the Lancashire cotton industry put pressure upon British trading companies in China to sell more of their products than before. Because of the fall in the silver exchange rate, Lancashire wanted to collect the sales profits of the cotton cloth exported to silver-standard countries as quickly as possible so that they could reduce exchange losses. With the communications revolution, information concerning prices in London and Shanghai could be quickly transmitted between the two by telegraph, and commodities could be transported faster and safer by steamship via the Suez Canal. This made speculation unprofitable, and since the downward fluctuation in the exchange rate eroded the sales profit, they started to export their products to China by a new sales system called the 'to arrive' system. By the new system, shippers could sell cotton cloth to importers by telegraph even before it was produced; thus Lancashire could avoid any risks of exchange loss or oversupply. But the importers needed to make quick sales of British cotton cloth. Although they were ordered to make prompt remittance to Lancashire according to the 'to arrive' system, the imported cloth was not easily sold due to the limited demand in the China market, and they were forced to store much of it for a long time. Whether the imported cloth was sold quickly or not, they were required to pay the import duty to the Chinese Imperial Maritime Customs when the cloth was landed, so they looked for a way to reduce the burden. Even though it was impossible to refuse remittance to Lancashire or payment of the duty, it was possible to delay the latter until the cloth was sold to Chinese dealers. This could be done if the stock was placed in bonded warehouses.

Although the establishment of bonded warehouses had been permitted since 1869 and was mentioned in Article III of the Chinese–German Supplementary Treaty of 1881,[14] they were not set up then because of the expensive registration fee charged by the Qing government. Now, due to the change in the sales system, the bonded warehouse question became a great issue. So British trading companies requested the Zongli Yamen to permit bonded warehouses again at the port of Shanghai.[15]

In contrast to the eagerness of the British trading companies, the attitude of the Qing government to the issue was entirely passive. Ever since the conclusion of the Supplementary Treaty they had been split on the issue, and it was Robert Hart who approved the claim of the British trading companies in 1882. He was sent to Shanghai to investigate proper measures for the introduction of the bonded warehouse system there. Based upon his own investigations he proposed to designate the godowns of CMSNC and those of the Shanghai and Hongkew and Jardine's Associated Wharves (*shuntai matou*; hereafter the Associated Wharves) to be the officially permitted bonded warehouses, to which foreign goods could be bonded.[16]

Meanwhile, Li Hongzhang and his group, including CMSNC and the Shanghai Daotai, Shao Youlian, opposed Hart's plan. The reason for their opposition was the fear of a fall in income for the military budget. From 1882 the Qing government needed sufficient funds to reorganize the army and to send troops to Korea if military tension with Japan increased.[17] However, now that the Qing government had ratified the Supplementary Treaty, it was impossible for them to reject Hart's plan. Instead, they limited the number of bonded warehouses by granting the privilege only to the godowns of the CMSNC. The decision was probably influenced by advice from CMSNC. In a communication dated 5 March 1886, CMSNC pointed out that bonded warehouses were built and administered as public property in France and Germany whereas proper private godowns were utilized as bonded warehouses in Britain and America. Nevertheless, according to the communication, the system in the English-speaking countries, which was the model of Hart's plan, was inapplicable to China because it would enable another foreign wharf company (the German company, Siemssen & Co.), which also administered godowns, to claim equal status with Shanghai and Hongkew and Jardine's Associated Wharves.[18] Therefore, CMSNC proposed that they alone should have the monopoly of bonded warehouses.[19]

The intention of the Li Hongzhang group was concealed so well that even Robert Hart did not know of it until he received the declaration from the Zongli Yamen dated 5 May, which ordered him to revise the provisional general regulation for bonding.[20] Although Hart expressed his opposition by warning of the ill consequences of leasing Central & Lower Wharves to Siemssen & Co. and of CMSNC's refusal to pledge the title deeds of their warehouses to the China Imperial Maritime Customs on 15 May, the Zongli Yamen simply repeated their order to him to carry out the monopoly plan for bonded warehouses that they had arranged clandestinely on 9 October.[21]

When the monopoly plan was made public, it caused a sensation among Western residents in Shanghai.[22] Their resentment was channelled into a protest movement organized by Jardine, Matheson & Co. Having obtained from the Commissioner of Shanghai Customs, H. Elgar Hobson, the information that the monopoly plan would not be put into effect until the end of 1887,[23] Jardine, Matheson & Co. started their political movement to shatter the monopoly plan on 24 October.[24] John Keswick, a partner of the Shanghai branch, consulted with Robert Hart on this problem[25] and asked the British Consul, P.J. Hughes to forward their protest to John Walsham, the British envoy in Beijing.[26]

However, as their lone petition to the British diplomats had no effect, Jardine, Matheson & Co. strengthened their case by obtaining the support of the Shanghai General Chamber of Commerce.[27] At the special general meeting on 9 December, John Macgregor succeeded in having this prepared resolution adopted by the members of the Chamber:

That in the opinion of this Chamber any scheme for the establishment of Bonded Warehouses which does not permit the Bonding of all Wharves and Warehouses or such of them as are prepared to accept the conditions and regulations as may be required by the Imperial authorities is against public policy and constitutes an interference with trade and vested interests.[28]

This meant that the grievance of Jardine, Matheson & Co. had become that of all Western residents in Shanghai. With the support of an editorial in the *North China Herald*, E.H. Lavers, the chairman of the Shanghai General Chamber of Commerce, sent an official letter to the doyen of the foreign diplomats in Beijing, von Brandt, to ask for their help.[29] In consequence, the Imperial Maritime Customs, CMSNC and the foreign diplomats had to do something to redress their grievances.

THE CONTROVERSY

Among those who were called to redress the grievance, CMSNC responded to the protest movement first. They began with a letter to the *North China Herald* on 15 December by the director, Ma Jianzhong. He presented an argument based upon the following two points. First, just as no Chinese immigrants 'would be permitted to have control of bonded warehouses' in London or America, the bonded warehouses should be administered by 'a body consisting entirely of its own nationals and which was already entrusted with numerous duties by the State'. The fact of residing in China could not give any foreigners the right to interfere with the collection of duties by the Qing government as they saw fit. Second, even if the monopoly of bonded warehouses by CMSNC might damage the interests of the shareholders of Western wharf companies, such as Associated Wharves or the Pooting Wharf Company, it would not affect most foreign merchants. As long as the cotton trade was carried out by the 'to arrive' system, foreign importers had to sell imported goods as quickly as possible. Because of the current necessity for quick sales, foreign importers could not afford to store large amounts of imported goods in duty-free conditions for a long time. Therefore, he concluded, there would be no need to have as many bonded warehouses as had been claimed by foreigners.[30]

The editor of the *North China Herald* published a rebuttal. First of all, he emphasized that no foreigners wanted to 'control' or 'superintend' bonded warehouses in China; they just wanted to have their godown properties converted into bonded warehouses.[31] Next, he corrected Ma's idea on the British bonded warehouse system by pointing out that no English law prevented Chinese merchants buying or building warehouses in Britain so long as they complied with Customs regulations. Furthermore, he insisted that the control of bonded warehouses by the Qing government and foreign bonded warehouses properties could coexist, if CMSNC adopted the system used in England and elsewhere; that is to say, the bonded goods could not be withdrawn unless the doors of the bonded warehouses were opened by two kinds of key, one held by the owners of the goods and the other by the Customs agent.[32]

Reading the above controversy, the editor of the *North China Herald* seems to have defeated Ma Jianzhong. But although Ma made no reply to the critical comment of the editor, CMSNC ignored his proposal. For CMSNC, the monopoly of bonded warehouses was an important step towards the autonomy of the infrastructure of Shanghai, which they believed must be established whatever obstacles they might face. So, because of the political priorities of the Chinese, the victory of the *North China Herald* achieved nothing.

Just after the correspondence between Ma Jianzhong and the *North China Herald* ended, the general regulations for bonding, which consisted of twenty-nine rules, came into effect on 1 January, 1888 as 'Customs Notification no. 279' by H. Elgar Hobson.[33] Being fully aware that the bonded warehouses would be monopolized by CMSNC, Jardine, Matheson & Co. applied to the Shanghai Customs for permission to have their warehouses converted into bonded warehouses on 31 December, 1887; but their application was eventually turned down by Hobson on 3 January.[34] Because of the monopoly policy, a German company, Melches & Co., one of the customers of Associated Wharves, was obliged to send their mail steamship *Neckar* to the wharf of the CMSNC instead of that of Associated Wharves that very day. Jardine, Matheson & Co., again asked the British consul to request that the British Foreign Minister take some action.[35] Pacific & Ocean Co. also made the same request because they were compelled to incur many additional expenses in moving merchandise from the wharf where it was discharged to the bonded warehouse.[36]

The change of wharf by the German steamer *Neckar* shattered the final supposition of Western mercantile society that the general regulations for bonding would be impracticable. They had to examine whether any ill effects would arise from the new regulations and found that problems would result from the following three rules:

2. When the Consul's Report has been received, the Manifest handed

114

in, and Permits to land applied for and issued, the vessel will be allowed to discharge.

6. Foreign goods may, at the Importer's option, be either treated as before – i.e. pay duty and be released – or may be bonded. The Importer must state on his Import Application – in addition to the description, number of packages, weight, and value of the goods – on which goods he wishes to pay duty and on which he wishes to defer payment, in order that the Customs may know whether to issue a Duty Memo or a Bonding Permit.

Local Rule 1. – An application for General Discharge Permit will be held to be an application for importation on payment of duty.

12. The insurance of bonded goods, Warehouse charges and indemnity for fire or loss, are matters to be arranged between the proprietors of the Bonded Warehouses and the Importers, and do not concern the Customs.[37]

The first problem was the delay in discharge. Rules 2 and 6 stipulated that steamships were not allowed to discharge their cargo until all the importers had sent application forms to the Customs to state whether they desired to pay duty at once or to put their goods in bonded warehouses, and had described the full details of their goods. Also, British importers customarily made out application forms after they completed the sales of the import goods on ship to Chinese dealers, which took between three or four days to a week. Under the new system, the discharge of the cargo was delayed until after the sales to Chinese dealers and the application for permissions of landing had been made. This would cause great inconvenience to the steamship agents.

The second problem was the contradiction between the local rule attached to rule 6, and the function of the bonded warehouse system. According to the local rule, an application for a general permit was to be considered as a statement that the steamer agent intended to pay duty on the whole cargo, and no portion of it would be allowed to be bonded.

Finally, the third problem was the ambiguous wording of rule 12, which implied that owners of bonded goods could not claim compensation against the Imperial Maritime Customs or CMSNC for goods damaged or stolen.[38]

Confronted by such specific criticism, the Shanghai Customs was forced to make a concession. H.B. Morse, who had dealt with the general regulations since November 1887, removed one of the claimed inconveniences by revising rules 2 and 6. He enabled a steamer to discharge its cargo on the same day as it arrived in Shanghai, if at least a day before the arrival of the vessel each importer had delivered an import application in which was stated the amount of his consigned goods to be bonded by the Shanghai Customs.[39] Partial and insufficient though it was, it was the only victory British trading companies gained from the Imperial Maritime Customs.

While they were carefully examining each rule of the general regulations for bonding and criticizing the Imperial Maritime Customs, Jardine, Matheson & Co. prepared a third letter to the Consulate in Beijing asking for help. The resolution by the Shanghai Chamber of Commerce only resulted in brief replies from von Brandt and the British government, each of which reported that the diplomats in Beijing had requested the Qing government to permit foreign bonded warehouses in China.[40] Jardine, Matheson & Co. needed the help of greater authority to achieve any effect. This time, they gained the support of an Italian senior consul, Ferdinando de Luca. With his help, they prepared the draft of a third memorandum after their application on behalf of Associated Wharves had been turned down by Elgar Hobson.[41] In it they skilfully stressed that the monopoly of the bonded warehouses was 'interference with the freedom of the usual course of trade in the channels in which it had been customary to carry it on'.[42] Attaching seventy-three signatures of major Western trading companies and colonial banks to the printed copy of this document, ten leading members of the Western mercantile community in Shanghai sent it to Consul Hughes on January 30.[43] It was presented at the meeting of foreign consuls in Shanghai the next day and then sent to von Brandt in Beijing with the unanimous approval of those present.[44] However, replies from him and the British government were disappointing because both simply reported that there had been no reply from the Qing government since January. Furthermore, the reply from the British Foreign Office implied that since the monopoly of the bonded warehouses was not an apparent violation of any treaty, it could not be an issue settled by diplomatic negotiation unless it obviously did considerable harm to the import trade.[45]

So did the monopoly of bonded warehouses of CMSNC do genuine harm to the import trade activities of Western mercantile houses? The answer was partly yes, and partly no. As anticipated by Western merchants, the wharf and the bonded warehouses managed by CMSNC were quite unpopular with Western steamships and importers for various reasons. Apart from the insufficient capacity of the bonded warehouses, and the ill-defined responsibility of CMSNC for damage or loss of bonded goods, and despite the task of remitting import duty imposed upon Western wharf companies, it was the revised procedure for discharge that kept Western steamships and importers away from the wharf and the bonded warehouses managed by CMSNC. As steamships could discharge on the day of arrival, because of the revised rule, the steamers had to classify each item of their cargo into a group to be bonded and a group not to be bonded according to the forms for bonding submitted by the importers. As this required laborious and detailed work,[46] only small amounts of imported goods were bonded. For instance, although six cargo ships from Europe arrived in Shanghai in the first three weeks of 1888, only one ship discharged its cargo at the wharf of CMSNC, and less than half of the discharged goods were bonded as shown in Table 5.1. Moreover, Robert Hart reported that only 9,063 out of more than 300,000 items discharged by the thirty ships in the first half of 1888 were bonded.[47] The unpopularity of the CMSNC bonded warehouse system established in China meant that British trading companies could not delay the payment of duty on cotton cloth. None the less, because they failed to get the bonded warehouse system they desired, British trading companies found another way to avoid the exchange risk and the possibility of over-supplying the market.

THE INTRODUCTION OF THE INDENT SYSTEM

Even though Western merchants failed to achieve the bonded warehouse system they had hoped for, they found they could avoid being left in an unfavourable position in the cotton cloth trade by changing the sales system. By doing so, they eventually succeeded in

Table 5.1 Imported and bonded cotton goods, 1–19 January 1888

Items	Declared for import	Bonded
Grey shirtings	67,471 pieces	1,520 pieces
White shirtings	19,402 pieces	4,000 pieces
English drills	2,580 pieces	900 pieces
T-cloths	16,430 pieces	11,500 pieces
Cotton yarn	522 piculs	228 piculs

Source: *North China Herald*, 3 Feb. 1888, 116.

laying all the risks of oversupply and exchange fluctuation on the shoulders of the Chinese dealers and colonial banks.

At first, the change of the sales system was irrelevant to the bonded warehouse question. It started with the introduction of a public auction system in the early 1880s, according to which, cotton piece-goods were sold at an auction which was held four or five times a week. The public auction system was met with the 'almost universal reprobation' of the importers. After a while, however, Western merchants learned by experience what amount and what kinds of cotton piece-goods they could safely offer at each auction, and they saw that auction prices did not fall much below the cost of imported goods.[48] Since the content of the annual consular report of 1887, which recorded the above information, was made public by the *North China Herald*,[49] they must have realized by August 1888 that they could avoid oversupply and the payment of duty for stored goods by carrying on business by the public auction system. But despite the effort of the British trading companies to maintain the equilibrium of the cotton cloth market by this system, it was immediately destabilized by Chinese dealers, who made large orders and disregarded the balance between demand and supply. For instance, in the 1888 season, they ordered much more cotton cloth than the market demanded, bringing about great losses to both Chinese and Western merchants and a remarkable increase of stock, as shown in Table 5.2.

Since the public auction system was not able to control the commercial activities of Chinese dealers, a new, more effective sales system was required to eliminate the defect. Although no record concerning the conception and introduction of it is available, the Indent System was probably established in this context. The operation of the

Table 5.2 The estimated stock of cotton piece-goods (pieces)

Items	At beginning of 1888	At beginning of 1889
Grey shirtings	922,520	982,013
White shirtings	218,227	601,764
T-cloths, 32 in.	288,130	434,425
T-cloths, 36 in.	69,582	145,092
Sheetings (English)	216,022	499,944
Sheetings (American)	144,695	700,745

Source: *Irish University Press, Area Studies, British Parliamentary Papers, Embassy and Consular Reports*, 16, 438.

system was described in the annual consular report of 1892 by N.A. Hannen as follows:

> Instead of holding goods on stock or to arrive to meet the requirements of the market, merchants prefer to sell to the native dealers before ordering the goods in England. They settle the price in silver and the exchange at the same time, and then transmit their orders by telegraph to Manchester. The buying (from Manchester) and selling (in China) and fixing the rate of exchange are thus practically simultaneous operations; the bank takes the risk of exchange and the foreign importer has no further interest in the transaction than simply earning his commission, which he deducts when he hands over the goods and gets paid by the Chinaman ...[50]

As a result of the introduction of the Indent System, the 'to arrive' sales systems, which enabled Lancashire to undertake speculation, was no longer possible. By fixing the sales prices in China and the exchange rate at the same time, British trading companies were at last liberated from the risks of oversupply and exchange loss. On the other hand, Chinese dealers had to shoulder the risk of oversupply because it was they who determined the quality and quantity of the cotton cloth imported, and colonial banks had to take the risk of losing on the exchanges. Only by offloading their risks on to others could British trading companies be freed from the burden they had carried.

CONCLUSION

Despite repeated requests and petitions for permission for their own bonded warehouse system, British trading companies only obtained a small revision in the procedure, and as a result there was a decrease in bonding. The monopoly of the bonded warehouses by CMSNC was so skilfully achieved by the Li Hongzhang group that foreigners could not persuade the Qing government to abandon the decision. This was because the monopoly did not violate any treaty, which was the most persuasive argument for Western diplomats to use to influence the policy of the Qing government. Putting the decision into effect, the Qing government succeeded in obtaining some autonomy for the port of Shanghai. However, it brought about little profit for them because most steamships disliked the complicated procedure for bonding, and preferred to discharge at the wharves administered by Western wharf companies.

Table 5.3 Prices of certain fabrics, based on actual sales by private firms, 1888–93 (Shanghai *taels*)

Articles	1888	1889	1890	1891	1892	Jan. 1893	Dec. 1894
Medium, 8¼ lb. shirtings	1.72	1.74	1.57	1.57	1.63	1.70	2.12
10 lb. shirtings	2.20	2.22	2.18	2.21	2.23	2.30	2.75
12 lb. shirtings	2.55	2.55	2.54	2.54	2.62	2.70	3.00
64-reed white shirtings	1.89	1.90	1.80	1.73	1.82	1.95	2.45
72-reed white shirtings	2.03	2.04	1.96	1.92	2.02	2.10	2.65
Medium, Irish-fold, white shirtings	2.59	2.59	2.52	2.53	2.62	2.75	3.40

Source: Irish University Press, Area Studies, British Parliamentary Papers, China, Embassy and Consular Reports, 18, 532.

Table 5.4 Proportional variations in local prices of ten standard cotton fabrics of English manufacture, based on prices realized at public auction (1882 = 1,000)

Year	Prices
1882, average year	1,000
1883, prices in June	987
1884, prices in June	995
1885, prices in June	990
1886, prices in June	994
1887, prices in June	1,036
1888, prices in June	1,080
1889, prices in June	1,084
1890, prices in June	1,006
1891, prices in June	952
1892, prices in June	979
1893, prices in January	1,135
1893, prices in June	1,154
1894, prices in January	1,394

Source: Irish University Press, Area Studies, British Parliamentary Papers, China, Embassy and Consular Reports, 18, 532.

Meanwhile, the Indent System did not relieve the depression in the British cotton cloth trade. Although it was introduced after several attempts and changes, it brought nothing but harmful effects for the trade. First of all, the Indent System arbitrarily ruled that Chinese dealers were 'the real merchants' because they shared with colonial banks all the risk of exchange rate fluctuations and oversupply and only they could decide how much and what kinds of British cotton cloth were to be imported; British merchants were in effect merely their agents.[51] They lost the power to control British cotton cloth sales in return for being liberated from the risks of exchange loss and oversupply.

However, Chinese dealers themselves did not want to take any risks, in spite of the hopes of the British. A year after the Indent System was introduced, they started to carry out business by contracts guaranteeing future delivery, in order to avoid exchange loss.[52] Chinese dealers could therefore receive cotton cloth before remitting to Manchester. If they fixed the rate of exchange as high as possible at the time of mailing the order, they could remit the sales price at the fixed rate. Moreover, because of the Indent System, the prices of import goods in silver were determined at the same time as the rate of exchange was fixed. If the Lancashire cotton industry held the price of cotton cloth in gold at this level, they must have received less and less in remittances as the silver exchange rate fell. In fact, they put up the prices in gold to guard their own profit. In consequence, as shown in Tables 5.3 and 5.4, the price of British cotton cloth in Shanghai started to rise after 1892, which led to further decreases in the imports of British cotton cloth.

Furthermore, as a result of relying upon Chinese dealers to look after their interests, British trading companies were confronted by another risk; irresponsible behaviour by Chinese brokers. The new trouble between the British merchants and the Chinese merchants arose from unreliable contracts:

> Seldom in the history of the (Mixed) court have there been so few cases set down under the civil list as during 1895. Trade has been flourishing generally, and native dealers who enter into engagements under what may be called the 'indent' system, have thus been enabled to clear their goods on arrival. At the same time the disastrous experiences of 1893 and 1894 have compelled caution on the part of the foreign importer, and eliminated the crowd of irresponsible native brokers who figured so frequently in the Mixed Court during those years ... Between Chinese, in respect

121

to their own dealings, all documents are regularly stamped with the chop or seal of their Hongs, thereby making the agreement binding on all the partners. A practice, however, appears to have sprung up, among Europeans, of accepting a mere signature of the Hong's name by the native broker, often in pencil, with the consequence that on a failing market, the contract is repudiated. Under such circumstances the British merchant has no remedy or redress, except against the native broker, who generally has no capital, and of course, is unable to carry out the contract.[53]

So the Indent System could protect the profit of British merchants from exchange fluctuations but it further damaged the trade in British cotton cloth, and caused new disputes with the Chinese merchants. Neither British trading companies nor the Qing government received any benefits from the commercial conflicts after 1886. It ended with the fatal decline of the British cotton cloth trade.

Now that they could no longer control the inland market for themselves, British enterprises made a final attempt to secure a profit from their commercial activities in China. They tried to alter the system and the rules of trade in their favour by using their political power. However, as shown in this case study, their attempt did not bring about a favourable outcome. Since their political ploys always stimulated the opposition of the Chinese authorities, they had to compromise with them. In consequence, the outcome was always unsatisfactory for them. Now that their last attempt had ended in failure, they had only one option to secure profit from trade activity in China: to declare war to subjugate the Chinese authorities. Otherwise they had to give up the Chinese market or be controlled by the Chinese mercantile class which had emerged during the decade. The outbreak of the Sino–British war and the Boxer uprising gave them great opportunities. Yet even the reorganization of China's foreign relations which started with the Treaty of Shimonseki did not bring about a favourable result. It reorganized the British commercial presence in China and deprived the British mercantile houses of the leadership of Western enterprise in China. After the Boxer rebellion, this leadership role passed to foreign banks, such as the Hongkong & Shanghai Bank. From then on, the system and rules of trade in China were mainly subject to the influence of these foreign banks.

Not only the trade but also the currency system was administered by the foreign banks. However attracted they are to the importance of Asian trade and the strength of the overseas Chinese, historians should not underestimate the political power of Western enterprise in China. Whether positive or negative, it could still influence trade and investment after the 1890s in Asia in general and even in Japan.

NOTES

1. *Shakai-Keizais-Shigaku* (Socio-economic History), 51(1), (1985).
2. Kanji Ishii, 'Igirisu shokuminchi gingkōgun no saihen-1870–1880 nendai no nihon chūgoku wo chūshin ni-' (The reorganization of the British colonial banks group in China and Japan during the 1870s and 80s), *Keizaigaku ronshū*, 45(1), (April 1979), 19–60; 45(3), (October 1979), 17–46; Kanji Ishii and Hisashi Seikiguchi (eds), *Sekai shijō to bakumatsu kaikō* (The World Market and the Opening of late Tokugawa Japan), Tokyo: University of Tokyo Press, 1982; Ishii Kanji, *Kindai nihon to igirisu shihon- jādin maseson shōkai wo chūsihn ni-* (Modern Japan and the British Enterprise with the special relationship of Jardine, Matheson & Co.), Tokyo: University of Tokyo Press, 1984; Mayako Ishii, 'Jyūkyū seiki kōhan no chūgoku ni okeru igirisu shihon no katsudō-jādin maseson shōkai no baai-' (Activities of the British enterprise in China in the latter half of the ninenteenth century as found in the documents of Jardine, Matheson & Company), *Shakai-Keizai-Shigaku*, 45(4), (Dec. 1979), 1–33; Michiaki Miyata, 'Shinmatsu ni okeru gaikoku bōekihin ryūtsū kiko no ichi kōsatsu-girudo no ryūtsū shihai wo chūsin to shite-' (A study on the foreign trade organization in late Qing China), *Sundai Shigaku*, no. 52 (Mar. 1981), 73–102; Eiichi Motono, 'Arō sensō igo no kachū no shinyō kōzō to sekai shijō' (The credit system of Central China after the Arrow War and the world market), *Shigaku Zasshi*, 93(10), (Oct. 1984), 35–67; Motono, '"The traffic revolution": remaking the export sales system in China, 1866–1875', *Modern China*, 12(1), (Jan. 1986), 75–102; Motono, '1870 nendai no chūgoku kinyū shijō to zaika gaikoku shōnin no chūgoku tsūka seido kaikaku undō' (The financial market in China during the 1870s and the currency reform movement by the foreigners in China), *Tochi seido shigaku*, no. 114 (Jan. 1987), 13–31; Motono, 'Anshō Yūkō yōkō tai shanhai chōkei kaikan jiken-chīfu kyōtei go no ahen bōeki funsō ni kansuru ichi kōsatsu-' (The Swatow Opium Guild case: a study of the opium trade conflict after the Chefoo Convention), *Chūgoku-kindaishi-kenkyū*, 6, (Sept. 1988), 33–64; Motono, '1860 nendai shanhai ni okeru baiben tōroku seido no zasetsu to yushutsu torihiki kikō no kaihen-jādin maseson shōkai no katsudō wo chūsin ni-' (The failure of the comprador registration system and the change of the export sales system in Shanghai) *Shigaku Zasshi*, 99(7), (July 1990), 1–41.
3. Shinya Sugiyama, 'Higashi ajia ni okeru "gaiatsu" no kōzō' (The structure of 'foreign pressure' in East Asia), *Rekishigaku Kenkyū*, no. 560, (Oct. 1986), 128–38.
4. Kaoru Sugihara, 'Ajia kan bōeki no keisei to kōzō' (Patterns and development of intra-Asian trade), *Shakai-Keizai-Shigaku* 51(1), (April 1985), 17–53; Takeshi Hamashita, 'Kindai ajia bōekiken ni okeru gin

ryūtsū' (Silver circulation in the modern Asian trade network), ibid., 54–90; Heita Kawakatsu, 'Ajia momen shijō no kōzō to tenkai' (The evolving structures of Asian markets for cotton goods), ibid., 91–125; Sakae Tsunoyama, 'Ajia kan kome bōeki to nihon' (Intra-Asian trade of rice and Japan in the later nineteenth century), ibid., 126–40; Hitoshi Kojima, *Nihon no kinhon'isei jidai (1897–1917)* (Japan's gold-standard era, 1897–1917), Tokyo: Nihon keizai hyōronsha, 1981; Michiaki Miyata, 'Kaikō ikō ni okeru suwatō kō no ryūtsū jōkyō to chiiki keiza' (The circulation circumstance of Shantou after its 'opening' and the economy of its surrounding district), paper delivered at the Sixth Modern and Contemporary Chinese Economic History Symposium, Tokyo, *Gakushi Kaikan bekkan*, 21 July 1990.

5. Kojima, *Nihon no kinhonisei jidai*; Shinya Sugiyama, 'International circumstance and foreign trade', in Mataji Umemura and Yūzō Yamamoto (eds) *Nihon keizaishi*, vol. 3: *Kaikō to Ishin* (Economic History of Japan, vol. 3: The Opening of Japan and Meiji Restoration), Tokyo: Iwanami shoten, 1989; Naoto Kagotani, '1880 nendai no ajia karano "shōgeki" to nihon no hannō-chūgokujin bōekishō no ugoki ni chūmokushite-' (The Asian impact during the 1880s and Japan's response to it with the special relationship with the activities of Chinese merchants), *Rekishigaku kenkyū*, no. 608, (July 1990), 1–18.

6. From the 1860s, Western mercantile enterprises led by British merchant houses had struggled with the Chinese local authorities consisting of Chinese merchants' guilds and local officials to control the inland market. The alteration of the trade rules and the abolition of the inland tax were the major issues in the disputes between the parties. The commercial struggles between the parties in Shanghai from the end of the 1870s to the end of the Qing Dynasty and their results are the theme of my D.Phil. Thesis, in progress.

7. A well-known attempt by British mercantile enterprises to avoid exchange loss on British cotton cloth was the import of machinery to produce cotton cloth with the native raw cotton. This created conflict with the native industry supported by the Chinese authorities. With regard to the conflict, see Yoshihiro Hatano, *Chūgoku kindai kōgyōshi no kenkyū* (The study of the early industrialization of China), Kyoto: Dōhōsha, 1961, ch. 4; and Masatoshi Tanaka, 'Nisshin sensō go no shanhai kindai "gaishō" bōsekigyō to chūgoku shijō' (Modern cotton-spinning industry managed by foreign merchants in post Sino-Japanese War Shanghai and the Chinese market), in Hideo Yamada (ed.) *Shokuminchi keizaishi no shomondai* (Problems of Economic History of Colonies), Tokyo: Ajia keizai kenkyūjo 1973, 10–34.

8. Stanley F. Wright, *China's Struggle for Tariff Autonomy*, Shanghai: Kelly & Walsh, 1938, 292–5; *Zhaoshangjushi* (History of China Merchant Steam Navigation Company), Beijing: Renmin jiaotong chubanshe, 1988, 175–8; Xue Pengzhi, 'Zhongguo jindai baoshui guanzhan de qiyuan he sheli' (The origin and the establishment of the bonded warehouses in modern China), paper delivered at the Second International Conference on the History of Chinese Customs, Xiamen, August 1990.

9. Takeshi Hamashita, 'Jyūkyū seiki matsu ni okeru ginka hendō to shanhai

kinyū shijō' (The fluctuations of silver rate and Shanghai financial market in late nineteenth century), *Hitotsubashi ronsō*, 87(4), (1982), 21–6; Hamashita, *Chūgoku kindai keizaishi kenkyū-kaikan zaisei to kaikōjō shijōken* (The study of modern Chinese economic history: Finance of the Imperial Maritime Customs in late Qing China and the market zone of treaty ports), Tokyo: Kyūko shoin, 1989, 122–6.

10. In this article, I have used recently published Chinese documents and English documents I found in the Jardine, Matheson Archives in the manuscript room of Cambridge University Library, and Great Britain Foreign Office Consular archives (FO228) in the Public Record Office in London. The quotation in this paper from the unpublished Crown Copyright material in the Public Record Office is with the permission of the Controller of Her Majesty's Stationery Office.

11. With regard to the trade conflicts before the 1880s, see my previous articles cited in note 2.

12. Heita Kawakatsu, 'Jyūkyū seiki matuyō ni okeru eikoku mengyō to higashi ajia shijō' (British cotton industry and the East Asian market in late nineteenth century), *Shakai -Keizai -Shigaku*, 47(2), (June 1981), 1–32; Kawakatsu, 'Jyūkyū seiki matsuyō no momen shijō-genmen wo chūshin ni-' (The cotton market in the late nineteenth century with special relation to raw cotton), *Yokohama kaikō shiryōkan kiyō*, 2 (Mar. 1984), 1–33.

13. Masaaki Oyama, 'Shinmatsu chūgoku ni okeru gaikoku menseihin no ryū nyū' (The pouring of foreign cotton piece-goods into late Qing China), in *Kindai chūgoku kenkyū iinkai* (Committee of Research of Modern Chinese History) (ed.) *Kindai chūgoku kenkyū* (The Study of Modern China), vol. 4, Tokyo: University of Tokyo Press, 1960), 1–108; Tanaka Masa-toshi, 'Nisshin sensō go no shanhai kindai gaishō bōsekigyō to chūgoku shijō'.

14. The English translation of the article is as follows:

> In all the open ports of China where it is considered desirable by the foreign trading community and the local circumstances appear to render it practicable, the Chinese Commissioner of Customs and the other officials concerned shall themselves take in hand the erection of entrepôts [bonded warehouses] and at the same time prepare the requisite regulations.
>
> *North China Herald*, 17 June, 1881, 581

15. *North China Herald*, 10 March 1886, 253–4.

16. Circular no. 395 (Second Series): 'Bonded Warehouses: system to be introduced at Shanghai; General Regulations and I.G.'s instructions', in China Imperial Maritime Customs Service Series no. 69: *Documents Illustrative of the Origin, Development, and Activities of the Chinese Customs Service*, vol. 1: *Inspector General's Circulars, 1861 to 1892* (hereafter CIMC Service Series no. 69), Shanghai: Statistical Department of the Inspectorate General of Customs, 1937, 531; 'Shao Youlian to Xu Run', *Zhongguo jindai hangyunshi ziliao di yizhou* (The Collection of History of Modern Transportation to China, vol. 1, hereafter *hangyunshi ziliao*), Shanghai: shanghai renmin chubanshe, 1983, 1134. After receiving Hart's proposal, the Zongli Yamen ordered the Shanghai Daotai, Shao

Youlian, to reinvestigate the condition of the godowns of CMSNC, Associated Wharves, and other Chinese merchants. Shao entrusted this task to a famous compradore, Xu Run (Hsü Jun), but unfortunately Xu's reply was not included in *hangyunshi ziliao*.

17. Since the soldiers' rebellion of 1882 (*Im-o byōn*), which was diplomatically settled with Japan by the treaty of Je-mul-pho, Japan and China had stationed troops in Korea to administer the Korean government. Their rivalry finally broke out in the Sino-Japanese War in 1894 (See Tomoo Suzuki, 'Kindai sangyō no ishoku to Rikōshō- 1882 nen no Shōyūren ate shokan no kōsatsu' (The transplantation of modern industry and Li Hongzhang: a study on Li Hongzhang's two letters in 1882 addressed to Shao Youlian), in Shingai Kakumei Kenkyūkai (The Society for the Study of the 1911 Revolution in China) (eds) *Kikuchi Takaharu Sensei Tsuitō Ronshū* (Essays on Modern and Contemporary Chinese History in Memory of the Late Professor Kikuchi Takaharu), Tokyo: Kyūko shoin, 1985, 88, 93.

18. The 'another foreign wharf company' whose claim for equal status worried CMSNC was a German company, Siemssen & Co. From the beginning of 1886, Siemssen & Co. competed with Jardine, Matheson & Co. for the lease of Central & Lower Wharves from CMSNC for five years. With help from Ma Jianzhong, one of the directors of CMSNC, and Hosea Ballou Morse, Siemssen won the competition ('J. Keswick to A. Michie', Jardine, Matheson Archives (hereafter *JMA*)–Press Copy Letter Book [hereafter *PCLB*] C42/2, 11 Jan. 1886; 'J. Keswick to W. Keswick', ibid., C41/8, 12, 13, Jan. 1886, 3 Feb. 1886). A year after, however, Morse proposed joint management of Central & Lower Wharves by Associated Wharves and China Merchants' Central & Lower Wharves [Siemssen & Co.] for some unknown reason. This proposal was turned down by Jardine, Matheson & Co. for its infeasibility ('J. Keswick to H.B. Morse', *JMA–PCLB* C43/2 14, 19 Feb. 1887).

19. 'CMSNC to Shao Youlian [?]', *Hangyunshi Ziliao*, 1134–5, 5 Mar. 1886. This letter did not indicate to whom it was addressed.

20. *CIMC Service Series no. 69*, 539.

21. Ibid., 540–6. Hart was prohibited from arguing for the lease of Central & Lower Wharves and against the refusal to pledge the title deeds of the bonded warehouses by the Imperial Commissioner in the South [Nanyang dachen], Ceng Guoquan, for some unknown reason.

22. *North China Herald*, 27 Oct. 1887, 451.

23. Although Jardine, Matheson & Co. had been promised by Robert Hart that they would be provided with any informatoin about the bonded warehouse question after 29 Jan. 1886 ('J. Keswick to W. Keswick', *JMA–PCLB*, C41/8 3 Feb. 1886), they could not get any valuable information until October 1887. Hart does not seem to have leaked the provisional general regulation of bonding even while it was being circulated within the Imperial Maritime Customs and the Zongli Yamen from May to October, 1887.

24. Although they initiated the protest movement, Jardine, Matheson & Co. believed they could not succeed in shattering the monopoly plan by themselves. In his letter to J.B. Irving on 2 November 1887, J. Macgregor confessed:

We will of course fight for the privilege of Bonded Warehouses being
extended to the Assocted [*sic*] Wharves, but if the work came to the
worst we mean to be even with the CMSN & Co's [*sic*] undertake to
pay Duties [*sic*] for Importers [*sic*], giving the same or greater privileges as the bonded godowns. We do not give to currency this
however keeping it in reserve as a trump card to be only played in
the last moment! (*JMA–PCLB* C41/10)

26. What was talked about by J. Keswick and Robert Hart was not recorded
('J. Macgregor to J.B. Irving', *JMA–PCLB* C41/10 24 Oct. 1887). Several
weeks after the meeting, however, H.B. Morse came from Tianjin to deal
with the bonded warehouse question. In his reply to the enquiry from
Shanghai General Chamber of Commerce on 21 November 1887, Elgar
Hobson revealed that Morse's visit was sanctioned by Hart. In fact, as I
reveal later, he came to revise the provisional general regulation for
bonding ('J. Macgregor to J.B. Irving', *JMA–PCLB* C41/10 2 Nov. 1887;
North China Herald, 14 Dec. 1887, 650.

26. 'John Macgregor to J.B. Irving', *JMA–PCLB* C41/10, 24, 29 Oct. 1887; 'J.
Macgregor to P.J. Hughes', *JMA–PCLB* C43/2, 28 Oct. 1887; FO 228/
854 'P.J. Hughes to J. Walsham, no. 65', 28 Oct. 1887.

27. 'J.Macgregor to J.B. Irving', *JMA–PCLB* C41/10 7, 10, 28 Nov. 1887;
North China Herald, 14 Dec. 1887, 649–51.

28. *North China Herald*, 14 Dec. 1887, 650.

29. 'J. Macgregor to J.B. Irving', *JMA–PCLB* C41/10, 28 Dec. 1887; *North
China Herald*, 28 Dec. 1887, 704.

30. *North China Herald*, 22 Dec. 1887, 680–1. In this letter, Ma Jianzhong
also proved that the special meeting of the Shanghai General Chamber of
Commerce on December was a political pantomime produced by J.
Macgregor in order to pass the resolution he had prepared. As evidence of
it, he pointed out that the number of those who attended the meeting was
so small that they had great difficulty in forming a quorum.

31. On the meaning of the 'control' or 'superintendency' of the bonded
warehouses, Ma and the editor of the *North China Herald* had a fierce
controversy. While the editor rejected the implication of arbitrary
collection of duties from the bonded goods by CMSNC, Ma denied the
implication. From their controversy, it was still uncertain what Ma
Jianzhong meant by 'the control of the Bonded Warehouses'.

32. *North China Herald*, 28 Dec. 1887, 698.

33. FO 228/866, 'Enclosure no. 1 in Mr. Consul-General Hughes' Despatch
No. 1 of 1888'; *North China Herald*, 6 Jan. 1888, 18–19.

34. FO228/866, 'Enclosures no. 3 and no. 4 in Mr. Consul-General Hughes'
Despatch no. 1 of 1888'.

35. FO228/866, 'Enclosure no. 2 and no. 5 in Mr. Consul-General Hughes'
Despatch no. 1 of 1888'.

36. FO228/866, 'Enclosure no. 6 in Mr. Consul-General Hughes' Despatch
no. 1 of 1888'.

37. FO228/866, 'Enclosure no. 1 in Mr. Consul-General Hughes' Despatch
no. 1 of 1888'.

38. *North China Herald*, 6 Jan. 1888, 6–7.

39. *North China Herald*, 11 Jan. 1888, 34.
40. *North China Herald*, 3 Feb. 1888, 130. Before sending the third letter to Beijing, W. Keswick sent a personal letter to the British Foreign Office to request them to put pressure upon the Qing government to permit Associated Wharves to keep bonded warehouses (*North China Herald*, 4 May 1888, 507).
41. 'J. Macgregor to J.B. Irving', *JMA–PCLB* C41/10, 4 Jan. 1888; 'J. Macgregor to Maclellan', ibid. C43/2, 6 Jan. 1888.
42. 'J. Macgregor to de Luca', ibid. C43/2, 6 Jan. 1888.
43. 'J. Macgregor to de Luca', ibid. C43/2, 24 Jan. 1888; 'J. Macgregor to J.B. Irving', ibid., C41/10, 30 Jan. 1888; *North China Herald*, 23 Feb. 1888: 124–5.
44. FO228/866 'P.J. Hughes to J. Walsham No. 6 of 1888', 2 Feb. 1888. Two weeks later, Jardine, Matheson & Co. sent another memo to Hughes (FO 228/866 'P.J. Hughes to J. Walsham, no. 8', 16 Feb. 1888). The text of the letter was not recorded in the despatch. Although they intended to send a further protest addressed to J. Walsham ('J. Macgregor to J.B. Irving' *JMA–PCLB* C41/10, 23 Apr. 1888), no letter from Jardine, Matheson & Co. was recorded in British consular archives after March 1888.
45. *North China Herald*, 16 Mar. 1888, 310; 14 May 1888, 507.
46. 'Robert Hart to the Zongli Yamen, Aug. 9, 1888', *Hangyunshi Ziliao*, 1145–50.
47. Ibid. In the letter to Sheng Xuanhuai, CMSNC criticized the analysis by Hart. They claimed that even the few ships as the 30 which discharged their cargos would not have come to their wharf if Associated Wharves had been allowed to keep bonded warehouses, and that the defects pointed out by Hart would not have been removed if permission had been issued to Associated Wharves ('CMSNC to Sheng Xuanhuai, Feb. 1889', *Hangyunshi Ziliao*, 1150–2).
48. *Irish University Press, Area Studies Series, British Parliamentary Papers, China, Embassy and Consular Reports*, 16, 182–3.
49. *North China Herald*, 6 Jan. 1888, 1–2; 24 Aug. 1888, 209–10.
50. *Irish University Press, Area Studies Series, British Parliamentary Papers, China, Embassy and Consular Reports*, 18, 196.
51. Ibid., 196–7.
52. Ibid., 532–3.
53. Ibid., 19, 482–3.

6

CHINESE MERCHANTS AND CHINESE INTER-PORT TRADE

Hajime Kose

The Chinese economy has often been analysed from the viewpoint of her entire national economy. This chapter, however, focuses on local economies within various regions and relations between those regions. The chapter therefore discusses the structure of internal trade in China. The Chinese domestic market was one of the most important parts of the Asian market and Chinese merchants were critical to the dynamism of both markets. Shanghai was not only a significant port in the Chinese internal market, but also an important centre in the network of intra-Asia trade, together with Singapore and Hong Kong (See Figure 6.1).

Many historians have examined relations between China and foreign capitalist countries in the nineteenth century, especially in the period after 1842. But as regards Chinese internal trade, there is much work to be done. It has been said that Chinese internal trade prospered in the years following the Ch'ing dynasty but was badly affected by the opening of China to the external world, particularly in the 1890s. Yet on examination it seems that the growth of foreign trade and the development of internal trade were interdependent. The purpose of this chapter is to examine the structure of Chinese commerce in the late nineteenth century, mainly by using the statistics of the Imperial Maritime Customs. It also tries to shed light on economic relations between China and Japan.

THE INTERNAL FLOW OF GOODS IN CHINA

Here are some basic data on Chinese internal trade from the 1890s to the early twentieth century. The shipments of some commodities (during the period 1876–1904) are given in Tables 6.1–6.4.[1]

Table 6.1 shows the distribution of raw cotton. It has been said that

Figure 6.1 Chinese open ports

the Lower Yangtze was the centre of cotton production and that raw cotton was carried from the Lower Yangtze to south China.[2] But from the 1890s north China began to export raw cotton and south China reduced its import of Yangtze raw cotton. Moreover, according to this table, from 1904 the Middle Yangtze began to export cotton to Shanghai. This raw cotton was re-exported mainly to Japan.

Table 6.2 shows the distribution of beancake. Soybeans were produced mainly in Manchuria and beancake was one of Manchuria's leading products. Yingkow, the main port in Manchuria before Dairen was opened to foreign trade, was the leading port for the export of beancake. From the table it can be seen that beancake was exported from Manchuria to south China. But the volume of beancake shipments

130

Table 6.1 Cotton exports (including re-exports) and imports in the internal market in China (in 1,000 piculs)

	1876		1890		1899		1904	
	Imports	Exports	Imports	Exports	Imports	Exports	Imports	Exports
Yingkow	3	–	59	–	52		52	
Tientsin	10	–	11	–	2	4		8
Chefoo	7	–	12		9	–	9	3
Kiaochow					6	2	15	1
Chungking					38		2	
Ichang				8	42	38	–	5
Shasi								11
Hankow	157	–	116	8	105	45	11	375
Kiukiang	6		30		4	3		28
Wuhu				11		5		14
Chinking					–	–		
Shanghai	22	270	26	279	79	201	627	98
Hangchow								20
Ningpo		22		25		65	1	124
Foochow	1		–		–		1	–
Amoy	25	–	5		7		5	
Swatow	35	–	11		5		12	–
Canton	10		5		7		22	
Total	276	292	283	323	356	361	758	685

Source: China, Imperial Maritime Customs Service, *Annual Reports*.

from Manchuria shrank after 1904. The decline in the demand for beancake in south China was due to the increase in its price and result of exports to Japan.[3]

Table 6.3 shows the distribution of brown sugar. Sugar was shipped from south China to north and middle China. The quantity of sugar shipments did not change much from 1876 to 1899. But sugar movements to middle China declined during that period. In the Shanghai sugar market the volume of south China sugar purchases decreased from 1890s, due to an increase of imports from Java and the Philippines.

Table 6.4 shows the distribution of domestic cotton cloth. Cotton cloth was one of the most important handicraft goods in late Imperial China. It has been argued that the Lower Yangtze was the centre of handicraft cotton cloth production. This table shows that Shanghai, Hankow and Swatow were the main export centres of domestic cotton cloth.[4] The main import ports were Tientsin, Yingkow and Canton.

Table 6.2 Beancake exports (including re-exports) and imports in the internal market in China (in 1,000 piculs)

	1876		1890		1899		1904	
	Imports	Exports	Imports	Exports	Imports	Exports	Imports	Exports
Yingkow		758		2,544		2,031		1,726
Chefoo		821		1,071		917		465
Kiaochow					3		29	2
Hankow				1		554		533
Wuhu							2	2
Chinking					6	49		488
Shanghai	105	36	627	293	911	865	636	582
Hangchow							197	
Ningpo	21			5		6		
Foochow	29			22				
Amoy	352	16	546		643	20	590	
Swatow	1,206		2,873		2,604	3	2,228	
Canton						39		211
Total	1,713	1,627	4,074	3,909	4,206	4,445	3,891	3,798

Source: China, Imperial Maritime Customs Service, *Annual Reports*.

Domestic cotton cloth competed with foreign cloth in domestic markets but it is remarkable that more domestic cloth was moved even as foreign cloth imports increased.

From this data it can be seen that, although the volume of some commodities decreased after the 1900s, the volume and movement of domestic goods did not change much.

In Figure 6.2 we can see the flow of domestic and foreign goods in 1899. As regards foreign goods, Shanghai was the centre of trade in north and middle China. Large volumes of foreign goods were shipped via Shanghai to other ports in north and middle China and even outer ports. The majority of all directly imported goods were Japanese. The quantity of foreign goods re-exported via Shanghai to north and middle China increased rapidly in the last years of the century. By contrast, south China was not deeply involved in these linkages. In south China, Hong Kong was the leading commercial centre. As for domestic goods, the most important trade relationship was between Shanghai and Hankow. The volume of shipments between these cities increased by 197 per cent between 1876 and 1899. Large volumes of locally produced goods from the Middle Yangtze were shipped from Hankow

Table 6.3 Brown sugar exports (including re-exports) and imports in the internal market in China (in 1,000 piculs)

	1876		1890		1899		1904	
	Imports	Exports	Imports	Exports	Imports	Exports	Imports	Exports
Yingkow	105	2	105	–	76	–	27	
Tientsin	193	–	248	3	167		70	
Chefoo	238	23	185		85	–	41	2
Kiaochow					6		2	
Ichang					10	9	4	3
Hankow	164	–	185		230		133	1
Kiukiang	17		20		6			
Wuhu			30	–	34		26	
Chinking	64		296	1	218	2	81	
Shanghai	595	260	705	784	500	61	359	171
Hangchow							121	
Ningpo	10	1	45		8		5	
Wenchow							1	
Foochow				1	–		1	
Amoy	18	108		120		139		40
Swatow		539		752		977		593
Canton		115		89		121		61
Total	1,404	1,048	1,822	1,749	1,341	1,308	870	871

Source: China, Imperial Maritime Customs Service, *Annual Reports*.

to Shanghai and most were exported to foreign markets. Imported foreign goods were shipped from Shanghai to Hankow in exchange. Tea was transferred from Hankow to Tientsin and finally exported to Russia. It was between Tientsin and Shanghai that the commercial growth was most remarkable. The volume of shipments between these ports increased by 358 per cent from 1876 to 1899. The Tientsin area was a great market for goods shipped through Shanghai. The trade in domestically produced goods between Yingkow and Shanghai was balanced. But south China markets were also important for Yingkow's balance of trade. The volume of domestic goods shipped between south China and Shanghai showed steady growth. On the other hand, Hong Kong was an important market for domestic goods from Guangchow. There was substantial trade between Wuhu and Swatow and Canton. Rice was the most important item in these transactions from Wuhu to south China.

The open ports can be classified into two groups: those who were

Table 6.4 Domestic cloth exports (including re-exports) and imports in the internal market in China (in 100 piculs)

	1876 Imports	1876 Exports	1890 Imports	1890 Exports	1899 Imports	1899 Exports	1904 Imports	1904 Exports
Yingkow	1		22		164	–	771	1
Tientsin	35		40	–	71	2	43	2
Chefoo	1		2	8	22	1	53	25
Kiaochow					–	–	5	–
Chungking					–		–	
Ichang			–		1	–	2	–
Shasi							–	8
Hankow	1	17	1	135	2	137	18	112
Kiukiang	4		13		13	–	6	–
Wuhu			105	2	119	1	70	–
Chinking	3		28	–	30	–	28	–
Shanghai	35	165	66	201	121	463	60	1,032
Ningpo	3		9		3			2
Wenchow								7
Foochow	5		17	–	21		33	–
Amoy	1	2	2	–	9		12	–
Swatow	17	19	22	64	27	135	25	60
Canton	96		71	1	136	3	124	–
Total	202	203	397	411	738	742	1,257	1,244

Source: China, Imperial Maritime Customs Service, *Annual Reports*.

developing due to the increase of imports, and those whose development was based on an increase in exports. In 1899 more than 50 per cent of the gross value of trade at Shanghai, Hankow and Wuhu was for export. These ports produced their own particular local products. For example, in Wuhu in 1899 the ratio of rice exports to total exports was 77 per cent. In Foochow and Kiukiang the ratio of tea exports to total exports was 80 per cent and 56 per cent, respectively. And at Amoy, Chinking, Ichang and Tientsin, the ratio of imports to the gross value of trade was comparatively high. The development of these ports was dependent on transportation improvements. At Tientsin and Chinking the ratio of imported cotton goods to total imports was over 30 per cent. In south China, for example, in Amoy and Swatow, the ratio of foodstuffs imported to total imports was relatively high.

There were two main trade areas in China: north and middle China, and south China. In north and middle China, Shanghai was the most

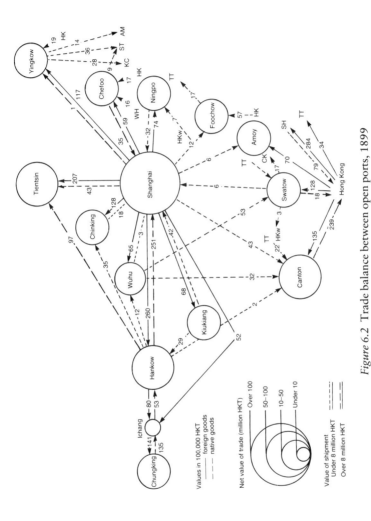

Figure 6.2 Trade balance between open ports, 1899

Source: China, Imperial Maritime Customs Service, *Annual Report, 1899*.

important transit port importing from middle China to Shanghai and re-exporting from Shanghai to north China. As a result silver flowed from north China to Shanghai and from Shanghai to middle China. On the other hand, south China had close trade relations with Hong Kong and South-East Asia. So in the late nineteenth century there was no single unified market, but two regional self-sufficient markets in China. Canton Maritime Customs remarked:

> Probably these imports (from the northern ports) which are thus in excess of our Exports coastwise, our Exports to Hongkong which are in excess of the Imports from that place and Hongkong's Exports to the coast ports, are parts of the same circle of changes.[5]

These regional economies were involved in a multilateral trade network.

The next topic is the relation between the growth of foreign trade and the development of the flow of domestic goods. We shall examine the beancake and cotton cloth trade in the Yingkow market. It is said that trade between Manchuria and southern China began at the time of the Ch'ing dynasty even though some of it was officially prohibited. At that time soybeans and bean products were shipped from Manchuria to southern China. Raw cotton, cotton products, silks and silk products were shipped from the Lower Yangtze to Manchuria, and sugar was carried from south China to Manchuria. But the quantity of Yinkow's trade was dependent upon the purchasing power generated by Manchuria's export activities.

Beancake was one of the most important goods for the Yingkow export trade. It was consumed mainly in south China. That area had been Manchuria's main beancake customer until Japan started to purchase it. In south China beancake was used chiefly as a fertilizer for sugar and corn cultivation, so the quantity of beancake exports from Yingkow was dependent on the state of sugar production in south China. Table 6.5 shows the value of sugar exports from Swatow to foreign and internal markets, and Table 6.6 shows the quantity of beancake exported from Yingkow to foreign countries and internal markets. According to the tables, these two commodities were mainly for domestic consumption and we can see the correlation between beancake exports at Yingkow and sugar exports at Swatow. After 1899 more and more Yingkow beancake was exported to foreign countries, particularly Japan, but it should be noted that the internal market was still of importance until the Russo-Japanese War. A lot of beancake was consumed in Japan in the 1890s. At that time it was still being sold in

Table 6.5 Swatow sugar exports (in 1,000 piculs)

	Brown sugar	White sugar	Foreign countries	Chinese ports	Total
1881	62	62	29	94	123
1882	61	66	29	98	127
1883	70	78	43	105	148
1884	82	100	44	138	182
1885	74	76	17	133	150
1886	65	66	7	124	131
1887	79	72	6	151	157
1888	76	66	7	134	141
1889	74	70	11	133	144
1890	75	74	1	149	149
1891	83	83	1	165	166
1892	63	56	1	118	119
1893	55	47	0	102	102
1894	46	46	0	92	92
1895	69	61	2	128	130
1896	70	63	1	132	133
1897	70	63	0	133	133
1898	79	67	2	143	146
1899	103	82	5	177	183
1900	85	53			138
1901	81	57			135
1902	64	45			109
1903	59	42			101
1904	59	47			107
1905	49	31			80
1906	33	23			56
1907	57	32			89
1908	48	35			83
1909	30	20			50
1910	64	22			86

Source: China, Imperial Maritime Customs Service, *Annual Reports*.

both southern China and Japan in large quantities.

As for the Yingkow import trade, Table 6.7 shows the value of American sheeting, the most popular foreign cotton cloth in Manchuria; the value of imports of cloth from the Yangtze region also increased. Before foreign trade expanded, cotton cloth imports from America depended on purchasing power based on the Yingkow region beancake exports to southern China. It was the increase in purchasing

Table 6.6 Yingkow beancake exports (in 10,000 piculs)

	Foreign countries	Chinese ports	Total
1881	–	144	144
1882	3	159	162
1883	1	171	172
1884	–	188	188
1885	2	179	181
1886	–	148	148
1887	5	198	203
1888	4	182	186
1889	8	181	189
1890	8	254	262
1891	22	285	307
1892	52	230	283
1893	34	199	233
1894	37	229	266
1895	31	50	81
1896	150	123	273
1897	168	163	331
1898	176	194	370
1899	235	203	438
1900	158	134	292
1901	267	166	433
1902	361	103	464
1903	324	131	455
1904	26	173	199
1905	152	20	172
1906	300	66	366
1907	290	77	267
1908	370	88	458
1909	467	55	522
1910	337	138	475

Source: China, Imperial Maritime Customs Service, *Annual Reports*.

power, based on the growth of the foreign export trade in beancake, which made possible the simultaneous increase in imports of Yangtze cotton cloth and American cloth. From the data shown above, it appears that foreign trade expansion and the development of internal trade were closely interrelated.

Table 6.7 Yingkow cotton sheeting imports (in 10,000 pieces; native cloth in 100 piculs)

	American sheeting	Native cloth via MC[a]	Native cloth via native customs
1881	3	18	
1882	6	28	
1883	7	7	
1884	15	8	
1885	19	22	
1886	22	49	
1887	26	54	
1888	19	16	
1889	20	21	
1890	41	22	
1891	46	20	
1892	37	17	
1893	25	24	
1894	29	19	
1895	14	57	
1896	38	84	
1897	57	98	
1898	63	134	
1899	110	164	
1900	43	76	
1901	98	240	
1902	109	196	1,728
1903	103	156	1,461
1904	114	769	827
1905	225	1,250	1,080
1906	34	938	1,064
1907	26	169	698
1908	52	202	1,239
1909	60	329	1,859
1910	33	278	1,189

Note: [a] MC = Maritime Customs
Source: China, Imperial Maritime Customs Service, *Annual Reports*.

CHINESE MERCHANTS AND INTERNAL MARKETS

The internal flow of goods was entirely controlled by Chinese merchants. Apart from locally produced goods, American and European goods were distributed by Chinese merchants, who were very active in the trade with Japan.

In internal trade Chinese merchants benefited from their settlement system, which owed its origin to the shortage of currency. Yingkow's settlement system was reported thus:

It [the Yingkow settlement system] may be briefly described thus: – a merchant selling Imports of any kind, although selling nominally for cash, must – unless he wishes to engage in the export trade, or is willing to submit to a discount of from one to five per cent – accept in payment for his goods what is known as 'market money' which is simply a credit placed to his name at a local native bank. All transactions are done through this bank and generally without even the passing of cheques or other documents between the parties. The buyer and seller go together to the bank and the former directs that the amount due the other be debited to his own account and placed to the credit of the seller. They may see the entry made in the books of the bank and both parties will keep a record of the transaction in their own private accounts; but, unless specially asked for, nothing in the form of a cheque or bill passes between them. The bank also, if requested, gives a certificate of credit to the seller, although this is not common. A credit thus placed means it is available at fourteen days' sight. Now this credit can only be used at par, in the purchase of other produce. If the seller desires actual sycee, he must pay for it the current premium, which, as just stated, may be from one to five per cent.[6]

This settlement system was profitable for the Chinese import–export merchants and promoted bartering. It made trade expansion possible even when little silver cash was available. There were many similar regional settlement systems all over China. This system functioned on the condition that merchants' credits offset each other. If the value of trade decreased sharply, the silver cash supply was not equal to demand and the settlement systems ceased to work. The system was not adaptable to fluctuations in the value of trade. If the settlement system had worked better, the trade could have become larger. As it was, the larger the trade grew, the more unstable it became. The main basis of these settlement systems was the fact that regional certificates of credit could be exchanged for a draft on Shanghai. As for the relations between internal trade and the settlement system, Japanese reports said: 'It is easy to remit money to Hong Kong or Shanghai with which

Table 6.8 Yingkow foreign trade value (in
1,000 HKT)

	Imports	Exports
1901	17,148	18,742
1902	18,316	17,525
1903	20,483	19,982
1904	19,298	12,159
1905	31,180	12,031
1906	14,029	14,790
1907	10,961	15,712
1908	15,334	19,609

Source: China, Imperial Maritime Customs Service,
Annual Reports.

Tientsin has close trade relations. But it is difficult to remit money to Newchwang [Yingkow] or Chefoo, especially Newchwang, because there are few transactions between Tientsin and Newchwang.'[7] 'Chinese banks can remit money to internal places, but they cannot send money to foreign countries, so it is easier for merchants to import foreign goods via Shanghai.'[8] Interregional trade and the settlement system were closely related to each other. Shanghai was the centre of settlement as well as of trade.

Foreign merchants did not have locally produced Chinese goods which could be exchanged together with their goods. When they wanted to get their profit in silver sycee, they were obliged to reduce their income. This placed foreign merchants at a disadvantage, and in the late nineteenth century foreign merchants withdrew from local ports to trading centres at Shanghai or Hong Kong.

As mentioned above, Chinese internal trade, including trade in foreign goods, was carried out by Chinese merchants, and although a few Japanese firms tried to achieve direct trade with the internal markets, the results of their attempts fell short of their expectations. So Japanese goods were also distributed from Shanghai to the internal market. After the Russo-Japanese war, the settlement system was disrupted by heavy fluctuations of trade in north China. Table 6.8 shows Yingkow's trade from 1901 to 1908. The munition boom at Yingkow and its collapse can be clearly seen. As a result, there was commercial panic there in 1907. This disturbance stopped shipments from Shanghai to Manchuria. Meanwhile, the direct import of goods

141

Table 6.9 Yingkow foreign cotton cloth imports (in 1,000 pieces)

| | Sheeting | | Drill | |
	American	Japanese	American	Japanese
1903	1033	71	570	3
1904	1141	2	442	4
1905	2252	60	975	12
1906	337	2	66	–
1907	258	99	131	9
1908	515	151	195	52
1909	602	186	302	102
1910	326	245	171	150
1911	309	370	138	186

Source: China, Imperial Maritime Customs Service, *Annual Reports*.

from Japan increased after the war. The rise in imports of Japanese cotton goods created competition with American cotton cloth shipped via Shanghai. This meant competition between the Chinese and Japanese merchants.

Table 6.9 shows the quantity of Japanese and American cotton cloth imported to Yingkow. After the Russo-Japanese War, Japanese products exceeded American goods.[9] The establishment of the Japanese Cotton Export Guild in 1906 is considered to be the principal reason for the increase in imports of Japanese cloth. The Guild was founded by five Japanese cotton mills, with Mitsui Bussan as a central figure. It sought to produce cotton cloth of uniform quality and to promote sales. It can be assumed that the collapse of the settlement system, due to the Russo-Japanese war, provided the opportunity for Japanese merchants to expand their sales in northern China.

From 1907 to 1910 there occurred many commercial crises in China. These crises, each of which had its own local origin, influenced each other. For example, a crisis in north China affected the Shanghai economy and caused a crisis there. The Shanghai transit trade was also disturbed by a regional economic depression caused by the Russo-Japanese War and the depreciation of the copper currency in the Middle Yangtze. During this difficult period Chinese interregional linkages changed. Table 6.10 shows Shanghai's trade. The ratio of foreign goods in transit to gross trade fell gradually. Meanwhile, the movement of local produce to internal markets increased, and so did the value of trade with Hanow and Tientsin, and so on.

Table 6.10 Shanghai trade value (in million HKT)

	Foreign goods			Domestic produce			Domestic produce of local origin	
	Imports	Re-exports		Imports	Re-exports		Exports	
		Foreign countries	Chinese ports		Foreign countries	Chinese ports	Foreign countries	Chinese ports
1900	127	7	81	67	45	13	34	17
1905	260	10	157	112	69	30	39	33
1910	200	9	138	177	113	39	63	32
1915	206	15	126	239	155	45	46	58
1920	390	15	150	218	105	59	89	144

Source: China, Imperial Maritime Customs Service, *Annual Reports*.

CONCLUSION

The strength of the Chinese merchants was based on their mercantile network. It should be noted that the expansion of Japanese sales in Asia was one of the most significant factors in Japanese industrialization. That expansion caused conflict between Chinese and Japanese merchants who tried to penetrate into the existing Chinese market network. Economic disturbances in China helped Japan expand her market and she increased her market share. But Japanese merchants were not completely successful. Chinese merchants continued to control the trade in many items.

NOTES

1. There were some changes in the Maritime Customs statistical series. See Hsiao Liang-lin, *China's Foreign Trade Statistics, 1864–1949*. Cambridge, Mass.: Harvard University Press, 1974, Introduction and 266–7. There is some difficulty when we examine Chinese internal trade. Customs statistics do not include domestic movements of Chinese junks.
2. Lower Yangtze includes Shanghai, Ningpo, Hangchou, etc. Middle Yangtze includes Hankow, Kiukiang, Wuhu, etc. North China includes Tienstin, Yingkow, Chefoo, etc. South China includes Swatow, Foochow, Canton, Amoy, etc.
3. According to the China Maritime Customs Decennial Reports, the beancake price per picul increased from HKT 0.76 (average 1882–91) to HKT 2.06 (average 1902–11).
4. Swatow's native cloth was actually native-dyed foreign cloth. See China

Maritime Customs, *Returns of Trade and Trade Reports, 1879: Swatow*, 211.

5. China Maritime Customs, *Returns of Trade and Trade Reports, 1890*, Part II: *Canton*, 413.

6. China Maritime Customs, *Reports on Trade, 1871–2: Newchwang*, 5.

7. Yuki Yamakawa, *Shinkoku Shutchō Fukumeisho* (Report on China), Tokyo, 1899, 104.

8. Japan, Foreign Office, *Manshu Jijo* (Report on North-eastern China), Tokyo, 1910, II, 110.

9. Kang Chao, 'The Chinese–American cotton-textile trade, 1830–1930', in Ernest R. May and John K. Fairbank (eds) *America's China Trade in Historical Perspective*, Cambridge, Mass.: Harvard University Press, 1986, 119–25.

7

THE DYNAMICS OF INTRA-ASIAN TRADE, 1868–1913

The Great Entrepôts of Singapore and Hong Kong

A.J.H.Latham

The network of intra-Asian trade in the late nineteenth century is only now being fully researched. This chapter will examine the trade of the two great redistribution centres of the East, Singapore and Hong Kong, and assess their role in the dynamic growth of commerce there in these years.

I

One of the first points which must be recognized is that although Singapore and Hong Kong were British colonies, much of their importance lay not in distributing British goods in Asia, but in re-directing and re-allocating Asian goods within Asia. They were the twin hubs of intra-Asian trading activity, not merely British trading outposts. British control of these two great ports ensured the maintenance of relatively free movement of trade in the Malacca and Sunda Straits, and the South China Sea, which was more important for the trade of East Asia than it was for the trade of Britain or the British Empire. But it did ensure access for British goods within the network of intra-Asian trade to those countries of Asia not part of the British Empire, whether they were French, like Indo-China, Dutch like Java and Sumatra, Spanish-American like the Philippines, or independent like Siam, China or Japan.

India provided Britain with her fastest-growing market in this period, but it is now understood that her position in international trade was more important than this. She had surpluses on her trade with America and continental Europe, but she also had a massive surplus on her trade with the rest of Asia, which despite her deficit with Britain gave her overall a massive trade surplus that resulted in a continuous inflow of gold and silver.[1] It was her relationship with the rest of Asia, and in particular China and Japan, which was the key to her success in the international economy. Recent work by Latham, Kawakatsu and Sugihara has concentrated on investigating more fully the intricacies of the web of intra-Asian trade which was opened up by this early work on India's trading surplus.

A key commodity in intra-Asian trade was rice, and understanding the movement of rice by sea in Asia is crucial to understanding the mesh of commerce there, and the forces which lay behind the dynamism of economic growth which manifested itself in this period. Rice was exported from Burma, then part of British India, and Siam and Indo-China to the rice deficit parts of Asia such as Singapore and the Malay Peninsula, Java and Sumatra, Borneo, the Philippines, and Hong Kong and the southern provinces of China. The trade was organized by Indian and Chinese merchants, using junks, *prahus* and other local shipping, a large proportion of these rice movements passing through either Singapore or Hong Kong.[2] It was the income gained by the capitalistic peasant producers of exported rice which enabled them to purchase textiles produced by the emerging manufacturing industries of Asia in Bombay, Shanghai and Osaka. Kawakatsu argues convincingly that industrialization in the cotton textile industry in Asia was possible because yarn and cloth could be produced there, using Asian cotton, at lower prices than the rival and more expensive products from Lancashire, which were made from American cotton. Asia continued to import up-market British cottons, but industrialized on the basis of down-market Asian products sold to rice-growing peasants.[3]

Similarly Sugihara, investigating Asia's integration into the world economy at this time, has argued that Japan's industrialization and the development of South-East Asia's rice exporting economies were very much two sides of the same coin. Rice producers bought yarn and textiles from Japan with the money they had obtained from growing and selling rice, some of which was actually supplied to Japan to feed the textile workers.[4] The implication is that perhaps there was dynamism in East Asia which did not owe its origin to trade with Europe and the West, but from growing specialization and incomes in Asia itself. Maybe there was an internal dynamism in the East entirely independent of market forces in the West.

II

It is within the context of the concept of an expanding intra-Asian economy that this chapter will examine the trade of Singapore and Hong Kong. For Singapore the trade figures of the Straits Settlements are used, which include Singapore's satellites Penang and Malacca. In constructing these figures the official sterling values given in the

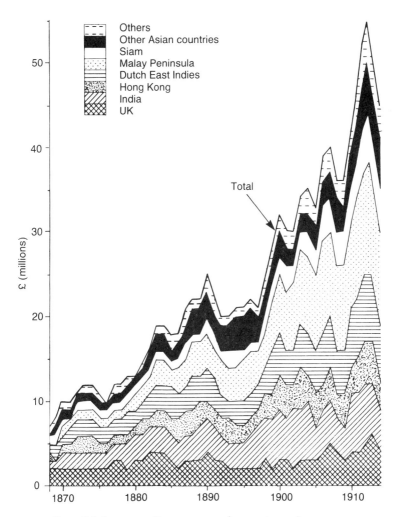

Figure 7.1 Imports to Singapore, etc., from major trading partners
Source: Appendix 7.1.

147

Table 7.1 Imports to Singapore, etc. (%)

	1868	1870	1880	1890	1900	1910	1913
UK	29.08	25.55	26.04	15.98	10.47	10.74	11.04
India	15.28	12.72	17.49	17.01	18.56	15.19	11.33
Hong Kong	10.31	11.12	12.15	9.94	11.88	9.10	8.33
Dutch East Indies	11.04	13.12	15.89	15.85	16.84	15.61	14.67
Malay Peninsula	5.22	9.40	8.25	14.92	20.69	23.87	23.76
Siam	7.17	8.14	9.60	7.28	6.28	8.85	9.72
Other Asia	9.75	10.95	5.26	12.72	9.24	9.28	10.44
Others	12.12	8.96	5.28	6.26	6.01	7.32	10.18
Total	99.97	99.96	99.96	99.96	99.97	99.96	99.97

Source: Appendix 7.1.

Statistical Abstract for British Colonies were used, but because these were erratically adjusted for the decline in the value of the silver Straits Settlements dollar, they were converted into £ sterling by using Shirras's figures for the value of silver per ounce, and then adjusting this to the weight of the dollar. An ounce of silver weighed 480.36 grains, and a Straits Settlement dollar weighed 417.44 grains.[5] This parallels the method used for adjusting the figures for India's trade with Hong Kong later in the chapter.

Table 7.2 Growth rates of Singapore, etc.: imports and exports, 1868–1913 (% per annum)

	Imports	Exports
UK	2.20	4.73
India	3.73	2.78
Hong Kong	4.07	1.23
Dutch East Indies	5.09	4.03
Malay Peninsula	8.00	6.54
Siam	5.10	1.79
Other Asia	4.49	2.24
All Asia	5.11	3.48
US	–	5.90
Others	4.02	4.73 (not inc. US)
		5.18 (inc. US)
Total	4.43	4.09

Source: Appendices 7.1, 7.2.

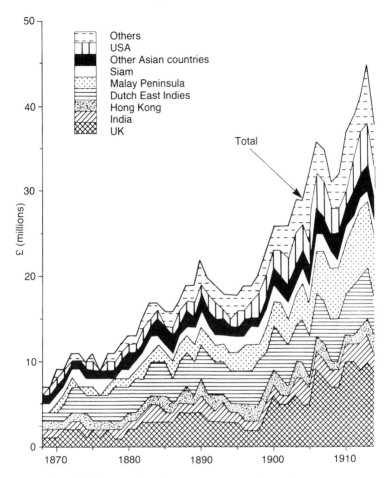

Figure 7.2 Exports from Singapore, etc., to major trading partners
Source: Appendix 7.2.

Figure 7.1 shows the value of imports going to Singapore etc. from her major trading partners. Table 7.1 gives the percentage of her imports from these countries at ten-year intervals. What is immediately obvious is that Singapore's imports from the countries of Asia are far more important than her imports from Britain, which never even reach 30 per cent of the total, and decline steadily as a percentage over the period to just over 10 per cent. Imports from India, Hong Kong, Dutch East Indies, Malay Peninsula, Siam and other parts of Asia vastly overwhelm those from Britain. Imports from Asia grew from

Table 7.3 Exports from Singapore, etc. (%)

	1868	1870	1880	1890	1900	1910	1913
UK	18.01	19.95	16.67	19.37	23.00	26.94	23.68
India	11.46	10.33	6.80	9.71	5.01	5.08	6.47
Hong Kong	11.99	8.67	7.25	7.89	6.03	3.06	3.41
Dutch East Indies	14.03	14.41	27.52	17.47	19.10	14.06	13.65
Malay Peninsula	6.26	7.47	7.15	11.53	13.01	15.67	17.87
Siam	8.65	10.07	7.59	9.15	4.95	4.00	3.16
Other Asia	13.47	13.02	11.31	8.33	7.94	7.07	6.01
US	5.37	8.89	8.60	6.57	10.29	9.11	11.64
Others	10.70	7.15	7.07	9.94	10.62	14.96	14.06
Total	99.94	99.96	99.96	99.96	99.95	99.95	99.95

Source: Appendix 7.2.

£4,672,876 to £44,062,055, a growth rate of 5.11 per cent over the 45 years, whilst imports from Britain only grew from £2,312,275 to £6,175,526, a growth rate of only 2.20 per cent. To make the point about Asia's importance in Singapore's imports even more strongly, it can be pointed out that in 1868 58 per cent of Singapore's imports came from Asia, but in 1913 that figure had increased to 78 per cent. Imports from other non-Asian countries accounted for only 12 per cent of the total in 1868 and 10 per cent in 1913. Table 7.2 gives the growth rates of imports and exports between Singapore, etc., and her major trading partners, from which it emerges that imports from the Malay Peninsula grew the fastest at 8 per cent per year, which is only to be expected as Singapore, Penang and Malacca were essentially the main ports serving the Peninsula. As we shall see, imports of tin were largely responsible for this expansion of trade, and also at the very end of the period, imports of rubber. Imports from the Dutch East Indies also grew very rapidly, because Singapore was a port of transhipment for many products of Java and Sumatra, in which tin and rubber again featured strongly, and also sugar. Imports increased substantially from Siam, due to purchases of rice, not only to feed Chinese migrants in Singapore and the Malay Peninsula, where they worked in the mines and plantations, but also in the Dutch East Indies, to which rice was transhipped. Imports grew fairly quickly from Hong Kong, partly due to specialist Chinese foodstuffs and artifacts, and less quickly from India, where opium, cottons, and rice from Burma featured. From the more detailed statistics given in Appendix 7.1 it can be seen that there was substantial trade with Indo-China, a French territory, largely because of imports of rice, and also imports from China. Japan does not feature until 1882, and though imports from there grew swiftly, they were too small to have accounted for the dynamism of Singapore's import structure. Nor can they have been particularly important to Japan's exports, except in so far as they were growing positively.

When we turn to exports, shown on Figure 7.2 and in Table 7.3, we can see that the West was a more important destination for Singapore's exports than she had been as a source of her imports. In 1868 the West took just over one-third of her exports, and in 1913 half of a much larger total. British imports grew from £1,342,496 to £10,745,269, at an average annual growth rate of 4.73 per cent. But the development of tin mining and rubber in the Malay Peninsula and the Dutch East Indies, much of which passed through Singapore for export, meant that other Western countries increased their share of Singapore's exports. By 1913, when Britain was taking 23 per cent of her exports, other Western countries were taking an additional 25 per cent, the US taking 11 per cent alone. Exports to the US grew at 5.18 per cent.

But if half Singapore's exports were going to the West, the other half went to Asian countries, with the Malay Peninsula itself taking 17 per cent. Exports to the Peninsula grew at 6.54 per cent, due in part to purchases of development material, but also supplies of rice, fish and other foodstuffs, utensils and hardware for the Chinese and Indian workers. The Dutch East Indies figures strongly with 13 per cent of the total in 1913, and a growth rate of 4.03 per cent for similar reasons. Exports to Siam, however, declined to 3 per cent of the total, with a low growth rate, and exports to both India and Hong Kong, and to other parts of Asia, declined in share and experienced low rates of growth. This suggests that the dynamism which Asian imports to Singapore enjoyed was not reflected in Singapore's exports to Asia. Indeed, on reflection, it seems that the dynamic element in Singapore's trade was Western purchases of tin and rubber, which drew imports to Singapore which were then re-exported West. The purchasing power which was thus transmitted to Singapore and Asia was not then channelled back to Britain, America and other Western countries, but retained in Asia where it was spent to a considerable extent on rice and other foodstuffs, and the manufactures of Asia's emergent industries. What is more, despite the increase in exports to the West, Singapore was generally in deficit on her trade account. In 1868 there was a deficit of £498,855, and this had grown to £10,561,340 by 1913. But as she was in surplus with non-Asian countries excluding Britain throughout the period, and in surplus even with Britain from about 1885, it is clear that her deficits lay in her trade with Asia. The dynamism of Singapore's trade did not originate in the East, but in the West. There is little evidence here of an internal dynamic in the East. On the contrary, dynamism was transmitted to the East from Singapore's Western sales.

K.G. Tregonning's *Home Port Singapore: A History of the Straits Steamship Company Ltd*[6] gives a fascinating impression of Singapore's South-East Asian trading connections, but the key study of Straits Settlement trade is by Chiang Hai Ding,[7] although he does not analyse imports or exports by country in detail. He does, however, confirm the importance of intra-Asian trade. At Singapore harbour Western manufactures were imported, and South-East Asian produce exported, whilst at the nearby Singapore river the native junks, *prahus* and other craft clustered, bringing rice, fish, areca nuts, gutta percha, rattans and the produce of the East, and taking away salt, opium, cotton piece goods and Western manufactures. Chinese middlemen linked the two emporia together, shifting goods between the new Harbour wharves, Raffles Place and Boat Quay on the Singapore river by bullock cart. English was the language of commerce for the foreign market, and Malay the language of the bazaar. The intra-Asian trade centred on Boat Quay, and was controlled by Chinese merchants whose trading networks spread far and wide across South-East Asia.[8]

Some insight into the complexities of Singapore's rice trade, the most important item in the intra-Asian trade, can be gained from Latham and Neal's paper of 1983.[9] This shows that rice came from Siam, Burma and French Indo-China, listed in order of importance, and was re-exported to the Malay Peninsula and the Dutch East Indies, with countries like Borneo taking the rest. Chiang confirms that other Asian foodstuffs such as fish and areca nuts were distributed in a similar way, but his breakdown of Straits Settlements imports and exports shows rice to have been the leading item of intra-Asian trade, comprising about 10 per cent of both imports and exports throughout the period. Opium was the next most important item of intra-Asian trade, but it fell from about 9 per cent of imports to 5 per cent between 1870 and 1910, with a corresponding fall in exports. Fish was much less important, constituting only about 2 per cent in each direction in 1910. Whilst rice was the dominant item of intra-Asian trade, it was only the second most important item in Singapore's total trade over the period as a whole. Tin led the way with imports rising from 10 per cent in 1870 to 19 per cent in 1910, and exports rising likewise from 13 per cent to 24 per cent. Rubber, that other vital Malayan product only became important after

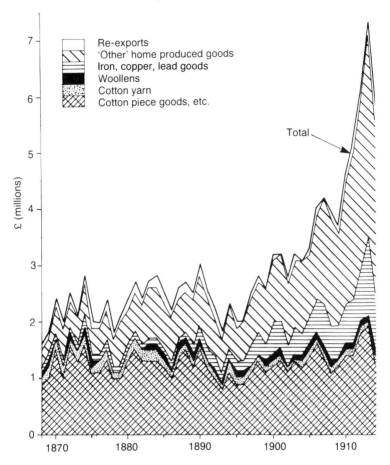

Figure 7.3 British exports to Singapore, etc.
Source: Appendix 7.3.

1905, but by 1910 was already contributing nearly 5 per cent of imports and 8 per cent of exports. By contrast, cottons dropped from about 20 per cent of imports in 1870 to less than 5 per cent in 1910, and from 18 per cent of exports to under 3 per cent. Tin and rubber were imported to Singapore for re-export to Britain and the West, but sufficient cottons did not move in the opposite direction. Clearly, an imbalance had developed.[10]

In understanding the trade of Singapore and Hong Kong in these years, it is necessary to have some insight into their trade with Britain,

Table 7.4 British exports to Singapore, etc. (%)

	1868	1870	1880	1890	1900	1910	1913
Cotton piece-goods	57.65	62.70	55.09	50.77	40.42	31.78	26.40
Cotton yarn	7.59	8.97	6.69	4.18	2.05	2.11	1.46
Woollens	4.62	2.04	2.21	1.91	1.49	1.61	1.47
Iron, copper, and lead manufactures	8.08	4.97	4.44	6.63	18.69	15.28	18.94
Others	16.63	17.69	23.77	31.81	35.57	46.67	48.82
Re-exports	5.41	3.59	7.76	4.67	1.75	2.51	2.88
Total	99.98	99.96	99.96	99.97	99.97	99.96	99.97

Source: Appendix 7.3.

and it has already been established that Singapore's imports from Britain grew only sluggishly. Cottons were the major item in imports from Britain. Figure 7.3 and Table 7.4 show the pattern of British exports to Singapore, etc., drawn from the *Annual Statement of Trade of the United Kingdom*. These show an annual growth rate of 3.41 per cent, rather higher than that for British imports to Singapore, a puzzling fact which may be partly explained by the fall in freight rates over the period. British exports were valued FOB (Full on Board), the price at which they were loaded on ship, but imports to Singapore were valued CIF (Cost Insurance and Freight), so the decline in freight rates would mean a progressive relative fall in the value of British cargoes arriving at Singapore.

Cotton piece-goods were by far the most important item, but as the figure shows, growth was negligible, at 1.64 per cent. In quantity terms exports grew from 56,974,235 yards to 131,298,100 yards, but this only represents an annual average growth of 1.87 per cent. Clearly, the piece goods trade was expanding less quickly than other sections of British trade.

The other major items of British export were cotton yarn, woollens and manufactures of iron, copper and lead. Apart from these there was also a miscellany of minor items, including apparel and haberdashery, arms and ammunition, beer and ale, coal, cinders and fuel, earthen- and chinaware, glass manufactures, hardware and cutlery, linens, machinery, telegraphic wires and apparatus, umbrellas and parasols, and so on. In 1868 cotton piece-goods contributed nearly 58 per cent of exports, but by 1913 they were only 26 per cent of the total, whilst

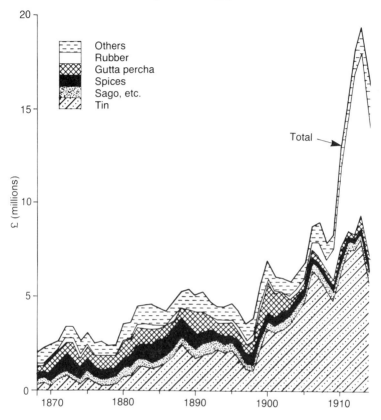

Figure 7.4 British imports from Singapore, etc.
Source: Appendix 7.4.

metal manufactures had increased from 8 per cent to 19 per cent.

The other category which showed considerable increase was the miscellaneous section, which increased from about 17 per cent to 49 per cent. The very slow increase in the value of British cottons exported to Singapore must be seen in the context of the relative decline of cottons as a percentage of Singapore's exports as a whole. It would be interesting to examine the composition of cotton imports in general to Singapore, and see what proportion of these were Indian or Japanese, but the figures are not to hand. Part of the explanation of the poor British performance may lie in the fact that to begin with Singapore imported British cottons to re-export to other parts of Asia, but later, cottons were sent direct to Asian countries by-passing Singapore

Table 7.5 British imports from Singapore, etc. (%)

	1868	1870	1880	1890	1900	1910	1913
Tin	18.52	11.56	19.08	33.64	47.88	48.06	41.82
Sago	13.04	11.13	13.99	10.60	5.94	3.68	1.90
Spices	13.96	15.52	12.58	13.64	6.60	1.80	0.87
Cutch & Gambier	16.93	14.04	12.67	10.16	3.71	1.16	0.62
Gutta percha	2.66	15.93	13.67	13.80	19.65	3.38	2.85
Rubber	3.71	2.86	3.10	1.19	2.65	34.69	45.57
Others	31.13	28.93	24.87	16.93	13.52	7.20	6.34
Total	99.95	99.97	99.96	99.96	99.95	99.97	99.97

Source: Appendix 7.4.

altogether. But probably more to the point is that Japanese cottons went direct to these markets.

None the less, it has been established that Singapore's rice imports from Siam, French Indo-China and Burma were considerable, and among the mix of goods which moved to those countries in exchange for rice were British cottons and manufactures. In 1894 the British Consul in Siam stated that 82 per cent of Bangkok's imports came from Singapore, Hong Kong and Bombay, of which Singapore was the most important, and that therefore British manufactures must have been a substantial part of this trade.[11] However, the Consul seems not to have understood Singapore's role in redistributing intra-Asian trade, and was apparently unaware how relatively unimportant British goods were in Singapore's range of imports and exports.

As for Britain's imports from Singapore, they are shown on Figure 7.4 and Table 7.5. The figure has had to be drawn on a different scale than Figure 7.3 because imports were so much bigger than exports. The figure reveals the overwhelming importance of tin in British imports, rising from over 18 per cent in 1868 to nearly 42 per cent in 1913. Even so, by then it was overshadowed by the dramatic increase in rubber which supplied nearly 4 per cent in 1868, less than 3 per cent in 1900, but over 45 per cent in 1913. It must of course be remembered that the establishment of plantation rubber in Malaya from the 1890s was one of the triumphs of the colonial period, with its heroes Clements Markham, Henry Wickham and 'mad' Henry Ridley.[12]

Another feature worth mentioning is that many of the items were classified as manufactured goods, because they had undergone some

156

form of processing. Tin of course was paramount here, as it was exported in blocks, ingots, bars and slabs after smelting. Prior to 1886 the Straits Settlements imported only smelted tin, and no ores, because the Malay States prohibited the export of ore. Then the Straits Trading Company was granted permission by the Selangor government to buy tin ore for a number of years, and they obtained concessions from other parts of the Peninsula, including Perak in 1889. They built a smelting works on an island in New Harbour, Singapore, and by 1896 were drawing ores away from rival Chinese operations in the Malay States. By this time five-sixths of the world's supply of tin came from Malaya. In 1900 Singapore had the largest smelting works in the world. A Chinese smelting works had been built in Penang in 1897, so in 1902 the Straits Trading Company built one of their own there, to compete with it. That they were able to do so is notable, as by 1914 three-quarters of Malayan tin came from Chinese mining operations.[13]

Cutch and gambier, which were extracts used for tanning, were also classified as manufactured items, so the Straits Settlements cannot be said to have been a mere supplier of raw materials to the metropolitan centre. There were also rice mills in Singapore and Penang, and rice milling was as important an industry for the industrialization of the East as flour milling was for the United States, although the output of these mills was distributed throughout Asia rather than to Britain.[14] Other items exported to Britain were things such as coffee, gum (lac, seed, stick and dye), untanned hides, horns and hoofs, isinglass, chemical oil (essential and perfumed), rice not in the husk, rum, unrefined sugar and hewn wood, all in too small a quantity to be separately itemized here.

Britain had a considerable trade deficit with Singapore in most years, and this deficit grew as purchases of tin and rubber increased. By 1913 British exports to Singapore were £7,388,201, when imports stood at £19,373,146, a deficit of £11,984,945. The deficit was greater than the total export value. The British deficit, or rather the Singapore surplus with Britain, does not show in the Straits Settlements figures until 1885, but this must be attributed to the freight and insurance charges included in the Straits Settlements import figures, but not in the British export figures. Shipping charges would have been payable to British companies for the most part. This British deficit with Singapore differs markedly from British experience with India where she had a considerable surplus. India had a deficit with Britain which she was able to pay for from the overall surplus on her trade with Asia and the rest of the world. But the opposite was true of Singapore which had a surplus with Britain which helped meet her overall deficit with Asia.[15] In 1913 British exports to the Straits stood at £7.3 million, but exports to India were nearly ten times as great at £71.7 million. Imports from the Straits were £19.3 million while those from India were more than double at £48.4 million. On this basis the British surplus with India was £23.3 million by comparison with the deficit with Singapore etc. of £11.9 million. In a wider context, Britain had a surplus with Asia in general that year of £35.7 million from exports of £128.3 million and imports of £92.6 million. Her Asian surplus was reduced by her deficit with the Straits.[16]

III

Now we can turn to the vexed question of Hong Kong, the most difficult and exploratory part of this chapter. Unlike Singapore, there are no trade figures for Hong Kong at all. It is said that they were never recorded or collected, as the Governor General was of the opinion they would only be misinterpreted by scholars in later generations. So the absence of figures leaves a gap in our understanding; without them it is difficult to begin to understand the economic mesh of the Far East. What follows is a highly conjectural exercise in reconstructing what the trade figures for Hong Kong might have looked like in these years. The technique adopted, admittedly elementary, is to make the assumption that one country's exports are another country's imports, and vice versa. Thus, if we have figures for China's exports to Hong Kong, and we do, then we have a rough estimate for Hong Kong's imports from China. The reverse is also true, and we use China's imports from Hong Kong as a proxy for Hong Kong's exports to China. The same principle is applied to Hong Kong's other trading partners as far as they can be established. Awkward questions like insurance and freight charges are skated over. None the less a rough picture emerges which has some plausibility. Others will doubtless see more sophisticated ways of tackling the problem, but at least this can be seen as a first attempt. It was certainly a time-consuming exercise, because obtaining figures for important trading partners such as Bangkok, French Indo-China and the Philippines required considerable detective work, and when figures were obtained they had, of course, to be converted into sterling. For Indo-China we still only have figures for rice exports to Hong Kong, but as this was the major item of trade from Indo-China they serve reasonably well. The Singapore exercise was used as a model for Hong Kong.

Figure 7.5 gives the graph for Hong Kong's imports. What is immediately obvious is that, as in the case of Singapore, Britain was not

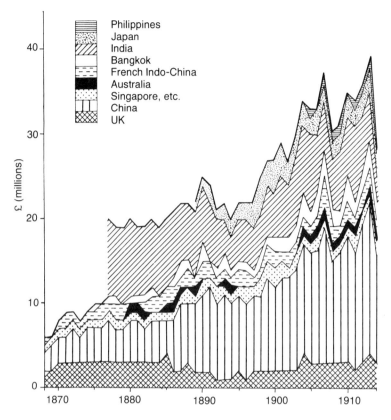

Figure 7.5 Imports to Hong Kong
Source: Appendix 7.5.

a very important trading partner although she was the colonial power. Imports from Britain grew hardly at all during these years, contributing nearly 18 per cent of imports in 1877, the first year for which we have reasonably full figures, and just less than 12 per cent in 1913. In these circumstances growth figures are almost meaningless, as anyone can see, but for the record, the rate from 1868 to 1913 is 1.52 per cent per annum. Table 7.6 shows the percentage of imports coming from the various countries, and Table 7.7 the rate of growth of trade with each country. Not surprisingly, it is China which is the chief supplier of Hong Kong's imports, providing 22 per cent of the total in 1877, and 45 per cent in 1913, the growth rate being a dynamic 4.37.

This contrasts sharply with the experience of India, Hong Kong's

Table 7.6 Imports to Hong Kong (%)

	1877[a]	1880[a]	1890[b]	1900	1910	1913
UK	17.63	19.40	10.57	10.78	10.73	11.66
China	22.13	23.55	32.92	36.22	40.98	45.28
Singapore, etc.	3.89	4.68	6.72	5.91	3.24	3.96
Australia	0.85	1.26	1.59	1.41	1.94	2.19
French Indo-China	8.06	4.52	7.68	7.25	5.23	5.42
Bangkok	4.16	2.49	6.44	4.23	8.17	7.30
India	43.24	44.06	27.95	19.69	22.08	13.78
Japan	–	–	6.09	14.46	6.96	8.74
Philippines	–	–	–	–	0.63	1.62
Total	99.96	99.96	99.96	99.95	99.96	99.95

Notes
[a] Excluding Japan and Philippines
[b] Excluding Philippines
Source: Appendix 7.5.

other major trading partner. In 1877 India supplied 43 per cent of the colony's imports, but this had fallen to less than 14 per cent in 1913. The growth rate over the period was actually negative at −1.41 per cent. One reason for this was the decline in the opium trade, India's

Table 7.7 Growth rates of Hong Kong imports and exports, 1868–1913

	Imports	*Exports*
UK	1.52	2.36
China	4.37	3.98
Singapore	1.23	4.07
Australia	4.44	1.62
French Indo-China	5.31	–
Bangkok (from 1870)	3.42	2.91
India (from 1877)	−1.41	−3.45
Japan (from 1889)	4.70	−6.77
Philippines (from 1903)	7.91	2.63
Total from 1877 (not including Japan and Philippines)	1.47	2.26
Total from 1877 (including Japan and Philippines)	1.78	2.28

Source: Appendices 7.5, 7.6.

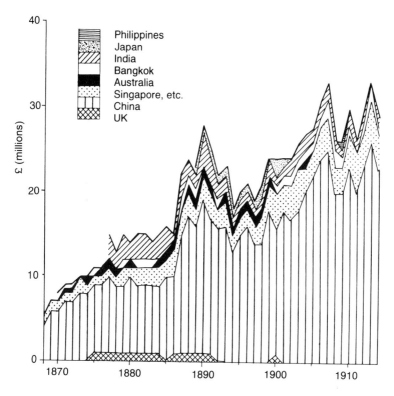

Figure 7.6 Exports from Hong Kong
Source: Appendix 7.6.

principal export to China in general.[17] The negative rate of growth of imports from India must have considerably lowered the overall rate of growth of imports into Hong Kong since 1877, which comes out at 1.78 per cent. Compare this with the rate of growth of imports into Singapore, etc., at 4.43 per cent.

Yet the structure of trade into Hong Kong was quite different from that into Singapore. There was virtually no inflow of tin and rubber into Hong Kong for re-export West. So the high rate of growth of imports from China was all the more remarkable. Nor did rice, that vital item of intra-Asian trade, come into Hong Kong from China, because China was a rice-deficit country and the people of her southern provinces had to import rice to live. Most of this rice came via Hong Kong, which imported it from other parts of Asia and re-exported it to China. Many observers reported rice to be the most important item of trade of the

Table 7.8 Exports from Hong Kong (%)

	1877[a]	*1880*[a]	*1890*[b]	*1900*[b]	*1910*	*1913*
UK	12.55	8.51	4.28	4.43	1.94	1.98
China	54.85	59.63	65.32	64.73	75.28	76.15
Singapore, etc.	10.72	11.48	8.84	15.87	12.62	14.51
Australia	2.25	3.07	2.43	1.17	0.79	1.07
Bangkok	1.98	2.18	2.71	2.84	3.74	3.27
India	17.62	15.09	13.16	6.44	4.99	2.30
Japan	–	–	3.24	4.48	0.22	0.38
Philippines	–	–	–	–	0.38	0.31
Total	99.97	99.96	99.98	99.96	99.96	99.97

Notes
[a] Excluding Japan and Philippines
[b] Excluding Philippines
Source: Appendix 7.6.

colony, importing it from Bangkok and French Indo-China, and redistributing it not only to China, but even to Japan, Hawaii and California. China was the main purchaser.[18] It is the import of rice which largely accounts for the high rate of growth of imports from French Indo-China, at 5.31 per cent, and from Bangkok, at 3.42 per cent, these being the two leading suppliers. Between them they were supplying nearly 13 per cent of Hong Kong's imports by 1913. Singapore was a relatively unimportant supplier of imports, and they showed little growth.

Japanese imports are not recorded before 1889, and in 1880 accounted for about 6 per cent of the total but, significantly for Asian development, they grew quickly at 4.70 per cent per annum, and in 1913 accounted for nearly 9 per cent of total imports. Clearly, Japan was on the move as an Asian trading nation, although still behind Britain as a supplier of goods to Hong Kong.

Other imports into Hong Kong from her various suppliers included sugar, flour, cotton piece goods and yarn, beans, hemp, kerosine, lead, opium, rattan, sandalwood, sulphur, tea, timber and general merchandise, and of course there was a large transit trade of which little is known.[19]

Details of Hong Kong exports are shown on Figure 7.6 and Table 7.8. Overwhelmingly exports were to China; so much so that, given the importance of China as a supplier of Hong Kong's imports, one is tempted to suggest that really Hong Kong was simply just a port of southern China which happened to be administered by the British. Hong Kong must have been a redistribution point for goods within China itself, goods going there to be sent on to other Chinese ports. Still, that cannot have been Hong Kong's only function because, as we have already seen, less than half of her imports came from China. Hong Kong was clearly also a funnel through which foreign goods passed on into China. Rice from Siam and Indo-China was one of these commodities, and opium from India another.

In return for the rice coming into Hong Kong, goods must have flowed the other way. Although we do not have details of the colony's exports to French Indo-China, the British Consul in neighbouring Siam listed piece-goods, earthenware, brass-ware, silk piece-goods, other silk goods, tea, paper, American flour, vegetables, matches, liquid sugar and molasses as coming from Hong Kong. Most of Bangkok's external trade was with Hong Kong and Singapore, and it was through these ports therefore that British manufactures would find their way to that country's markets.[20] Yet many of these listed items were not of British origin, underlining the relatively low percentage of British goods in Hong Kong's overall import structure, and Hong Kong's role as a redistributor of Asian goods in general. Many of the items, such as silks, tea and hardware, must have come from China and were going to Bangkok to supply the substantial Chinese community there, and similar items would have gone to Indo-China for the same reason. This trade in ethnic Chinese goods is also marked in Hong Kong's trade with Singapore.

To what extent Japanese goods were also re-distributed to Asian countries from Hong Kong is a cause for conjecture. If exports to China grew from 55 per cent to 76 per cent between 1877 and 1913, at a growth rate of 3.98 per cent, exports to Britain declined from less than 13 per cent to about 2 per cent of the total. Although a moderate rate of expansion at 2.36 per cent is revealed, a cursory examination of the figures shows this to be frankly meaningless. This was nothing like the rapid expansion of Singapore's exports to Britain in this period, but then Hong Kong's natural hinterland China was not producing tin and rubber like Singapore's hinterland, the Malay Peninsula and the Dutch East Indies.

Surprisingly, the second most important destination for Hong Kong's exports after China was Singapore, the percentage rising from nearly 11 per cent to over 14 per cent, with a growth rate of 4.07 per cent, the highest rate of growth of all Hong Kong's trading partners. In the absence of informed eye-witness accounts, one can only suppose that much of this trade was in Chinese ethnic consumer goods: silks, porcelains, teas and foodstuffs for the substantial Chinese migrant community at the mines and rubber plantations in the Malayan Peninsula and Java and Sumatra.[21] If this trade was a strong tie of intra-Asian trade, it must be remembered that imports from Singapore to Hong Kong do not show this vitality, and that in any case the Chinese community which was being served had been attracted to the mines and rubber plantations by Western economic forces. None the less Hong Kong earned a substantial surplus on her trade with Singapore, in 1913 exporting £4,939,638 but importing only £1,550,341, a surplus of £3,389,297.

Contrasting strongly with Singapore's experience was India, which took nearly 18 per cent of Hong Kong's exports in 1877, but just over 2 per cent in 1913. Presumably this reflects the catastrophic decline in India's opium exports to Hong Kong.

Other destinations for the colony's exports were of little significance, although it is worth noting that despite a growth rate of 4.70 per cent in imports from Japan, her exports to that country declined at a negative rate of −6.77. By 1913 Japan was importing only £88,653 from Hong Kong, but exporting £3,367,639, a surplus of £3,278,986. There can be no doubt that Japan was receiving a substantial boost to her economic development and industrialization from this trade link. One of the ways in which she integrated into the intra-Asian trade network was via Hong Kong. Her trade there was much more important to her than her trade with Singapore, although even there she had a surplus, as already noted. However, her surplus with China, which had built up rapidly from about 1899, was far greater. These surpluses were particularly important for Japan, as she had a deficit on her Asian trade in general due to heavy deficits with British India throughout, the Dutch East Indies from 1898, and smaller deficits with Siam, French Indo-China and the Philippines from about the 1890s. She was also in deficit with Europe to a very similar extent, due to deficits with Britain and Germany in particular, and despite surpluses with France and Italy from the 1870s. The only other country in Europe of any significance that she enjoyed a surplus with was Russia from 1894. It was with North America in general, and the United States in particular that she enjoyed her biggest surpluses, but even so apart from good years in the 1880s and early 1890s she was in overall deficit most years, 1906 and 1909 being exceptions. In this context the surpluses with Hong Kong and Singapore must have been all the more welcome. But her deficits with so many Asian countries clearly were important for the development of their export trades, whether it was rice from Siam and French Indo-China, sugar from the Dutch East Indies, or hemp and sugar from the Philippines.[22]

Returning again to Hong Kong, it can be noted that imports from Australia also experienced a high rate of growth, whilst exports there did not grow anything like so quickly, although they did not actually decline like those to Japan.

Before moving to a more detailed examination of British trade with Hong Kong, some consideration must be given to Hong Kong's overall balance of trade in so far as these figures can be relied on. Hong Kong appears to have run an overall trade deficit between 1877 and 1913, in 1913 exports being £34,032,063, but imports £39,054,905, a deficit of £5,022,842. She was however normally in surplus with her main trading partner, China. She was also usually in surplus with Singapore, etc. Her deficits therefore came from her trade with Britain and India while she had smaller deficits with Bangkok and Japan, and also Australia and the Philippines. We have no figures for Hong Kong's exports to French Indo-China but it is a fair assumption that she had a deficit there as well, as the trade with Indo-China was very similar to that with Bangkok, chiefly involving imports of rice. The fact that imports from French Indo-China are included in the overall figures, but not exports to that country, does of course exaggerate the total deficit, but not enough to render the whole outline invalid. So it appears that Hong Kong, like Singapore, was in deficit. But unlike Singapore, which had a surplus on her trade with Britain, she was in deficit with London.

It must be remembered that Hong Kong appears to have had a substantial trade with Germany, but there are no figures for this trade so far available. We know from the numbers of ships listed as visiting Hong Kong in the early years of the century that Germany was the second most important shipping nation in terms of steamships, usually sending about half as many ships as the British, the Japanese sending about half as many as the Germans. US shipping was negligible, at about 50 ships a year to Britain's 2,000. The absence of German figures is the biggest single omission from these figures, and it is not clear how they would have affected our assessment.[23]

The other significant omission is the Dutch East Indies, and this is because there is no convenient source of these statistics. Figures are available, but they are broken down by item and country. To obtain overall trade figures with particular countries it would be necessary to add each item going to every country for every year between 1868 and

1913. This is not an impossible task, but not one practical for the purposes of this paper.[24] Trade with Hong Kong may have been of some size, because the majority of the Netherlands Indies exports of sugar and other items were consumed in Asia, not the West, as we have already seen from the Japanese deficit with these countries.[25]

Now British trade with Hong Kong can be dealt with, and it must be said immediately that it reveals some strange characteristics. British exports to Hong Kong are shown on Figure 7.7. The relative lack of dynamism has already been mentioned, and this can be seen at a glance. Exports fell steadily in value from the 1880s through the 1890s, and if a new peak was hit in 1904, it fell away again, before recovering to a new peak in 1913. A long-term growth rate has no meaning in these circumstances. In the early days exports to Hong Kong were greater than those to Singapore, but from about the 1890s exports to Singapore rose swiftly and by 1913 their value was £7,388,201 to Hong Kong's £4,554,590. The types of goods exported to each colony were similar, as can be seen from Table 7.9. Cotton piece-goods were of course the major item, with cotton yarn, woollens, iron, copper and lead manufactures as other large categories. Note that woollens were more important than in the trade to Singapore, reflecting Hong Kong's cooler winters. The miscellaneous category 'others' increased to both colonies as the products available diversified over the years, and as development needs expanded. The impact of Japanese and Indian cottons on the Hong Kong market is not as marked as one might imagine, except that it may well be the penetration of these competitors in the China market that eroded the dynamism of British exports overall. Even in 1913, 51 per cent of British exports to Hong Kong were cotton piece-goods. Indian and Japanese competition may have been more marked in the yarn trade, as yarn contributed 16 per cent of exports in 1868 but less than 2 per cent in 1913.

When British imports from Hong Kong are examined, a truly remarkable picture emerges. Figure 7.8 is drawn on a different scale than Figure 7.7 because British imports from Hong Kong were so few. The peak year was 1877, after which they declined continuously. The pattern of imports can only be described as bizarre. Table 7.10 shows tea to have been the leading import in 1868, with nearly 67 per cent of the total, but by 1913 the figure was under 1 per cent. Silk knubs, etc., rose from 3 per cent to nearly 12 per cent. Hemp, presumably imported through Hong Kong from the Philippines, does not appear on the import schedules until the 1880s, rising to nearly 41 per cent in 1900, then collapsing to just over 1 per cent in 1913. 'Others' rose from about

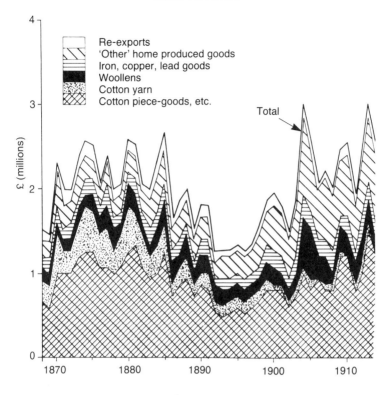

Figure 7.7 British exports to Hong Kong
Source: Appendix 7.7.

30 per cent in 1868 to 86 per cent in 1913. This category consisted of fruit, spices, sugar, bristles, canes, feathers and down, hair, hides, nuts and kernels, essential oil, arms and ammunition, chinaware, earthen-ware and pottery, curios, drugs, mats and matting, tin in blocks, ingots, bars and slabs, parcel post, and other items. As for the demise of tea, direct trade with China must have been responsible for this, as in 1910 Britain imported 18,782,200 pounds of tea, worth £645,810 direct from China.

The other feature of British trade with Hong Kong which requires comment is the fact which has already been established: that Hong Kong was in deficit with Britain throughout the period. By 1913, when imports stood at £675,276, exports to Hong Kong were £4,554,590, a surplus of £3,879,314. So she was in deficit with Britain, and in deficit overall. Put another way, Britain's surplus on her trade with Hong Kong

167

Table 7.9 British exports to Hong Kong (%)

	1868	1870	1880	1890	1900	1910	1913
Cotton piece-goods	44.60	44.65	49.92	47.94	43.11	48.27	51.46
Cotton yarn	16.22	18.42	18.73	9.81	1.89	0.58	1.72
Woollens	10.04	6.63	9.88	9.82	9.47	10.52	8.80
Iron, copper, and lead manufactures	9.85	7.54	6.33	9.18	12.30	8.20	8.28
Others	14.10	18.17	10.34	15.44	26.67	26.76	25.31
Re-exports	5.16	4.55	4.77	7.77	6.54	5.64	4.40
Total	99.97	99.96	99.97	99.96	99.98	99.97	99.97

Source: Appendix 7.7.

of £3,879,314 went some way to cover her deficit on her trade with Singapore of £11,984,945. What is more, Hong Kong's deficit with Britain that year amounted to nearly six times the value of her export trade to Britain. All in all, Britain's surplus with Hong Kong was a useful addition to her overall surplus with her trade in Asia. A further point worth making is that British exports to Hong Kong made up about a quarter of British exports to China as a whole, some 26 per cent in 1868 and 23 per cent in 1913.[26] What is more, China herself was in deficit with Britain from the mid-1880s, on the evidence of the Chinese figures.[27] China and India were the main source of Britain's Asian surplus, to which Hong Kong also contributed, but Singapore reduced it.

So from this chapter it emerges that the concept of a dynamic intra-Asian market economy is more complex than one might originally imagine. As far as Singapore is concerned, it was her Western sales of tin and rubber which were crucial to the growth of her trade. But she was in surplus with the West and in deficit with Asia, so her purchases of Asian products such as rice from Siam and Indo-China were important to the peasants of those countries. Her imports from Hong Kong were another important link in intra-Asian trade, and she was in deficit here presumably due to purchases of the paraphernalia of Chinese domestic life, from silks and tea to porcelain. Yet the Chinese who were purchasing them in the Malay Peninsula were only there because of Western demands for primary products. None the less, the producers of these items in Hong Kong's hinterland were clearly benefiting.

As for Hong Kong, it is difficult to argue that she owed the dynamism of her trade to Western demands, as she appears to have been

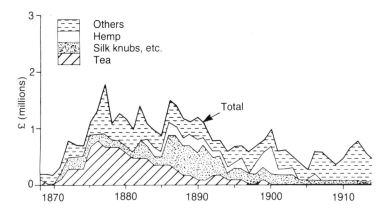

Figure 7.8 British imports from Hong Kong
Source: Appendix 7.8.

in deficit overall, and was certainly in deficit with Britain, her major Western trading partner. Unlike Singapore, Hong Kong did not have a hinterland producing tin and rubber, or indeed any other major primary good in demand in the West. Her sales to Britain were almost laughable. She was in deficit with Bangkok and probably with Indo-China, due to rice purchases, but much of this rice was for transhipment to the provinces of southern China, normally in deficit and often in dearth.

She was also in growing deficit with Japan, who must have benefited considerably from her trade surplus there. Japan, it must be noted, also had a large surplus with China and a smaller one with Singapore, these Asian surpluses being important to her as she was in deficit with the rest of Asia, and indeed in overall deficit. The remaining bright light in Japan's trading balance was her surplus with the United States. Indeed

Table 7.10 British imports from Hong Kong (%)

	1868	1870	1880	1890	1900	1910	1913
Tea	66.96	33.58	50.99	15.86	6.60	0.78	0.75
Silk knubs, etc.	3.13	18.31	9.81	40.32	20.52	27.73	11.98
Hemp	–	–	–	16.13	40.95	2.53	1.18
Others	29.90	48.10	39.19	27.66	31.90	68.95	86.06
Total	99.99	99.99	99.99	99.97	99.97	99.99	99.97

Source: Appendix 7.8.

169

this trading surplus which Japan had with the United States was another important Western input to the Asian trading network.

But the crucial element in Hong Kong's trade was her relationship with China with whom she had a surplus, which went a long way to meeting her deficits with Asia in general, and with the rest of the world. She also had an important surplus with Singapore. It is in China that the true nature of the changes taking place in Asia may be revealed. China constituted such a large part of intra-Asian trade, and it is there that the growth of trade reveals fundamental changes taking place. Even away from the great industrial city of Shanghai, specialization of function and exchange must have been resulting in increased productivity.[28] These changes can hardly have been due to Western demands. It is China which holds the key to the dynamism of the intra-Asian trading network, providing crucial sales for Bangkok and Indo-China through Hong Kong, and also for Japan. It is there that attention must now be centred.

NOTES

1. A.J.H. Latham, *The International Economy and the Undeveloped World, 1865–1914*, London: Croom Helm, 1978 and 1983, 67–83; A.J.H. Latham, 'Merchandise trade imbalances and uneven economic development in India and China', *Journal of European Economic History*, 7 (1978), 33–60.

2. A.J.H. Latham and Larry Neal, 'The international market in rice and wheat, 1868–1914', *Economic History Review*, 36 (1983), 260–79; A.J.H. Latham, 'The international trade in rice and wheat since 1868: a study in market integration', in Wolfram Fischer, R. Marvin McInnis and Jurgen Schneider (eds) *The Emergence of a World Economy, 1500–1914*, Part Ii, 1850–1914, Wiesbaden: Franz Steiner Verlag, 1986, 645–63; A.J.H. Latham, 'Ethnic Chinese multinationals in the international grain trade before the Second World War', *South African Journal of Economic History*, 1 (1986), 4–18; A.J.H. Latham, 'From competition to constraint: the international rice trade in the nineteenth and twentieth centuries', *Business and Economic History*, Second Series, 17 (1988), 91–102.

3. H. Kawakatsu, 'International competition in cotton goods in the late nineteenth century: Britain versus India and East Asia', in Fischer *et al.* (eds) *Emergence of a World Economy*, 619–43; Peter Mathias, 'The emergence of a world economy, 1500–1914', *Vierteljahrschrift für Sozial- und Wirtschaftsgeschichte*, 74 Band, Heft 1 (1987), 7–8.

4. K. Sugihara, 'Patterns of Asia's integration into the world economy, 1880–1913', in Fischer *et al.* (eds) *Emergence of a World Economy*, 709–28.

5. G.F. Shirras, *Indian Finance and Banking*, London: Macmillan, 1919, 466; *Straits Settlements Bluebook 1876*.

6. K.G. Tregonning, *Home Port Singapore: A History of the Straits Steamship Company Ltd, 1890–1965*, Singapore: Oxford University Press, 1967.
7. Chiang Hai Ding, *A History of Straits Settlements Foreign Trade, 1870–1915*, Singapore: National Museum, 1978.
8. Ibid., 47, 51, 58.
9. Latham and Neal, 'Market in rice and wheat', 264–5, 279–80.
10. Chiang, *Straits Settlements Foreign Trade*, 106–19; Warren Dean, *Brazil and the Struggle for Rubber: A Study in Environmental History*, Cambridge: Cambridge University Press, 1987, 24–35.
11. British Parliamentary Papers: *Accounts and Papers*, LXXXVIII, no. 1653 (483–492), 485–6, 489.
12. Dean, *Brazil and the Struggle for Rubber*, 7–35.
13. Chiang, *Straits Settlements Foreign Trade*, 74, 92, 109–13.
14. Latham, 'Chinese multinationals', 4–18.
15. Latham, *International Economy*, 68–81; Latham, 'Merchandise trade imbalances', 33–60.
16. B.R. Mitchell and Phyllis Deane, *Abstract of British Historical Statistics*, Cambridge: Cambridge University Press, 1971, 318–30, 324–6.
17. Latham, *International Economy*, 75, 81, 88–90.
18. Latham, 'Trade in Rice and Wheat', 647; British Parliamentary Papers: *Accounts and Papers* 1895 C no. 1520 (329–); British Parliamentary Papers: *Accounts and Papers*, 1896 LXXXVIII no. 1653 (483–); British Parliamentary Papers: *Accounts and Papers*, 1900 LIV cd 3–5 (487–); British Parliamentary Papers: *Accounts and Papers*, 1902 LXV cd 788–10 (1–).
19. British Parliamentary Papers: *Accounts and Papers*, 1902 LXV cd 788–39.
20. British Parliamentary Papers: *Accounts and Papers*, 1892 LXXXIV no. 938 (35–); British Parliamentary Papers: *Accounts and Papers*, 1897 XCIII no. 1787 (295–).
21. A.J.H. Latham, 'Migration in South East Asia: a preliminary survey, 1800–1914', in Luigi de Rosa and Ira A. Glazier (eds) *Migration Across Time and Nations: Population Mobility in Historical Contexts*, New York: Holmes & Meier, 1986, 11–29.
22. Tanzan Ishibashi (ed.) *Foreign Trade of Japan: A Statistical Survey*, Tokyo: Oriental Economist, 1935, 22–3, 349–68.
23. British Parliamentary Papers: *Accounts and Papers*, 1903 cd 1388–17, XLIII (251–); British Parliamentary Papers: *Accounts and Papers*, 1904 cd 1768–26, LVI (467–).
24. *Statistiek van den handel de scheepvart en de in-en uitvoerregten op Java en Madura in Nederlandsche Indie*, Batavia, 1877–1915.
25. Hiroyoshi Kano, 'Javanese sugar industry in the 1920s: a historical case of "dependent" industrial development', unpublished paper presented at Workshop 34 on 'Development Theory and Comparative Approaches to the Economic History of the Third World', Bern, Switzerland, 24–29 August, 1986.
26. British Parliamentary Papers. Accounts and Papers: Trade and Navigation (United Kingdom), *Annual Statement of Trade*, London, various years.
27. Latham, *International Economy*, 81–92, 201.
28. Ibid., 156–7.

APPENDICES

Appendix 7.1

Straits Settlements imports (£)

Year	(1) UK	(2) India	(3) Hong Kong	(4) Dutch East Indies	(5) Malay Peninsula	(6) Siam	(7)c (Other Asia) Labuan, Borneo, Sarawak, Indo-China, China, Japan, Ceylon, Philippines, Mauritius	(8) Other total minus (1)–(7) includes Russia, Germany Holland, France, etc.	Total
1868	2,312,275	1,215,045	819,619	877,617	415,163	570,163	775,269	963,925	7,949,080
1869	2,046,217	1,159,368	747,934	1,170,844	731,131	713,503	862,903	969,024	8,400,927
1870	2,682,550	1,336,155	1,167,589	1,377,601	987,824	855,232	1,150,395	940,761	10,498,110
1871	2,446,991	2,083,744	1,060,659	1,432,508	999,454	804,796	856,171	789,197	10,473,522
1872	2,421,166	2,488,045	1,140,819	2,170,961	1,292,430	911,507	846,073	499,252	11,770,257
1873	2,640,844	2,030,065	1,398,635	2,535,997	851,149	1,247,587	983,182	545,497	12,232,960
1874	2,536,252	2,080,705	1,634,401	2,224,454	898,323	1,200,304	966,190	571,105	12,111,739
1875	2,151,411	2,012,119	1,033,436	2,148,616	1,040,894	1,086,686	1,074,071	631,249	11,178,486
1876	2,373,626	2,081,555	1,333,821	1,557,709	904,140	1,090,496	843,886	528,893	10,714,130
1877	3,277,555	1,792,990	1,618,422	2,058,041	1,003,546	1,049,249	873,246	576,065	12,249,118
1878	3,216,420	2,316,285	1,438,127	1,985,195	1,033,705	794,529	750,302	482,139	12,016,704
1879	2,990,445	2,072,782	1,869,218	2,365,381	1,123,511	1,142,399	1,097,465	613,403	13,274,608
1880	3,621,738	2,433,075	1,690,348	2,209,488	1,147,259	1,335,503	732,718	734,355	13,904,489
1881	3,828,383	2,736,501	1,668,959	2,733,950	1,746,989	1,088,349	1,030,817	995,122	15,829,074

Year									
1882	4,148,947	3,035,568	1,718,807	2,813,467	2,270,318	900,207	1,233,327	873,663	16,994,306
1883	4,760,803	2,844,444	2,151,649	3,231,666	2,168,141	1,545,241	1,392,784	1,058,694	19,153,425
1884	4,381,427	2,816,654	2,138,479	3,440,372	2,259,065	1,525,047	1,561,750	983,534	19,106,331
1885	3,514,438	2,792,955	2,132,098	3,607,644	2,165,668	1,327,840	1,425,923	1,167,737	18,134,306
1886	2,897,691	2,992,498	2,204,308	3,583,667	2,477,081	1,275,048	1,962,762	1,084,630	18,477,689
1887	3,531,194	3,119,503	2,735,778	3,374,016	3,188,614	1,283,875	2,711,487	1,106,939	21,051,410
1888	3,853,446	2,773,281	3,224,187	3,966,835	3,407,159	1,310,713	2,894,545	1,367,484	22,797,654
1889	3,883,618	3,624,638	2,595,212	3,710,064	3,355,186	1,810,347	2,072,515	1,531,233	22,582,816
1890	4,066,573	4,328,282	2,528,596	4,031,644	3,796,180	1,851,663	3,237,248	1,593,147	25,433,336
1891	3,507,365	3,833,992	2,642,572	3,691,335	3,288,818	1,575,066	2,181,895	1,444,756	22,165,802
1892	3,213,271	3,159,721	2,232,169	3,071,712	3,736,332	1,455,520	2,464,730	1,048,784	20,382,243
1893	2,854,463	2,934,215	2,258,856	2,850,320	4,028,947	1,808,435	2,730,371	1,194,429	20,660,038
1894	2,917,535	2,929,494	1,843,908	3,194,987	4,040,882	1,500,740	4,554,682	947,624	21,929,855
1895	2,336,306	3,405,921	1,924,147	3,110,818	4,462,301	1,538,223	3,672,031	989,927	21,439,678
1896	2,414,330	3,744,555	2,308,472	3,253,891	4,315,870	1,690,891	3,482,544	1,210,781	22,421,336
1897	2,840,459	4,219,891	2,193,442	3,165,720	3,643,810	1,860,719	2,767,671	1,252,768	21,944,483
1898	3,111,905	5,597,030	2,305,203	3,671,311	3,975,340	1,828,678	2,259,196	1,451,830	24,200,496
1899	2,919,560	5,937,607	3,060,042	4,539,401	5,788,281	1,950,275	2,302,081	1,709,766	28,207,017
1900	3,363,089	5,963,276	3,816,431	5,408,529	6,646,673	2,018,280	2,967,903	1,931,505	32,115,688
1901	3,200,516	5,743,220	3,118,101	4,675,096	7,044,458	2,428,356	2,275,919	2,059,321	30,544,991
1902	2,957,065	6,418,232	3,178,013	4,283,917	7,583,395	2,300,767	2,182,126	1,704,469	30,607,989
1903	3,598,414	5,817,841	5,049,256	4,622,762	8,919,837	2,328,045	2,570,054	2,045,345	34,951,557
1904	3,122,483	7,356,190	3,213,118	5,074,644	8,849,006	2,739,746	2,501,673	2,363,872	35,220,736
1905	3,423,628	4,561,078	3,042,838	5,044,127	9,208,564	3,129,257	2,707,687	2,325,473	33,442,656
1906	4,108,127	4,893,404	3,606,756	5,979,178	10,427,442	3,996,830	3,413,101	3,161,129	39,585,967
1907	5,767,415	4,941,388	3,763,690	5,794,323	10,231,574	3,521,101	3,487,088	3,393,278	40,899,857
1908	4,385,785	4,037,990	2,964,594	5,433,557	9,389,533	4,380,355	3,434,343	2,886,703	36,912,860
1909	3,892,124	4,028,068	3,214,934	5,716,097	9,162,151	4,033,666	3,836,588	2,674,855	36,558,483
1910	4,568,615	6,462,253	3,869,878	6,640,065	10,151,688	3,765,449	3,949,424	3,114,204	42,521,576
1911	4,759,063	6,414,151	4,389,033	6,795,588	11,883,817	4,216,545	4,045,707	3,933,445	46,437,349
1912	5,452,740	7,304,860	4,247,562	8,083,104	12,682,270	4,399,425	5,067,570	5,267,021	52,504,552
1913	6,175,526	6,338,647	4,939,638	8,205,978	13,291,542	5,440,781	5,845,319	5,699,041	55,936,471
1914	4,888,499	4,256,929	3,538,270	6,770,949	11,379,949	5,056,385	5,592,917	4,176,300	45,660,198

Straits Settlements imports (£)

Year	French Indo-China	China	Japan	Brunei, Brit. N. Borneo, Sarawak, Labuan	Philippines
1868	278,832	221,064	—	203,504	71,868
1869	298,992	234,206	—	273,602	56,101
1870	347,044	224,243	—	483,924	95,183
1871	301,630	172,901	—	316,509	65,129
1872	211,036	332,628	—	173,604	128,803
1873	521,705	196,160	—	167,067	98,249
1874	465,017	256,814	—	153,193	91,164
1875	498,911	293,508	—	157,461	124,189
1876	327,283	270,990	—	155,825	89,786
1877	280,070	357,053	—	180,625	55,497
1878	210,712	285,517	—	179,606	74,465
1879	327,897	428,486	—	238,326	102,756
1880	196,911	244,210	—	196,589	95,006
1881	333,583	332,166	—	257,402	107,664
1882	282,308	390,682	167,399	219,354	173,582
1883	622,629	315,538	26,860	256,332	171,422
1884	639,078	435,149	90,752	216,356	180,414
1885	449,463	469,372	170,107	221,430	115,550
1886	348,275	447,258	788,439	254,683	124,105
1887	396,271	578,874	1,301,836	261,908	146,732
1888	718,503	889,271	852,813	280,724	138,440
1889	661,247	596,364	301,909	336,974	138,582
1890	618,540	775,874	1,219,898	369,703	182,618

Year					
1891	832,841	684,970	192,612	384,311	72,359
1892	1,138,924	688,207	124,199	354,455	80,401
1893	947,186	622,864	675,784	320,780	80,769
1894	752,685	498,624	2,901,115	263,715	102,542
1895	692,570	375,207	2,158,045	301,412	102,626
1896	765,779	444,650	1,777,880	347,652	76,651
1897	1,145,703	591,234	571,138	308,384	75,441
1898	678,428	534,807	503,752	363,440	75,640
1899	730,976	441,103	538,708	466,179	74,025
1900	857,458	612,328	766,525	497,664	190,053
1901	545,323	410,516	784,342	418,330	81,164
1902	497,534	414,463	640,325	456,448	113,058
1903	534,814	660,662	746,114	301,450	260,504
1904	500,366	562,282	754,913	542,380	85,000
1905	578,979	659,447	642,586	650,911	104,232
1906	698,795	751,772	588,666	752,126	102,878
1907	941,570	797,330	816,195	736,640	131,197
1908	1,134,756	723,275	784,837	629,789	105,429
1909	1,361,934	815,745	787,942	714,800	100,476
1910	1,022,237	972,684	982,362	762,531	150,679
1911	1,068,996	1,013,900	1,054,593	666,166	184,211
1912	1,522,206	1,134,929	1,247,612	795,232	199,663
1913	1,925,750	1,432,059	1,504,768	669,721	219,985
1914	2,056,955	1,257,540	1,410,723	627,283	182,854

Notes

The given exchange rate is used to convert £ to $ and then the exchange rate recalculated by taking the London price of silver per oz. from G.F. Shirras, *Indian Finance and Banking*, London, Macmillan, 1919, p. 458, and converting this to the value of the dollar by the formula $x/480.36 \times 417.44$ where x is the annual silver price per oz. 1 oz. = 480.36 grains; $1 = 417.44 grains (see *Straits Settlements Blue Book*, 1876).

a This column is the sum of the columns for French Indo-China, China, Japan, Brunei, British North Borneo, Sarawak, Labuan and the Philippines.

Source: Statistical abstract for British Colonies.

Appendix 7.2

Straits Settlements exports (£)

Year	(1) UK	(2) India	(3) Hong Kong	(4) Dutch East Indies	(5) Malay Peninsula	(6) Siam	(7)ª (Other Asia) Labuan, Borneo, Sarawak, Indo-China, China, Japan, Philippines, Ceylon, Mauritius	(8) US	(9) Others	(10) Total
1868	1,342,496	854,215	893,724	1,045,706	467,029	645,183	1,004,030	400,398	797,440	7,450,225
1869	1,604,945	919,277	645,299	1,134,495	599,670	763,116	931,010	552,290	728,716	7,878,823
1870	1,828,643	947,356	794,815	1,321,386	685,217	923,026	1,193,995	815,400	655,925	9,165,767
1871	2,184,807	700,353	1,009,847	1,626,089	892,101	940,110	1,070,506	877,021	405,306	9,706,145
1872	2,953,192	676,143	1,100,629	2,391,070	968,189	1,200,508	1,109,844	959,570	242,157	11,601,306
1873	2,598,910	672,094	1,101,036	2,837,678	753,092	1,237,669	1,349,779	543,872	313,299	11,407,432
1874	1,968,814	800,948	1,270,887	2,873,387	735,631	1,219,427	1,125,000	543,715	331,546	10,869,360
1875	2,125,465	583,876	969,793	3,104,012	840,035	1,225,698	1,045,955	651,664	599,601	11,146,103
1876	1,788,816	495,144	872,802	2,939,209	866,940	1,124,355	955,485	393,323	469,206	9,905,284
1877	2,036,213	729,314	804,851	3,327,748	679,308	982,053	1,077,653	604,880	1,153,027	11,395,052
1878	1,940,750	778,886	861,778	3,616,038	858,652	886,284	952,741	445,206	952,085	11,292,426
1879	1,973,269	842,505	992,215	3,765,305	949,134	1,061,004	1,135,797	841,721	1,084,529	12,645,484
1880	2,202,831	898,277	958,274	3,635,510	944,692	1,002,675	1,494,267	1,136,007	934,893	13,207,431
1881	2,696,970	896,288	1,082,570	3,378,669	1,246,767	890,709	1,246,768	806,426	801,330	13,046,502
1882	3,076,664	931,736	1,082,862	3,783,026	1,693,510	765,194	1,550,151	1,225,963	1,237,894	15,347,003

1883	3,919,336	1,099,921	1,202,241	1,635,619	1,351,612	1,627,052	1,173,325	1,618,542	17,592,067
1884	3,933,805	1,117,360	1,216,750	2,119,092	1,316,265	1,596,949	710,285	1,551,494	17,657,121
1885	3,602,629	937,376	1,610,771	1,706,671	1,179,909	1,192,476	621,789	1,821,243	16,625,897
1886	3,408,007	941,861	1,396,587	1,944,754	1,058,879	1,250,310	906,046	1,902,814	16,008,910
1887	4,274,482	1,047,482	1,374,681	2,035,202	1,451,577	1,164,365	1,081,329	1,683,660	17,716,626
1888	4,532,915	1,137,517	1,364,489	2,049,926	1,493,737	1,578,449	1,033,720	1,763,780	19,152,831
1889	4,213,100	1,116,670	1,000,569	2,317,682	1,254,935	1,586,986	1,398,088	2,071,558	19,073,904
1890	4,279,513	2,145,759	1,743,829	2,547,929	2,021,233	1,840,153	1,453,088	2,197,601	22,088,156
1891	3,997,183	1,479,011	1,121,777	2,367,487	971,345	2,077,660	1,421,490	2,388,059	20,521,476
1892	3,615,130	1,120,271	1,282,690	2,483,128	909,077	1,933,611	1,573,343	2,335,150	19,403,649
1893	3,908,139	1,214,696	1,162,604	2,315,114	1,158,090	1,532,465	831,778	2,329,098	18,674,447
1894	3,326,806	942,778	1,144,616	2,334,603	1,286,733	1,624,627	1,077,956	2,438,199	18,216,057
1895	3,251,588	963,829	1,151,925	2,462,834	1,396,757	1,499,744	1,494,269	2,342,236	18,709,403
1896	2,896,717	967,188	1,229,566	2,573,569	1,447,004	1,546,598	1,494,445	2,741,444	19,345,388
1897	2,587,079	1,230,458	1,334,958	2,966,823	1,588,107	1,644,840	1,849,424	1,523,342	19,088,407
1898	2,768,652	1,131,354	1,763,205	2,664,785	1,582,959	1,627,844	2,205,488	2,570,520	20,708,348
1899	4,670,562	1,134,680	1,569,789	2,933,286	1,295,096	1,725,954	2,979,395	2,988,817	23,748,095
1900	6,176,110	1,347,082	1,621,434	3,495,883	1,329,253	2,133,920	2,764,735	2,853,589	26,852,624
1901	5,336,594	1,359,958	1,674,452	3,457,051	1,427,525	1,824,905	3,235,242	2,741,578	26,231,840
1902	5,425,026	1,211,399	1,348,982	3,449,593	1,728,974	1,979,226	3,355,348	3,276,212	26,253,031
1903	6,011,224	2,416,437	1,589,426	3,896,048	1,479,927	2,150,550	3,790,259	3,575,543	29,100,619
1904	5,388,877	3,328,105	1,913,914	4,081,446	1,641,876	1,995,262	3,340,178	3,480,611	29,842,517
1905	5,759,248	1,352,906	1,501,864	4,475,560	1,668,934	1,773,051	3,652,779	3,643,223	28,482,823
1906	9,127,226	2,234,654	1,647,616	5,354,990	2,194,011	2,207,286	4,040,082	4,137,252	36,284,011
1907	8,823,000	2,080,769	1,462,917	5,669,648	2,162,638	2,423,257	3,320,224	4,355,530	35,618,556
1908	7,584,897	1,890,627	1,185,339	5,737,961	2,029,259	2,328,610	2,459,194	3,875,619	31,945,448
1909	7,488,633	1,962,826	1,242,128	5,441,805	1,730,095	2,380,649	3,664,278	3,984,565	32,804,686
1910	10,190,123	1,923,087	1,159,185	5,928,997	1,515,620	2,674,961	3,446,709	5,661,914	37,822,142
1911	10,022,759	2,196,792	1,433,047	6,861,365	1,399,757	2,458,596	4,268,526	5,538,962	39,887,146
1912	9,964,295	2,981,372	1,476,274	8,103,305	1,534,008	2,525,304	5,532,151	5,903,237	43,765,022
1913	10,745,269	2,938,641	1,550,341	8,111,723	1,434,376	2,730,484	5,284,974	6,383,476	45,375,132
1914	9,975,583	2,009,272	1,124,973	6,496,189	1,368,444	2,532,460	4,686,862	5,092,010	38,981,369

Straits Settlements exports (£)

Year	French Indo-China	China	Japan	Brunei, Brit. N. Borneo, Sarawak, Labuan	Philippines
1868	403,321	376,701	–	182,993	41,014
1869	401,863	247,923	–	254,536	26,686
1870	476,743	254,901	–	424,552	37,796
1871	563,564	221,314	–	246,550	39,076
1872	581,709	290,860	–	148,724	88,550
1873	789,771	365,377	–	144,331	50,298
1874	687,052	247,562	–	134,876	55,508
1875	593,074	259,340	–	143,700	49,839
1876	561,079	223,092	–	130,411	40,902
1877	624,337	283,263	–	129,768	40,284
1878	548,656	223,875	–	141,555	38,654
1879	732,265	203,021	–	137,958	62,551
1880	693,629	592,998	–	122,722	84,916
1881	674,238	369,517	–	89,074	113,938
1882	608,323	557,948	32,298	129,799	224,911
1883	772,481	380,046	21,694	166,528	286,300
1884	795,516	392,536	11,422	198,656	198,816
1885	522,419	369,827	1,931	156,152	142,146
1886	379,248	438,591	1,860	160,514	270,095
1887	370,959	330,014	18,883	186,942	212,876
1888	516,986	626,513	13,438	274,353	109,517
1889	385,482	657,994	5,001	314,106	154,886
1890	588,798	695,851	18,684	356,606	127,318

1891	790,377	578,448	213,097	366,841	115,580
1892	720,127	577,087	201,932	297,768	97,887
1893	474,307	594,901	58,746	261,617	78,071
1894	589,665	562,766	123,078	221,712	100,040
1895	347,689	494,883	298,224	245,104	88,403
1896	387,428	611,533	116,105	305,394	91,435
1897	345,266	367,423	510,854	280,807	69,835
1898	380,311	410,858	361,486	291,780	87,157
1899	288,894	631,511	93,994	382,671	270,879
1900	361,001	634,838	201,963	412,732	449,197
1901	359,156	419,275	151,267	364,033	408,781
1902	370,159	471,015	295,801	355,608	323,792
1903	248,366	735,291	465,574	375,557	215,825
1904	262,667	618,590	370,493	498,188	182,092
1905	237,711	411,672	245,088	633,929	191,478
1906	310,146	536,164	278,917	731,517	180,962
1907	354,369	540,889	302,733	741,300	200,555
1908	241,647	350,515	379,594	580,586	161,418
1909	234,474	421,134	313,479	584,271	167,625
1910	265,675	473,919	482,592	832,719	187,638
1911	234,751	565,978	483,699	736,190	183,336
1912	338,218	320,129	623,226	860,646	201,078
1913	410,639	327,413	633,429	729,594	187,434
1914	323,628	265,575	410,565	600,987	176,044

Notes and Source: As for Appendix 7.1.

Appendix 7.3

British exports to the Straits Settlements (Singapore, etc., including Malay States) (£)

Year	(1) Cotton yards etc.	(2) Cotton yarn	(3) Woollens	(4) Iron, copper, brass, lead etc. & manufactures	(5) Other home-produced goods	(6) Total home-produced goods	(7) Re-exports	(8) Total
1868	938,163	123,514	75,223	131,576	270,705	1,539,181	88,040	1,627,221
1869	1,085,899	144,342	83,183	137,856	286,995	1,738,275	92,096	1,830,371
1870	1,509,763	216,164	49,326	119,706	426,128	2,321,087	86,490	2,407,577
1871	1,064,232	164,152	49,988	92,503	562,460	1,933,335	140,642	2,073,977
1872	1,633,235	150,601	75,037	98,852	462,347	2,420,072	113,837	2,533,909
1873	1,360,963	153,761	55,555	116,185	418,759	2,105,223	66,596	2,171,819
1874	1,692,718	190,246	70,280	147,535	600,747	2,701,526	106,488	2,808,014
1875	1,139,334	143,794	67,465	103,960	507,081	1,961,634	132,543	2,094,177
1876	1,196,645	123,375	37,024	104,294	507,608	1,968,946	100,517	2,069,463
1877	1,371,770	157,529	54,567	135,973	555,750	2,275,589	134,239	2,409,828
1878	1,017,230	126,739	25,802	86,855	519,340	1,775,966	106,819	1,882,785
1879	1,064,236	92,510	33,181	87,719	751,372	2,029,018	153,619	2,182,637
1880	1,355,227	164,757	54,592	109,329	584,792	2,268,697	190,962	2,459,659
1881	1,520,872	198,415	58,337	109,913	676,291	2,563,828	179,690	2,743,518
1882	1,381,470	141,421	61,157	104,070	649,969	2,338,087	157,034	2,495,121
1883	1,364,107	169,425	71,742	133,010	885,717	2,624,001	169,105	2,793,106
1884	1,358,529	169,686	74,875	161,810	867,972	2,632,872	183,426	2,816,298
1885	1,226,113	147,614	70,622	139,105	761,648	2,345,102	179,633	2,524,735
1886	1,009,711	126,558	60,406	109,140	798,299	2,104,114	155,467	2,259,581
1887	1,432,145	118,328	90,631	135,461	704,967	2,481,532	177,087	2,658,619

1888	1,505,493	136,802	75,642	144,790	729,277	2,592,004	155,584	2,747,588
1889	1,226,295	150,154	53,394	214,974	757,657	2,402,474	124,423	2,526,897
1890	1,535,773	126,539	57,929	200,637	962,366	2,883,244	141,411	3,024,655
1891	1,209,833	135,102	53,919	185,536	879,153	2,463,543	125,719	2,589,262
1892	1,080,902	106,306	42,415	196,235	666,628	2,092,486	112,933	2,205,419
1893	832,335	56,533	53,398	192,589	621,682	1,756,537	92,185	1,848,722
1894	1,191,396	120,905	43,573	178,693	817,692	2,352,259	46,663	2,398,922
1895	956,586	122,931	39,644	224,615	652,130	1,995,906	36,914	2,032,820
1896	974,362	110,489	37,457	263,429	634,137	2,019,874	53,127	2,073,001
1897	1,120,002	114,670	33,604	355,217	873,402	2,496,895	42,021	2,538,916
1898	1,322,555	120,804	42,848	319,536	967,569	2,773,312	43,538	2,816,850
1899	1,170,227	87,948	44,054	354,700	955,452	2,612,381	47,518	2,659,899
1900	1,296,136	66,012	48,066	599,357	1,140,568	3,150,139	56,125	3,206,264
1901	1,352,466	118,753	41,691	490,723	1,199,878	3,203,511	79,217	3,282,728
1902	1,124,126	103,693	51,365	390,968	1,074,403	2,744,555	59,961	2,804,516
1903	1,311,048	87,623	59,026	456,489	1,211,759	3,125,945	74,324	3,200,269
1904	1,287,271	54,835	59,889	459,411	1,267,849	3,129,255	54,074	3,183,329
1905	1,483,546	95,898	55,359	465,466	1,163,929	3,264,198	56,995	3,321,193
1906	1,683,783	92,193	62,916	633,548	1,495,756	3,968,196	68,965	4,037,161
1907	1,455,828	71,028	105,441	760,954	1,819,358	4,212,609	75,568	4,288,177
1908	1,171,697	96,778	51,334	641,842	1,895,141	3,856,792	77,491	3,934,283
1909	1,273,837	72,775	40,628	610,348	1,671,114	3,668,702	73,172	3,741,874
1910	1,491,130	99,116	75,622	717,166	2,189,423	4,572,457	118,184	4,690,641
1911	1,496,114	82,916	95,870	753,526	2,587,301	5,015,727	123,693	5,139,420
1912	1,843,627	85,344	104,585	862,145	3,015,617	5,911,318	148,894	6,060,212
1913	1,950,738	108,186	108,863	1,399,807	3,607,281	7,174,875	213,326	7,388,201
1914	1,382,618	97,977	62,785	1,038,331	3,109,209	5,690,920	125,516	5,816,436

Source: Annual Statement of Trade of the United Kingdom.

Appendix 7.4

British imports from Singapore, etc. (£)

Year	(1) Tin	(2) Sago, etc.	(3) Spices	(4) Cutch & gambier	(5) Gutta percha	(6) Rubber	(7) Others	(8) Total
1868	379,883	267,453	286,363	347,277	54,733	76,104	638,350	2,050,163
1869	442,229	264,858	345,026	289,358	52,617	61,719	857,453	2,313,260
1870	294,504	283,586	395,524	357,799	405,908	72,954	737,045	2,547,320
1871	688,152	267,734	524,786	417,012	153,999	75,420	569,216	2,696,319
1872	876,250	318,403	793,811	446,636	225,789	140,798	703,427	3,505,114
1873	656,365	291,618	818,058	526,524	366,424	76,867	728,423	3,464,279
1874	406,719	286,319	553,117	411,457	217,513	52,878	676,851	2,604,854
1875	738,680	368,645	677,521	573,523	132,514	56,401	602,026	3,149,310
1876	569,090	311,680	461,319	460,416	144,849	48,875	645,717	2,641,946
1877	309,104	359,946	519,227	539,562	199,998	48,375	745,583	2,721,795
1878	368,288	400,832	435,216	425,040	280,887	35,574	591,121	2,536,958
1879	488,391	370,948	371,694	370,295	397,769	50,031	516,233	2,565,361
1880	705,745	517,429	465,462	468,502	505,821	114,989	919,676	3,697,624
1881	835,553	548,844	504,773	443,994	471,355	81,348	898,290	3,784,157
1882	1,347,604	424,604	644,920	524,877	505,430	128,132	1,004,932	4,580,499
1883	1,310,453	452,467	830,148	453,804	425,813	171,384	998,947	4,643,016
1884	1,202,150	391,305	888,351	538,902	416,394	89,980	1,085,332	4,612,414
1885	1,344,340	404,953	988,035	418,052	323,518	61,080	902,188	4,442,166
1886	1,512,886	403,375	892,832	477,856	244,617	47,185	793,871	4,372,622
1887	1,905,703	373,052	1,001,568	432,752	142,436	79,287	846,906	4,781,704
1888	2,572,093	420,655	892,553	396,000	151,804	49,759	868,458	5,351,322

1889	2,023,254	477,657	959,253	439,642	478,647	42,408	996,173	5,417,034
1890	1,745,412	550,062	707,874	527,336	716,412	61,973	878,732	5,187,801
1891	1,912,657	589,794	676,280	428,985	623,659	57,757	1,067,733	5,356,865
1892	2,081,831	574,348	544,351	371,582	453,093	42,017	801,067	4,868,289
1893	2,246,281	478,468	432,930	380,243	247,568	43,523	689,374	4,518,387
1894	2,116,516	469,608	373,188	386,938	391,510	63,934	783,089	4,584,783
1895	2,168,398	460,537	368,831	410,741	336,531	108,874	791,534	4,645,446
1896	1,831,523	425,853	355,855	368,613	304,606	117,155	906,242	4,309,847
1897	1,217,178	340,281	423,397	292,879	269,462	126,177	973,850	3,643,224
1898	1,100,126	380,394	558,579	226,339	529,306	276,433	870,732	3,941,909
1899	2,409,615	432,310	502,246	261,822	873,692	254,847	1,133,315	5,867,847
1900	3,364,718	417,902	464,032	261,196	1,381,179	186,802	950,170	7,025,999
1901	3,163,767	434,233	325,385	302,154	1,107,964	51,732	727,069	6,112,304
1902	3,296,998	486,010	427,759	249,446	868,282	39,825	684,410	6,052,730
1903	3,541,296	471,066	328,027	234,328	378,080	109,397	831,213	5,893,407
1904	4,113,006	400,328	387,012	210,689	133,576	214,082	825,127	6,283,820
1905	4,757,877	388,428	299,947	166,036	119,287	265,863	838,337	6,835,775
1906	6,427,697	480,785	279,986	165,452	233,658	401,623	845,339	8,834,540
1907	6,137,824	545,491	244,588	186,270	161,154	640,123	1,121,744	9,037,194
1908	5,460,118	530,068	206,452	192,022	67,414	602,362	911,776	7,970,212
1909	4,857,798	495,732	248,788	177,896	91,373	1,798,039	790,082	8,459,708
1910	6,294,052	482,418	236,683	152,055	442,854	4,543,926	943,833	13,095,821
1911	7,566,630	457,236	190,670	115,912	191,290	5,044,632	1,027,039	14,593,409
1912	7,501,484	490,951	138,111	113,428	153,301	8,628,278	1,212,286	18,237,839
1913	8,103,460	368,802	170,263	120,381	552,233	8,828,379	1,229,528	19,373,146
1914	5,840,806	347,167	380,206	156,272	171,903	7,761,234	1,730,788	16,388,376

Source: *Annual Statement of Trade of the United Kingdom*

Appendix 7.5

Hong Kong imports (£)

Year	(1) UK exports	(2) China exports	(3) Straits Settlements exports	(4) Australia exports	(5) French Indo-China exports	(6) Bangkok exports	(7) India exports	(8) Japan exports	(9) Philippine exports
1868	2,305,009	2,575,061	893,724	121,096	206,319	–			
1869	2,254,608	3,662,505	645,299	136,044	94,968	–			
1870	3,570,733	3,365,323	794,815	105,632	431,563	670,157			
1871	3,024,084	3,629,925	1,009,847	120,593	1,469,218	787,644	Statistics include some China figures to 1876	Hong Kong figures included in China before 1889	Hong Kong figures included in China before 1903
1872	3,099,244	4,015,301	1,100,629	148,116	1,167,423	–			
1873	3,610,265	2,511,222	1,101,036	168,722	626,142	357,218			
1874	3,909,246	3,584,498	1,270,887	210,716	306,815	463,413			
1875	3,839,136	3,940,097	969,793	201,502	895,494	704,540			
1876	3,261,805	4,306,907	872,802	150,707	1,602,435	732,335			
1877	3,645,068	4,576,800	804,851	177,634	1,668,067	861,798	8,940,944		
1878	3,041,329	4,462,244	861,778	156,323	1,704,851	900,095	8,445,334		
1879	3,128,227	4,601,041	992,215	239,480	1,104,166	654,691	8,685,626		
1880	3,967,792	4,818,270	958,274	259,418	924,869	510,685	9,011,798		
1881	3,800,189	4,892,097	1,082,570	318,658	870,577	572,736	7,834,541		
1882	3,143,674	4,705,675	1,082,862	303,580	1,691,872	600,643	8,086,754		
1883	3,047,470	5,282,330	1,202,241	314,645	1,745,936	575,767	7,953,914		
1884	3,587,487	4,811,684	1,216,750	351,206	1,042,092	640,184	7,656,221		
1885	4,062,182	4,197,615	1,610,771	352,369	1,939,682	725,709	7,269,941		
1886	2,559,766	5,649,526	1,396,587	444,677	2,726,386	971,632	7,797,446		
1887	2,803,561	7,619,081	1,374,681	348,659	1,661,849	1,484,064	7,297,020		

Year									
1888	3,003,379	7,878,009	1,364,489	365,025	1,451,988	1,168,330	7,506,443		
1889	2,378,197	8,318,206	1,000,569	402,273	961,687	794,544	7,485,458	1,133,704	
1890	2,741,404	8,539,008	1,743,829	413,948	1,993,919	1,671,992	7,248,277	1,580,112	
1891	2,732,157	9,268,626	1,121,777	458,986	1,544,979	711,103	6,416,091	2,022,654	
1892	1,972,935	8,860,607	1,282,690	431,427	1,264,055	495,571	5,775,262	1,909,563	
1893	1,935,419	9,503,472	1,162,604	558,303	1,363,745	2,061,248	3,985,722	2,006,607	
1894	1,980,227	8,116,881	1,144,616	786,892	1,173,669	963,494	4,435,168	1,700,945	
1895	2,044,616	8,955,549	1,151,925	305,115	1,810,282	1,157,254	4,748,056	1,935,439	
1896	1,959,209	9,005,229	1,229,566	313,512	1,765,939	1,392,438	5,059,716	2,162,306	
1897	2,079,951	8,993,857	1,334,958	291,117[a]	539,021	971,646	5,255,415	2,579,653	
1898	2,347,689	8,952,512	1,763,205	350,385	1,227,123	1,713,988	5,568,134	3,185,158	
1899	2,862,345	10,812,823	1,569,789	434,222	1,656,347	1,363,550	5,605,637	3,514,859	
1900	2,956,262	9,926,902	1,621,434	388,362	1,987,021[c]	1,161,324	5,397,882	3,964,758	
1901	2,797,978	10,579,523	1,674,452	413,711	1,176,385	1,703,708	6,700,818	4,245,523	
1902	2,274,217	10,745,410	1,348,982	390,178	1,566,245	2,117,898	6,474,510	2,652,296	
1903	2,891,710	11,764,952	1,589,426	390,564	1,270,010	1,851,136	7,500,937	3,031,918	296,737
1904	4,574,767	12,446,751	1,913,914	595,769	1,287,501	2,692,425	7,816,482	2,838,538	353,529
1905	3,841,735	12,250,531	1,501,864	796,539	926,956	2,322,426	9,027,706	2,053,852	560,810
1906	3,220,498	13,610,730	1,647,616	726,094	997,078	2,806,145	7,405,169	2,760,255	607,848
1907	3,355,403	15,799,225	1,462,917	859,946	4,099,873	2,575,931	5,953,867	2,487,245	464,983
1908	3,088,340	12,277,996	1,185,339	756,779	2,351,123	2,010,938	6,013,166	1,890,951	517,421
1909	3,713,852	12,589,778	1,242,128	569,933	974,832	2,613,333	6,996,116	2,210,914	432,817
1910	3,834,005	14,634,115	1,159,185	693,751	1,868,606	2,918,774	7,884,389	2,485,126	226,574
1911	2,985,812	13,922,881	1,433,047	730,924	1,575,455[d]	1,934,891	8,885,617	2,491,433	201,799
1912	3,761,337	15,776,398	1,476,274	856,313	1,760,444	1,908,386	7,338,260	2,928,716	321,294
1913	4,554,590	17,686,479	1,550,341	855,903	2,118,790	2,854,334	5,382,693	3,415,992	635,783
1914	3,710,016	12,880,115	1,124,973	452,114[b]	1,845,962	2,108,344	2,889,267	3,367,639	405,183

Notes and Sources:

Column (1): *Annual Statements of the Trade of the United Kingdom.*

Column (2): Liang-Lin, Hsiao, *China's Foreign Trade Statistics, 1864–1949*, Cambridge, Mass.: Harvard University Press, 1974, 148–51, 190–1.

Notes and Sources (continued)

Column (3): *Statistical Abstract for British Colonies.* These figures have been adjusted for the fall in the value of silver. See Straits Settlements Imports, pp. 172–5.

Column (4): [a]Includes Tasmania from this date; [b]six months ended 30 June; *Statistical Abstract for British Colonies.*

Column (5): [c]Cochin China only before this date; [d]Official valuation after this date. Albert Coquerel, *Paddys et Riz de Cochin chine*, Lyon: Imprimerie A. Ray, 1911, 203ff (Appendices); *Bulletin economique de l'Indochine*, 4(1902)–17(1915). Exchange rate from Hsiao, *China's Foreign Trade Statistics*, 190–1. Note: Figures are for rice only. The quantity for the year is multiplied by the average price. From 1900 the figures are for all Indo-China; but the same method is employed as the official valuation uses a constant franc conversion figure. From 1911 this official figure is used in the absence of reliable average values. Rice was the main item of trade with Hong Kong.

Column (6): Siam, Dept of Customs, Statistical Office, *Foreign Trade and Navigation of Port of Bangkok 1910–1912*, Bangkok, 1911–23; *British Parliamentary Papers.* Diplomatic and Consular reports on the Trade and Commerce of Bangkok (from 1870). Exchange rate from Owen (see Column (9)).

Column (7): *Statistical Abstract for British Colonies*; exchange rate from G.F. Shirras, *Indian Finance and Banking*, London: Macmillan, 1919, 466.

Column (8): Tanzan Ishibashi (ed.) *Foreign Trade of Japan: A Statistical Survey*, Tokyo: Oriental Economist, 1935, 349. Exchange rate: Govt of Japan. Dept of Finance, *Financial and Economic Annual of Japan*, vol. I, Tokyo, 1902, 108–9; vol. VII, Tokyo, 1907, 154–5; vol. XV, Tokyo, 1915, 148–9.

Column (9): *Statistical Bulletin of the Philippine Islands*, Manila, no. 2(1919), 99–100; no. 3(1921), 128–9; N.G. Owen, *Prosperity without Progress: Manila Hemp and Material Life in the Colonial Philippines*, Berkeley: University of California Press, 1984, 264–5, 273, 277; Hsiao, *China's Foreign Trade Statistics*, 190–1.

Appendix 7.6

Hong Kong exports (£)

Year	(1) UK imports	(2) China imports	(3) Straits Settlements imports	(4) Australia imports	(5) Bangkok imports	(6) India imports	(7) Japan imports	(8) Philippine imports
1868	235,804	4,473,876	819,619	177,075	—			
1869	281,932	6,375,914	747,934	201,228				
1870	281,159	6,350,760	1,167,589	170,228	324,108		Hong Kong figures included in China before 1889	Hong Kong figures included in China before 1903
1871	367,944	7,394,400	1,060,659	219,235	230,766	Statistics include some China figures to 1876		
1872	833,764	6,951,949	1,140,819	188,337	286,630			
1873	783,457	8,005,884	1,398,635	319,927	196,748			
1874	747,291	7,504,805	1,634,401	325,745	224,644			
1875	1,154,910	8,507,977	1,033,436	292,411	297,709			
1876	1,356,850	8,143,170	1,333,821	333,171	316,202			
1877	1,895,310	8,280,600	1,618,422	340,408	300,357	2,661,037		
1878	1,174,469	8,175,865	1,438,127	855,785	337,761	2,508,954		
1879	1,327,085	8,314,300	1,869,218	412,328	262,665	3,756,946		
1880	1,253,541	8,776,395	1,690,348	452,685	322,252	2,220,849		
1881	1,015,716	8,639,630	1,668,959	538,797	323,252	3,114,989		
1882	1,429,749	8,294,580	1,718,807	556,348	307,780	3,175,463		
1883	1,171,986	8,151,298	2,151,649	503,079	225,969	2,599,924		
1884	1,052,302	8,587,907	2,138,479	890,826	277,395	2,252,561		
1885	968,414	9,328,386	2,132,098	670,753	293,435	2,842,267		
1886	1,556,062	8,739,945	2,204,308	608,981	341,314	2,484,555		
1887	1,409,241	14,018,594	2,735,778	625,021	453,989	2,822,124		

Appendix 7.6 (continued)

	(1)	(2)	(3)	(4)	(5)	(6)	(7)	(8)
Year	UK imports	China imports	Straits Settlements imports	Australia imports	Bangkok imports	India imports	Japan imports	Philippine imports
1888	1,296,690	16,398,666	3,224,187	769,501	509,263	2,208,202	634,022	
1889	1,129,190	14,980,904	2,595,212	948,006	417,799	2,319,369	927,160	
1890	1,225,064	18,684,380	2,528,596	697,800	775,845	3,764,813	818,408	
1891	1,101,702	16,752,744	2,642,572	588,344	389,555	3,437,125	1,003,848	
1892	836,705	15,199,160	2,232,169	617,876	300,440	2,103,803	1,057,486	
1893	885,634	15,919,348	2,258,856	440,513	652,156	2,131,657	944,970	
1894	630,818	13,171,355	1,843,908	377,520	376,000	1,205,274	851,441	
1895	759,441	14,419,228	1,924,147	417,256	498,702	1,156,146	989,188	
1896	797,158	15,220,076	2,308,472	307,548	544,056	1,120,222	1,221,963	
1897	606,314	13,419,761	2,193,442	369,534[a]	593,733	1,405,886	1,609,532	
1898	726,637	14,018,258	2,305,203	328,852	773,307	1,381,363	752,191	
1899	883,126	17,773,448	3,060,203	302,453	719,265	1,326,137	1,078,777	
1900	1,066,048	15,565,054	3,816,431	282,042	684,074	1,550,691	1,132,005	
1901	602,841	17,820,873	3,118,101	285,010	637,886	1,273,990	251,625	
1902	610,398	17,358,120	3,178,013	320,385	786,280	1,931,379	177,452	
1903	582,764	18,006,988	5,049,256	309,555	1,007,104	1,428,990	251,537	81,606
1904	466,811	20,217,480	3,213,118	379,320	1,049,328	1,726,017	114,665	49,346
1905	386,440	22,269,878	3,042,838	277,038	927,175	1,413,207	69,843	45,299
1906	638,507	23,842,136	3,606,756	230,311	1,213,209	1,974,800	83,702	62,830
1907	600,109	25,291,825	3,763,690	260,792	1,584,468	1,991,283	113,784	75,390
1908	510,495	20,028,591	2,964,594	247,689	1,351,252	1,325,374	64,097	84,762
1909	455,674	19,546,182	3,214,934	241,533	1,150,887	1,358,341	68,544	88,039
1910	596,402	23,079,323	3,869,878	244,724	1,149,522	1,530,498		117,972

1911	734,628	19,909,840	4,389,033	302,762	660,183	859,260	71,285	165,068
1912	841,616	22,554,432	4,247,562	331,007	108,826	1,145,967	89,918	166,324
1913	675,276	25,917,036	4,939,638	365,607	1,114,111	782,958	131,546	105,891
1914	598,876	22,914,381	3,538,270	155,667[b]	1,157,092	662,558	88,653	59,429

Notes and Sources: As for Appendix 7.5.

Appendix 7.7

British exports to Hong Kong (£)

Year	(1) Cottons (piece-goods etc.)	(2) Cotton yarn	(3) Woollen (piece-goods etc.)	(4) Iron, copper, & lead & manufactures	(5) Others	(6) Total home-produced goods	(7) Re-exports	(8) Total
1868	1,028,184	373,913	231,574	227,192	325,109	2,185,972	119,037	2,305,009
1869	970,276	338,832	269,247	261,457	291,025	2,130,837	123,771	2,254,608
1870	1,594,574	657,956	236,891	269,442	649,067	3,407,930	162,803	3,570,733
1871	1,508,578	461,551	167,320	205,508	444,757	2,787,714	236,370	3,024,084
1872	1,529,035	423,758	227,414	228,415	464,051	2,872,673	226,571	3,099,244
1873	1,898,352	545,059	286,656	227,348	454,553	3,411,968	198,297	3,610,265
1874	1,959,187	748,779	277,921	262,582	402,494	3,650,963	258,283	3,909,246
1875	1,944,793	681,334	368,290	279,218	326,176	3,599,811	239,325	3,839,136
1876	1,691,786	530,835	286,175	256,185	315,395	3,080,376	181,429	3,261,805
1877	1,638,341	739,707	357,974	408,424	363,531	3,507,977	137,091	3,645,068
1878	1,576,989	402,852	366,741	224,249	299,965	2,870,796	170,533	3,041,329
1879	1,747,042	491,979	228,543	173,080	307,340	2,947,984	180,243	3,128,227
1880	1,981,007	743,442	392,187	251,203	410,362	3,778,201	189,591	3,967,792
1881	2,018,149	665,167	299,057	246,615	385,609	3,614,597	185,592	3,800,189
1882	1,642,581	558,461	254,814	243,067	333,397	3,032,320	111,354	3,143,674
1883	1,470,861	390,846	203,584	273,832	552,354	2,891,477	155,993	3,047,470
1884	1,583,563	492,191	313,629	240,342	589,221	3,218,946	368,541	3,587,487
1885	1,906,703	551,014	387,536	342,684	569,586	3,757,523	304,659	4,062,182
1886	1,173,476	215,769	324,321	238,670	358,296	2,310,532	249,234	2,559,766
1887	1,352,098	263,135	272,755	248,380	416,782	2,553,150	257,026	2,810,176

1888	1,464,399	374,910	367,357	209,662	396,650	2,812,978	198,618	3,011,596
1889	1,112,654	222,481	201,064	249,668	395,851	2,181,718	206,911	2,388,629
1890	1,314,473	269,022	269,422	251,844	423,451	2,528,212	213,192	2,741,404
1891	1,258,171	287,383	337,556	242,931	405,287	2,531,328	200,829	2,732,157
1892	890,953	182,333	259,379	161,530	305,617	1,799,812	173,123	1,972,935
1893	773,503	171,187	308,469	193,750	375,138	1,822,047	113,372	1,935,419
1894	842,072	192,033	208,312	174,721	392,056	1,809,194	171,083	1,980,277
1895	981,562	201,809	199,855	143,620	381,967	1,908,813	135,803	2,044,616
1896	885,343	143,184	229,108	192,718	371,684	1,822,037	137,172	1,959,209
1897	910,467	232,436	207,248	225,830	399,393	1,975,374	104,577	2,079,951
1898	1,015,356	208,802	226,675	236,093	538,189	2,225,115	122,574	2,347,689
1899	1,276,616	192,368	244,017	294,213	681,395	2,688,609	173,736	2,862,345
1900	1,274,732	56,013	280,045	363,641	788,451	2,762,882	193,380	2,956,262
1901	1,255,633	122,552	213,969	293,482	727,089	2,612,725	185,253	2,797,978
1902	946,902	92,546	167,540	247,654	681,560	2,136,202	138,015	2,274,217
1903	1,192,276	100,315	294,826	305,508	826,689	2,719,614	172,096	2,891,710
1904	1,596,175	68,855	923,768	381,725	1,365,434	4,335,957	238,810	4,574,767
1905	1,236,706	183,156	937,976	311,880	1,047,219	3,716,937	124,798	3,841,735
1906	1,419,877	53,118	344,567	313,034	934,553	3,065,149	155,349	3,220,498
1907	1,297,818	37,516	466,452	391,552	1,031,911	3,225,249	130,154	3,355,403
1908	1,211,561	91,455	280,947	317,339	1,000,163	2,901,465	186,875	3,088,340
1909	1,883,669	78,544	342,701	287,584	974,852	3,567,350	146,502	3,713,852
1910	1,850,999	22,516	403,663	314,456	1,026,094	3,617,728	216,277	3,834,005
1911	1,293,869	77,149	281,028	238,535	898,747	2,789,328	196,484	2,985,812
1912	1,556,887	64,486	505,833	272,847	1,130,709	3,530,762	230,575	3,761,337
1913	2,344,069	78,470	401,003	377,383	1,153,203	4,354,128	200,462	4,554,590
1914	1,812,786	50,957	309,725	293,582	1,162,359	3,629,409	80,607	3,710,016

Source: Annual Statement of Trade of the United Kingdom.

Appendix 7.8

British imports from Hong Kong (£)

Year	(1) Tea	(2) Silk knubs, husks & waste raw, & manufactures	(3) Hemp	(4) Others	(5) Total
1868	157,907	7,384	–	70,513	235,804
1869	48,964	23,589	–	209,379	281,932
1870	94,426	51,489	–	135,244	281,159
1871	144,541	122,128	–	101,275	367,944
1872	395,420	113,832	–	324,512	833,764
1873	396,184	172,014	–	215,259	783,457
1874	392,912	116,726	–	237,653	747,291
1875	766,001	194,819	–	194,090	1,154,910
1876	839,568	152,383	–	364,899	1,356,850
1877	735,394	218,236	–	941,680	1,895,310
1878	712,974	112,914	–	348,581	1,174,469
1879	746,774	134,884	–	445,427	1,327,085
1880	639,270	122,993	–	491,278	1,253,541
1881	544,060	75,885	–	395,771	1,015,716
1882	577,152	311,906	23	540,688	1,429,749
1883	558,680	177,591	97,570	338,145	1,171,986
1884	445,459	127,286	141,677	337,880	1,052,302
1885	403,406	108,374	89,016	367,618	968,414
1886	424,785	566,809	110,982	453,486	1,556,062
1887	342,517	619,791	125,940	320,993	1,409,241
1888	265,309	459,563	134,998	436,320	1,296,690

Year					
1889	203,115	546,092	156,338	223,645	1,129,190
1890	194,323	494,049	197,725	338,967	1,225,064
1891	195,526	505,356	100,426	300,394	1,101,702
1892	227,480	277,229	133,393	198,603	836,705
1893	208,807	309,324	103,346	264,157	885,634
1894	188,780	110,908	51,054	280,076	630,818
1895	165,632	141,536	105,790	346,483	759,441
1896	107,353	223,510	197,588	268,707	797,158
1897	92,243	157,694	47,201	309,176	606,314
1898	80,821	134,647	270,990	240,179	726,637
1899	112,837	199,814	333,138	237,337	883,126
1900	70,427	218,849	436,597	340,175	1,066,048
1901	61,071	168,497	136,583	236,690	602,841
1902	32,353	176,204	139,585	262,256	610,398
1903	50,213	201,566	120,036	210,949	582,764
1904	45,529	122,692	12,088	286,502	466,811
1905	18,481	118,915	250	248,794	386,440
1906	34,142	129,636	44,289	430,440	638,507
1907	18,801	121,658	42,822	435,579	618,860
1908	30,531	135,990	14,115	366,703	547,339
1909	6,750	175,249	8,218	265,457	455,674
1910	4,653	165,411	15,091	411,247	596,402
1911	14,003	176,104	9,246	535,275	734,628
1912	6,724	129,524	11,315	694,053	841,616
1913	5,117	80,953	8,026	581,180	675,276
1914	9,202	92,858	3,994	492,822	598,876

Source: Annual Statement of Trade of the United Kingdom.

8

SINO-JAPANESE TRADE AND JAPANESE INDUSTRIALIZATION

Sakae Tsunoyama

Kawakatsu has presented a new view of the process of Japanese industrialization, seeing it not as a copy of European industrialization, but a product of the dynamic forces of Asian economic history. These forces also account for the recent development of Newly Industrialized Economies (NIEs) and ASEAN which have quickly followed the success of Japan's industrialization. His idea is related to the work of Sugihara, who has argued that Japan's industrialization resulted from intra-Asian trade in the late nineteenth century.[1]

Kawakatsu emphasizes the importance of intra-Asian trade as a stimulus to Japanese industrial development rather than Western influences. This is probably correct. But the history of intra-Asian trade since the fifteenth century has not been studied by economic historians. When it is researched, it may be possible to answer the question raised by Kawakatsu concerning the success of Japan as a competitor in intra-Asian trade. This short paper contributes to this research; it shows the unique role of Japan's industries in intra-Asian trade by analysing Sino-Japanese trade in the Tokugawa period and early Meiji era.

It must be noted that there was a fundamental difference between Japan and the European countries in the circumstances in which early industrialization took place. European countries in the nineteenth century had national policies of protectionism with high tariffs and subsidies in order to foster their own infant industries, by saving them from the impact of British free trade policies. This nineteenth-century protectionism was successful in achieving industrialization in the backward European countries. But Japan, having opened its doors to the world in 1858, had no tariff autonomy to protect its industries from the impact of free trade. The same could be said of other Asian

194

countries. Under these circumstances it would be natural for a backward country to become an agricultural economy according to the law of the international division of labour, or to become a colony or a semi-colonial country. In fact, the history of Asia since the middle of the nineteenth century shows that world capitalism forced its countries to be dependent upon the advanced Western powers, with the sole exception of Japan.

How could Japan succeed in industrializing without protective policies such as high tariffs, and not be turned into an agricultural country? Japan's success seems a curious story for Europeans. The key point for this success is to be found in the structure of the Asian market, which was very different from the West in the pattern of the people's way of life. It worked as a sort of non-tariff barrier against Western merchants.

THE STRUCTURE OF INTRA-ASIAN TRADE IN THE SEVENTEENTH AND EIGHTEENTH CENTURIES

It is very difficult to find reliable statistical data on intra-Asian trade in the seventeenth and eighteenth centuries in Chinese official documents, though many Chinese junks were supposed to be active in the cross-trade between the Asian mainland and the islands of South-East Asia.[2] Their trade extended to Japan, and they were permitted to trade at Nagasaki after Japan's seclusion in 1639. The Tokugawa Bakufu strictly controlled Nagasaki trade, allowing only the ships of the Dutch and the Chinese. So luckily, we have Bakufu's official records of Sino-Japanese trade for about two hundred years, and they show the details of the most important route in intra-Asian trade.

In the Dutch–Japanese trade of the seventeenth century it was very profitable for the Dutch to import gold, silver and copper from Japan. But the Dutch leading export goods to Japan were not European commodities but the products of South China and South-East Asia, particularly raw silk, silk textiles and sugar. Japan bought them at very high prices, as mentioned by Montesquieu in his *De l'esprit des lois* (1748).[3] As a result, lots of silver and copper flowed out of Japan. The Dutch made big profits in the trade at Nagasaki, because they could use the most profitable route in intra-Asian trade to the best advantage. But, despite the glittering history of the Dutch–Japanese trade, in reality Chinese junks controlled the intra-Asian trade as a whole in the seventeenth and eighteenth centuries.[4]

Chinese junks arrived in Nagasaki with raw silk, silk textiles and sugar; but they carried from Japan not only silver and copper but also various necessary foods and things for their daily life, such as marine products, sake, soya bean sauce, rice, and so on. These were the most important exports from Japan in the seventeenth century and were increasing in variety towards the end of the eighteenth century.[5]

The structure of Japan's import trade, however, greatly changed in the eighteenth century with the development of import-substituting industries in Japan. The Bakufu in the seventeenth century particularly encouraged the expansion of sericulture, the silk textile industry and the cultivation of sugar cane, aiming at self-sufficiency in the supply of these import goods. The development of these import-replacement industries led to structural change in intra-Asian trade due to the decrease of exports of silver and copper from Japan. The most important consequence of this change was the decline of Dutch trade with Japan, because it was not as profitable as previously. The arrival of Dutch ships at Nagasaki became less and less in the eighteenth century: on average one or two ships per year as compared with seven or eight ships in the middle of the seventeenth century.

Chinese junks also decreased in number from the middle of the eighteenth century, but ever since the beginning of seclusion in 1641 the number of junks in the Japanese trade had been much greater than that

Table 8.1 Ships arriving at Nagasaki, 1641–1781

Year	Dutch	Chinese	Year	Dutch	Chinese
1641	9	97	1715	3	7
1650	7	70	1721	3	33
1655	4	45	1725	2	30
1661	11	39	1731	1	38
1665	12	36	1735	1	29
1671	7	38	1741	2	14
1675	4	29	1745	3	20
1681	4	30	1751	3	11
1685	4	73	1755	2	12
1691	3	70	1761	2	12
1695	5	60	1765	1	12
1701	4	65	1771	2	13
1705	4	80	1775	1	13
1711	4	57	1781	1	13

Source: Nichiran Gakkai (ed.) *Yōgakushi-Jiten* (Dictionary of the History of Western Learning), Tokyo: Yūshōdō-Shuppan, 1984, Appendix Table 2.

of Dutch ships, as shown in Table 8.1. These junks came to Nagasaki mostly from Shanghai, Ningpo, Foochow, Amoy, Canton and other ports in South China and even from Siam, and they were certainly engaged in intra-Asian trade.

It is worth noting that Japan in the eighteenth century imported from the Netherlands new intellectual information such as Western academic knowledge and technology (particularly astronomy, cartography and medical science) and also paintings, natural history and so on. This Western intellectual information was very useful for Japan's later modernization and industrialization, and the import of Chinese culture was held in less esteem.

THE IMPORT OF WESTERN CONSUMER GOODS AND INTRA-ASIAN TRADE

The opening of five ports in China by the Treaty of Nanking in 1842 and the further opening of eleven more ports in China after the Treaty of Tientsin in 1858 caused a great transformation in Asian trade. This had previously been carried on mainly by Chinese junks for more than two hundred years. At almost the same time Siam and Japan were forced to open their doors to the world by the pressure of the Western powers. As a result, intra-Asian trade was opened to Western merchants. They came to Asia with the commodities of Western civilization, which had been invented in the West to be used in the daily life of the people; for example, matches, soap, the Western style of umbrella, oil lamps, glassware, and so on. When they were imported, the people of Asia found them very convenient and usable. In the case of matches, people who previously used to get a spark by using a flint could now easily get a light merely by using a match. The same can be said of the umbrella, because until then their only protection from rain was a sheet of oiled paper to cover the head. The Western style of umbrella became a desirable good for Asians who found it both convenient and fashionable.[6]

However, although these were very desirable items, they were too expensive for most of the poor people in Asia to buy. So the Japanese tried to copy them for themselves. They were so skilful that they could soon make imitations of them. The Japanese copies were not as good but were much cheaper than the Western originals. They were exported to the Asian mainland by Chinese merchants (and soon also by Japanese merchants) to compete with the expensive Western goods.

Japanese matches, for example, were successful in driving out

European matches in Hong Kong as early as 1887. Though it is true that a Japanese consul reported in 1887 that the Japanese match was unpopular in Hong Kong because its label was a poor imitation and was of inferior quality, it is also true that the poor people preferred the Japanese match because of its cheapness.[7] Another example was cotton flannel, which was invented by a Japanese in Wakayama just after the Meiji restoration in 1868 as a substitute for imported woollen flannel. Japanese cotton flannels were exported to South China to meet the needs of poor people and made a remarkable advance in the 1890s against the competition of German cotton flannel.[8] There are other similar examples which cannot be listed in this short paper.[9] These convenient Western small wares are called in general *yoshiki zakka*, the Western style of merchandise; they were becoming popular in England in the middle of the nineteenth century.[10]

This revolution in living conditions in Europe came to Asia immediately after the opening of the Asian ports. The Western style of merchandise attracted Asians, even the poor. They wanted to have them. Therefore, a very large market was created for Western small wares in Asia. The success of Japan's industrialization and its growth in overseas trade was mainly dependent upon the large Asian market. This is the reason why so much importance must be placed on the intra-Asian trade by Chinese junks. Japanese overseas marketing performed by consuls must also be emphasized, as the reports to the government were passed on effectively through the domestic information network connecting central government, local governments, the chambers of commerce and the manufacturers, and so on.[11] Japanese consular reports from China contributed to the increased sales of Japanese goods to mainland Asia. According to the British government survey of Hong Kong in 1895 which commented upon the decline in sales of British goods, Japanese cotton rags, cleaning soda and sulphuric acid were already dominant in the Hong Kong market and some kinds of Japanese cotton cloth, linen cloth, towels, soap, paper and other cheap goods were competing with British goods. One of the reasons for the decline in the sales of British goods, as this survey pointed out, was that British manufacturers were idle in their market research into consumer taste in the region.[12]

The *Annual Trade Report in Hong Kong, 1899* (Japanese Consular Report, *Tsūshō Hōkoku*, no. 191, 1901) indicated that Japan's trade volume with Hong Kong ranked first in exports and second in imports; it was followed by the overseas junk trade, French Indo-China, Siam, Java and the East Indies Islands, Hainan and Tonkin Bay, and so on, in order of the volume of import trade. And in the volume of export trade from Hong Kong, the overseas junk trade ranked first, Japan second, followed by the China coast, India and the Settlement Colonies, the USA, and so on.

Hong Kong, the free port, was the centre of intra-Asian trade. Those who dominated Hong Kong's trade could dominate the Asian market. Chinese junks and Japan were dominant at the end of the nineteenth century; so it was inevitable that the two would compete vigorously with each other, and that this would lead eventually to military action. But the factor which determined the fate of trade competition between the two was Japan's success in industrializing.

As mentioned above, Japan's early industrialization began with the import-substituting industries of the eighteenth century. Through Japanese success in the production of raw silk, silk textiles and sugar, formerly major imports from China, the trend of Sino-Japanese trade changed during the eighteenth century. The export of various Japanese small wares increased towards the end of the Tokugawa period. It is interesting to find handicraft goods such as umbrellas, copper-ware, lacquered ware, earthenware, and so on, and also marine products among the export goods of early Meiji Japan. This shows that in China people's interest in Japanese goods was emerging. This tendency in Sino-Japanese trade continued, and was followed by the export of Japanese copies of Western small wares.

The development of Japanese industries making Western small wares was a response to the inflow of Western goods after the opening up of the country. We can call it the second stage in the development of Japanese import-substituting industry and it led to Japan's success in achieving modern industrialization. In Asia the word 'modernization' meant in most cases 'Westernization', which however does not always mean the import and use of Western things. Nevertheless, Asian people had a longing for the things of Western civilization such as matches, soap, umbrellas, and so on. Under these circumstances it was Japan which could supply them at prices cheap enough for the poor to buy, and so compete with Western countries. On this point it can be said that Japan's industrial civilization, even though it may be criticized, has played the role of transformer, converting Western high-powered electric current to local requirements.

NOTES

1. Kaoru Sugihara, 'Patterns and development of intra-Asian trade, 1880–1913' [in Japanese], *Socio-economic History*, 51(1), (1985); Heita Kawakatsu, 'Japan's industrial revolution in Asian history' [in Japanese], *Waseda Journal of Political Science and Economics*, nos 297–8 (1989).

2. Anthony Reid, *Southeast Asia in the Age of Commerce*, vol. 1: *The Lands below the Winds*, New Haven, Conn., and London: Yale University Press, 1988. This book hints at the history of South-East Asian Trade in the fifteenth and seventeenth centuries.

3. Montesquieu referred to Japan's import of sugar at very high prices. See Baron de Montesquieu, *De l'esprit des lois* (1748), Livre XX, ch. ix.

4. As for the Chinese junk, see Osamu Ōba, 'Scroll paintings of Chinese junks which sailed to Nagasaki in the 18th century and their equipment', *Mariners' Mirror*, 60(4), (1974).

5. Yōko Nagazumi (ed.) *Statistics of Export–Import Goods at Nagasaki by Chinese Junks, 1637–1833* [in Japanese], Tokyo: Sōbun-sha, 1987.

6. It is worth noting that from the end of the eighteenth century Chinese junks had already begun to import large numbers of Japanese style umbrellas, which looked like those of Western style but were made of paper and bamboo. For example, Chinese junk no. 3, which sailed from Nagasaki in 1799, carried out 3,000 umbrellas; no. 4 carried 2,550; no. 5 carried 7,000; no. 7 carried 270 and so on. In the year 1799–1800 it was recorded that more than 13,000 umbrellas were exported from Japan. Sakae Tsunoyama, 'Japan's industrialization and Asia', *Journal of Economics of Kwansei Gakuin University*, 44(2), (1990) 10.

7. Sakae Tsunoyama, *Information Strategy of Japanese Overseas Trade* [in Japanese], Tokyo: Nihon Hōsōshuppan-kai, 1988, 122–4.

8. Sakae Tsunoyama, 'Anglo-Japanese competition in South China market after the Sino-Japanese War', in Kei-ichiro Nakagawa (ed.) *Historical Studies in Business Management* [in Japanese], Tokyo: Iwanami-shoten, 1990.

9. Tsunoyama, 'Japan's industrialization and Asia'.

10. Asa Briggs, *Victorian Things*, London: Batsford, 1988, ch. 5.

11. Sakae Tsunoyama (ed.) *Studies in Japanese Consular Reports* [in Japanese], Tokyo: Dōbunkan-Shuppan, 1986, 3–39.

12. Tsunoyama, 'Anglo-Japanese competition in South China market after the Sino-Japanese War', in Nakagawa (ed.) *Historical Studies in Business Management*.

9

JAPAN'S EAST ASIA MARKET, 1870–1940

Peter Schran

Japan was drawn into the 'millstream' of modern economic development relatively late, in the mid-nineteenth century. As latecomers to this
experience, the Japanese became the most avid students not only of the
Western technology and commerce to which they were being exposed
(and of the civilization that had created them), but also of the
imperialistic politics which had made Tokugawa Japan submit to that
exposure. Moreover, in their efforts to emancipate themselves from
such impositions and to achieve for Japan eventually a status
comparable to that of the dominant powers of the time, the Japanese
began to emulate those powers – notably Britain, France, Germany,
Russia and the United States – by pursuing opportunities not only for
free trade but also for empire-building.

In the circumstances, these two approaches appeared sequentially
interdependent. In order to be able to assert themselves effectively at
some future time, the Japanese first had to modernize and develop to
some extent. This required Japan's participation in international trade
on Western terms, the domestic consequences of which could be and
were modified by government fiscal and regulatory intervention. The
acquisition of the new technology, which involved substantial outlays
for purchases of new producer goods in addition to payments for
purchases of new or cheaper consumer goods from abroad, depended
on earnings from the export of numerous traditional products.
Although the most prominent among those items, raw silk and tea, were
much in demand in both Europe and North America, other commodities
found more ready markets on the Asian mainland because cultural
similarities made them more attractive there. China in particular thus
became right away a customer as well as a source of primary products.
In that latter capacity more than in the former, it was soon joined by
British India.

As Japan's development progressed, both the composition and the direction of its trade began to change. In relative terms, exports of primary products diminished while their imports grew, and exports of finished goods rose while their imports fell. In this context, Japan also became less of a business partner and more of a competitor for the industrialized nations of the West, vying with them in third markets to sell more and more similar modern manufactures and to buy the raw materials for their production. The less-developed areas of Asia – in addition to China and India, especially South-East Asia and Oceania – became the principal arenas for this competition.

Whereas China thus appeared as merely one of several major markets, it held special promise, not so much because of its proximity and cultural affinity, but because of its potential for political dependency. By the mid-nineteenth century, China – like Japan – had been forced to accept 'unequal treaties' which limited its sovereignty. But the impositions were more far-reaching, and China coped with them much less effectively. As a consequence, it was forced time and again to cede territory and to give up claims to overlordship over adjacent states, beside forgoing tariff autonomy and allowing ever more foreign 'treaty port' enclaves on its territory as well as granting extra-territorial rights to the citizens of the Western treaty powers. By the late nineteenth century, when Japan felt sufficiently strong to realize imperial ambitions, the various treaty powers had begun to vie with each other for railroad concessions in related spheres of influence.

The treaty powers shared the privileges which each had extracted from China through the institution of the most-favoured-nation clause. Japan, which had failed earlier to obtain comparable concessions peaceably, remained disadvantaged until it waged war on China and defeated it in 1895. As the newest treaty power, it not only acceded to all previously imposed rights but added to them new Chinese concessions on inland navigation and treaty port industrialization. In addition, it forced China to cede Taiwan (Formosa) and to give up its claim to overlordship over Korea (Chosen). By its victory in the subsequent Russo-Japanese War, Japan in 1905 secured Russia's acquiescence in its colonization of Korea. Russia also had to transfer its rights to the Kwantung Leased Territory and to the southern section of the Chinese Eastern Railway Zone (renamed the South Manchuria Railway Zone), which it had prevented Japan from acquiring ten years earlier.

During the course of one decade, less than fifty years after its forcible opening, Japan thus managed both to emancipate itself and to establish its empire. By adding to the impositions on China, it asserted itself sufficiently to regain its territorial rights over foreigners and its tariff autonomy. At the same time that it acquired Taiwan and Korea as colonies, it therefore also possessed once again the power to practise protectionism overtly.

The Japanese used this power soon, not only to promote their further domestic industrialization *per se* but also to institutionalize preferences; for example, for Taiwanese sugar and Korean rice imports into Japan proper as well as for the export of Japanese manufactures to these colonies. As a consequence, the shares of Taiwan and Korea in Japan's total trade increased rapidly, and their development accelerated as well. Eventually, in the 1920s, imperial preferences were extended even to the Kwantung Leased Territory, evidently also in order to protect the intermediate position of Japan. The subsidization and regulation of shipping and ship-building facilitated this integration, assuring that most of the trade to and from Japan as well as within the empire was carried in Japanese bottoms.

While Japan thus followed the lead of most Western powers in forming and protecting strategic interests both at home and in its newly acquired possessions, China remained open perforce to almost all foreign trade and investment with hardly any restrictions, and the Japanese at once did their best to keep it that way. Because of this institutionalized inequality between countries, China's trade and investment were distorted as well, in inverse relation. To the extent that Japan – like other treaty powers – promoted exports relative to imports, and exports of manufactured consumer goods in exchange for imports of raw materials for industrial production, it induced China to conform by buying and selling accordingly without intervention. By implication, it also encouraged in China the (development of) production of exportable primary products relative to that of importable manufactures. The growth of import-substituting manufacturing in China required in such circumstances unusual product differentiation or cost advantages in order to proceed.

Although Japan competed with all other countries everywhere in China, it evidently developed regional interests and advantages, in accordance with its empire-building strategy. Hong Kong, as the entrepôt for South China, and the South China region generally were important trading partners during the pre-emancipation period but lost favour thereafter, as that region's trade tended to stagnate. Shanghai as the entrepôt of the Yangtze Valley and the Central China region retained its significance as the arena where Japan contended with the

United States and, secondarily, Britain for this largest and most dynamic part of the China market. North China and, even more so, Manchuria with their principal ports of Tientsin (Tianjin) and Dairen (Dalian), respectively, were the regions where the Japanese began to predominate after their success in the Russo-Japanese War. Under the law and order assured by the Kwantung Army and through the agency of the South Manchuria Railway Corporation, Japan developed not only the trade but the entire economy of the Kwantung Leased Territory, the railroad corridor and adjacent areas in forms that were not so different from its colonial practices, though tempered by the multilateralism of the treaty provisions.

In terms of its overall share of the China market, Japan surpassed most of its competitors – notably the US – in the late nineteenth century and began to rival Great Britain with its colony Hong Kong on the eve of the First World War. Japan's China trade, along with its trade and development generally and China's trade and development as well, received a boost during the war, when the Western powers' pre-occupation with it and the extraordinary increase in shipping costs made import substitution, export expansion and larger market shares easier to achieve. Setbacks followed with the competitors' return after the war, of course. More lasting threats arose in addition because of China's advancing political reconstitution, which resulted in its successful negotiation of tariff autonomy in 1928, thirty years after Japan had regained as much or more for itself. Japan at first accepted the change reluctantly, because it stood to lose more than the other powers from China's new protectionism – which resembled that practised by Japan, needless to say.

The coincidence of China's new protectionism with the Great Depression and its effects on trade was too much for the Kwantung Army to take. Instead of accommodating itself to China's eventual emancipation, as the Western powers did, Japan embarked on the opposite course of expanding its empire in order to preserve its established advantage. Manchuria, long dominated 'informally' within the treaty system, was redefined as a minority territory under Chinese rule since the overthrow of the Manchu dynasty and reconstituted as a separate country, Manchoukuo, in 1931. As a Japanese satellite, it was integrated into the Yen bloc and experienced under Japanese hegemony remarkable development, thanks to major Japanese resource commitments as well as policy revisions which had earlier appeared contrary to Japanese domestic interests.

The pattern of Japan's trade with Manchuria changed notably for these reasons. To be sure, the established exchange of various manufactured products (especially textiles, wheat flour and sugar) for various primary products (notably soya beans, bean cake and coal) continued and became more exclusive in response to tariff revisions. In addition, however, Japan now supplied large quantities of industrial investment goods, which in many instances were not yet fully competitive with Western products and consequently could not be sold profitably elsewhere. Their supply on capital account increased Japan's export surplus dramatically and turned Manchuria's small trade surplus overall into a very large trade deficit. Manchuria's trade with most other parts of the world tended to diminish unless it came to be conducted under bilateral agreements, as with Germany. But it continued until the onset of the Second World War and remained essential for the implementation of the development strategy, given Japan's techno-logical and resource limitations.

Japan's forcible creation of Manchoukuo did not provoke immediate war with China and did not keep Japan from continuing to exercise its remaining treaty power rights in the residual Chinese territory. That territory's trade declined in value during the early 1930s under the combined influence of the depression and the drastic rises in tariff rates. The quantity of imports decreased, and the share of producer goods among them increased. The quantity of exports increased, and other agricultural products (oil seeds, oil, eggs and egg products in particular) replaced soya beans and bean cake as the principal food-stuffs sold abroad. Japan's shares of the territory's exports and imports held fairly steady in relative terms and continued to yield a trade surplus, albeit of much smaller magnitude. But the relative constancy implied absolute declines in Japan's trade with North, Central and South China, which offset the advances in trade with Manchuria. The combined shares of Manchoukuo and the Republic of China in Japan's total trade contracted somewhat as a result.

Sino-Japanese trade relations changed more significantly soon thereafter, when Japan's determination to extend its hegemony over China further and to obtain for itself, as in Manchoukuo, privileges with respect to trade and investment finally brought on the Second Sino-Japanese War of 1937–45. Japan's military advances, resulting in the rapid occupation of most coastal provinces and the increasing isolation of 'Free China' in the interior, made it possible to impose those terms without much delay or consideration of the other treaty powers' interests. In response to such measures and the incorporation of the new North China Federal Reserve Bank system into the Yen bloc, Japan's exports to 'Occupied China' increased dramatically, while its imports from that territory declined in absolute and relative terms. At issue remains whether the consequent export surplus was actually unintended or a variant of the old policy of exporting more to China while importing more from other parts of the world, since China's currency remained convertible for some time and other countries, especially the United States, South-East Asia and India, sold more to 'Occupied China' than they bought from it. As a share of total Japanese imports, those from the entire mainland (Manchoukuo plus Occupied China) approached once again the previous common levels while exports to it exceeded any previously experienced percentage of total Japanese sales abroad.

The formerly internal trade between Manchuria and the rest of China passed through substantial changes in response to the initial political separation and subsequent reintegration within the Yen bloc. Because of the imposition of tariffs on both sides, the trade between the two entities declined very much during the early 1930s, exports from Manchuria to China falling even more than imports from China into it. With the Japanese occupation of north China in particular, exports to China increased once again and approached the level of the late 1920s by the late 1930s. Imports from China increased also, but not enough to prevent the re-emergence of a large export surplus, which had been characteristic of pre-Manchoukuo times as well. Manchuria thus contributed notably to the import surplus of 'Occupied China'. The pattern of exchange may not have been affected greatly by political events. Manchuria continued to export to China primarily coarse grains, soya beans, bean oil, bean cake and coal, while it imported from it primarily rice, wheat flour, tea, tobacco, cotton and paper.

On the eve of the Pacific War, Japan thus had succeeded in transforming most of East Asia – all of which had once been part of the Chinese Empire in name if not in fact – into a set of colonies, satellites and occupied territories. On all these entities – Taiwan, Korea, Kwantung Leased Territory and SMR Zone, Manchoukuo and even north China – Japan imposed institutions and regulations which biased their external trade flows in favour of the metropolitan territory as the ultimate or intermediate origin or destination. As a consequence, even the direct trade between dependencies appears to have remained or become smaller than it would have been in less-restricted circumstances, and the share of the entire empire in the total trade of all dependencies appeared correspondingly overly large. The benefits of free trade obviously could not materialize fully under such conditions, and the dependent populations in particular paid for that, involuntarily.

However, the biases which Japan imposed did not favour simply an exchange of Japanese-manufactured consumer goods for colonial raw materials. They also gave rise to a protected Empire-wide market for Japanese-made producer goods, which were not yet competitive in free markets. By supplying such goods to both the dependencies and the metropolitan territory, economies of scale could be realized in their production; and the production of primary products, as well as their processing, could be increased and improved in both locations. As a consequence, most dependencies experienced a process of 'dependent' development, which also was clearly 'second best' in their circumstances and not necessarily the choice of the dependent populations. At times, and especially during the 1930s, this process was accelerated by massive Japanese investments, which assured, for example, that the Manchurian economy grew from 1924 to 1941 at roughly the same 4 per cent per annum which the Japanese economy experienced. Korea and Taiwan also achieved similar growth rates at least since the time of the First World War.

Moreover, the integration of economic relations within the Empire proceeded gradually, and the Empire as a whole did not achieve a high degree of autarky – except for lack of alternatives during the final phase of the Pacific War. Until then, Japan as well as its dependencies continued to export to the rest of the world products which were competitive, in order to pay for imports which could not be produced internally on acceptable terms. As the intermediary in this process and as the territory that was most in need of inputs from the more-industrialized countries under the strategy, Japan resorted to trade with the world outside its Empire more than any of its dependencies did, with the exception of newly 'Occupied China' during the Second Sino-Japanese War. China then, as well as before its occupation, was one of the major markets where export surpluses were achieved by Japan, which helped to pay for its import surpluses from Europe and North America.

The following sections document this transformation of Japan's economic relations with the various parts of East Asia that need to be distinguished. They also discuss specific features of these relations in greater detail than this synopsis has done. The conclusion to the chapter will address in addition some of the evaluative issues which the Japan experience poses.

THE GROWTH AND STRUCTURAL TRANSFORMATION OF JAPAN'S TRADE

Japan's trade with the rest of the world has been reported systematically for the years since 1868. The reported data imply high rates of increase in the values of exports and imports not only *per se* but also relative to the value of national income, which grew rapidly as well (at approximately 4 per cent per annum in real terms) in comparison with the value of national income in other countries. Trade clearly appeared as the engine of growth, which increased more rapidly even than the value added by Japan's secondary (manufacturing plus) sector until the early post-First World War years.[1] Its share in national income fluctuated during the 1920s and declined slowly during the 1930s under the impact of the depression and all governments' responses to that event (Table 9.1).

At their height toward the end of the First World War, Japan's exports and imports each accounted for somewhat more than 20 per cent of its national income. Moreover, both exports and imports consisted of large varieties of goods with relatively small domestic market shares. Lockwood concluded for this reason that

> For most Japanese industries the export market played a subordinate role throughout the prewar (WWI) decades. Also, it tended to absorb goods not essentially dissimilar in character from those widely consumed at home. The pattern varied widely from industry to industry, however, and the total impact of world demand in intensifying the rate of Japanese industrialization was highly significant.[2]

Lockwood's generalization appears to fit even the most prominent export items, namely raw silk at all times, supplemented first by tea and subsequently by cotton yarn and cotton fabrics. The most prominent import items – textiles, sugar, raw cotton – seem to have been similarly marginal to domestic production:

> On the whole, however, the destructive impact of imported foreign manufactures on the traditional handicrafts seems to have been neither very pronounced, nor very widespread. It was slight by comparison with the inroads made in later years by Japan's own developing factory industries.[3]

The latters' effects on the structure of Japan's foreign trade are made evident in Table 9.2. The export shares of foodstuffs and raw materials,

Table 9.1 The share of international trade in Japan's national income
Unit: Percent of national income produced, as estimated by Kazushi Ohkawa

Period	All areas Exp.	All areas Imp.	Korea Exp.	Korea Imp.	Taiwan Exp.	Taiwan Imp.	China Exp.	China Imp.	Hong Kong Exp.	Hong Kong Imp.	East Asia Exp.	East Asia Imp.
1878–80	4.6	5.7					1.0	0.9			1.0	0.9
1881–85	5.5	4.6					1.0	1.0			1.0	1.0
1886–90	8.1	7.9					1.3[a]	1.2[a]			1.6	1.5
1891–95	10.1	9.3					0.8	1.6			2.3	2.3
1896–1900	10.4	13.9			0.3[b]	0.2[b]	1.6	1.6	1.5	0.7	3.7	2.4
1901–05	13.8	16.2			0.5	0.4	3.0	2.0	1.8	0.6	4.8	2.7
1906–10	14.9[c]	15.9[c]			0.7	1.0	3.4	2.2	1.3	0.2	4.9	3.3
1911–15	16.8	17.0	1.1	0.7	1.0	1.2	4.0	2.3	0.8	0.0	6.8	4.2
1916–20	21.3	20.1	1.3	1.3	0.9	1.3	4.8	3.5	0.7	0.0	7.6	6.2
1921–25	16.2	20.8	1.5	2.1	0.8	1.4	3.5	2.9	0.6	0.0	6.3	6.4
1926–30	18.1	20.4	2.2	2.4	1.0	1.7	3.5	2.8	0.5	0.0	7.1	6.9
1931–35	17.8	18.7	2.8	2.6	1.2	1.9	3.0	2.1	0.2	0.0	7.3	6.6
1936–40	17.6	16.6	3.9	2.6	1.3	1.7	4.9	2.2	0.1	0.0	10.2	6.5

Notes
[a] 1889–90: including, as before, Hong Kong
[b] Average, 1897–1900
[c] 1910: excluding Korea
Source: Derived from Bank of Japan, Statistics Department, *Hundred-year Statistics of the Japanese Economy*, July 1966, 32, 278–9, 290–2.

Table 9.2 Japan's international trade by category[a]
Unit: Percent of total exports/imports

Period	Food-stuffs Exp.	Food-stuffs Imp.	Raw materials Exp.	Raw materials Imp.	Fabricated raw materials Exp.	Fabricated raw materials Imp.	Finished goods Exp.	Finished goods Imp.	Other commodities Exp.	Other commodities Imp.
1868–70	32.2	44.3	24.9	4.3	40.9	18.6	1.2	31.1	1.9	1.7
1871–75	39.0	14.4	17.5	3.8	36.6	21.5	3.1	56.6	3.8	3.8
1876–80	38.0	13.5	11.8	3.7	41.5	27.6	4.8	51.9	3.8	3.4
1881–85	31.5	19.1	11.9	4.0	45.6	29.0	8.0	45.7	3.0	2.2
1886–90	26.5	19.7	11.7	7.5	45.0	28.6	13.1	42.3	3.7	1.9
1891–95	18.5	21.7	9.8	20.8	44.7	20.1	23.5	34.9	3.5	2.5
1896–1900	13.0	23.3	11.7	26.7	46.6	17.7	25.7	30.9	3.0	1.4
1901–05	12.2	24.8	9.4	32.9	46.1	15.5	29.6	25.3	2.7	1.5
1906–10	11.2	14.6	9.3	39.7	46.7	18.5	31.2	26.3	1.5	0.8
1911–15	10.8	12.1	7.8	51.9	49.4	18.2	30.6	17.1	1.4	0.7
1916–20	8.9	10.3	5.6	52.8	41.3	24.4	42.2	11.9	2.0	0.7
1921–25	6.3	14.2	6.1	49.9	47.9	17.6	38.4	17.7	1.3	0.7
1926–30	7.7	13.8	5.4	54.8	42.1	16.0	42.8	14.6	1.9	0.8
1931–35	8.1	9.2	4.2	60.2	29.4	17.1	55.7	12.7	2.7	0.8
1936–40	10.1	8.7	4.4	51.8	26.0	25.9	57.3	12.9	2.4	0.7

Note
[a] Excluding Korea and Taiwan, which are counted as Japanese territory
Source: Derived from Bank of Japan, Statistics Department, Hundred-year Statistics of the Japanese Economy, July 1966, 280–1.

which accounted for the major share of the export value in the beginning, declined almost continuously to less than 15 per cent of the total. The export share of fabricated raw materials, which consisted at first primarily, and after the turn of the century largely, of raw silk, fluctuated until the 1930s, when it declined notably, largely because of a fall in the export share of raw silk.[4] The export share of finished goods rose rapidly to offset the decline in the shares of food-stuffs and raw materials. Until the First World War, this rise appears to have been attributable primarily to the growth of textile goods sales abroad. In subsequent years and especially during the 1930s, it reflected mostly the increase in industrial producer goods exports.[5] The last development would be even more apparent if sales to Korea and Taiwan were included in the tabulation.

On the import side, this pattern of change was matched by an almost continuous fall of the share of finished goods and a similarly continuous rise in the share of raw materials. The import share of fabricated raw materials fluctuated as did their export share around a fairly constant trend, but at half the level. The import share of food-stuffs, which might have been expected to increase continuously as well, decreased after 1905. It would have continued to rise if purchases from Taiwan and Korea had been included.[6] But this change would not have been very pronounced, either, because of Japan's protection of domestic food production when that activity began to experience serious threats from foreign competition. Except for this retarding influence of protectionism, Japan's foreign trade evidently experienced a very rapid structural transformation during the course of its extraordinary growth.

THE SIZE AND CHARACTERISTICS OF JAPAN'S EAST ASIA TRADE

At the beginning of the Meiji Restoration, Japan's trade with China accounted for almost all of its East Asia trade, and the Bank of Japan one hundred years later reported it as such.[7] The trade with Hong Kong was counted as part of the China trade until 1889. The trade with Taiwan was also part of it until Taiwan became a Japanese colony, the statistical separation appearing in 1897.[8] The coverage of the trade with Korea prior to 1910, when Korea became a Japanese colony, is uncertain. Another source reports the percentage shares of Japan's total exports and imports for the pre-colonial period shown in Table 9.3.[9] The subtotals for 'East Asia' and 'Others' in Table 9.4 may have to be adjusted accordingly. The data for China after 1931 continue to include

Table 9.3 Korea's share of Japan's total exports and imports, 1877–1916

Period	Exports to Korea (%)	Imports from Korea (%)
1877–86	1.2	1.3
1887–96	1.9	3.0
1897–1906 (inferred)	5.0	2.6
1907–16 (inferred)	5.5	4.3

the exports and imports of the Kwantung Leased Territory and of Manchoukuo with the SMR Zone.[10]

The amendments and corrections to Table 9.4 may add to the relative size of Japan's East Asia market during the late nineteenth century, but they do not modify the table's indications greatly thereby. China, successively net of Hong Kong, Taiwan, possibly Korea, but not Manchuria, accounted, with some variations, fairly steadily for about 20 per cent of Japan's exports and 15 per cent of its imports. Hong Kong also was more important as a destination of sales than as a source of purchases, and it rivalled China in both respects during the late nineteenth century. But its importance as a place of trade for Japan was short-lived. Japan's trade with it declined rapidly, while the trade with the colonies expanded from very small beginnings to very substantial magnitudes. This protected market in Taiwan and Korea matched Japan's open market in China by the mid-1920s and surpassed it soon thereafter. Moreover, unlike the trade with China, the trade with Taiwan registered import surpluses until the end of the period and the trade with Korea exhibited such surpluses until the depression. Within China, the trade with Manchuria developed on the same pattern until the formation of Manchoukuo, when Japan began to invest heavily in the region.[11]

In combination, these developments accounted for an increasing share for East Asia in the total value of Japan's external trade, from about 20 per cent during the late 1870s to almost 50 per cent during the late 1930s, with spurts after the achievement of treaty power status in China, during the First World War, and during the Second Sino-Japanese War. Moreover, whereas Japan's total exports tended to fall short of its total imports more often than not, exports to East Asia exceeded imports from East Asia at most times, frequently by substantial fractions. Both relations are indicated by the data of Table 9.1, which gives an impression of East Asia's importance in terms of

Table 9.4 East Asia's share in Japan's international trade
Unit: Percent of exports/imports

Period	China Exp.	China Imp.	Hong Kong Exp.	Hong Kong Imp.	Taiwan Exp.	Taiwan Imp.	Korea Exp.	Korea Imp.	East Asia Exp.	East Asia Imp.	Others Exp.	Others Imp.
1873–75	21.8	32.8							21.8	32.8	78.2	67.2
1876–80	19.5	19.3							19.5	19.3	80.5	80.7
1881–85	18.5	21.1							18.5	21.1	81.5	78.9
1886–90	20.2	15.0	13.2[a]	6.5[a]			?	?	20.2	18.3	79.8	81.7
1891–95	7.4	16.8	14.9	8.0			?	?	22.3	24.8	77.7	75.2
1896–1900	15.3	11.7	16.9	4.6	2.7[b]	1.4[b]	?	?	35.0	17.5	65.0	82.5
1901–05	21.5	12.6	9.8	1.1	3.5	2.8	?	?	34.8	16.5	65.2	83.5
1906–10	22.6	14.1	5.2	0.2	4.9	6.1	?	?	32.7	20.4	67.3	79.6
1911–15	23.7	13.6	4.4	0.2	6.0	7.3	6.5	3.9	40.6	25.0	59.4	75.0
1916–20	22.5	17.6	2.9	0.1	4.0	6.7	6.1	6.3	35.5	30.7	64.5	69.3
1921–25	21.3	14.1	3.4	0.0	4.7	6.7	9.5	10.0	38.9	30.8	61.1	69.2
1926–30	19.3	13.7	2.5	0.0	5.5	8.2	12.1	11.8	39.4	33.7	60.6	66.3
1931–35	17.1	11.2	1.4	0.1	6.8	10.1	15.5	14.1	40.8	35.5	59.2	64.5
1936–40	27.9	13.5	0.8	0.1	7.3	10.3	21.8	15.6	57.8	39.5	42.2	60.5

Notes
[a] 1889–90
[b] 1897–1900

Source: Derived from Bank of Japan, Statistics Department, *Hundred-year Statistics of the Japanese Economy*, July 1966, 278–9, 290, 292.

national income shares. Exports to and imports from the area initially accounted for 1 per cent of Japan's national income each. They grew to 10.2 per cent and 6.5 per cent of it, respectively, during the co-prosperity years 1936–40.

Changes in the commodity composition of Japan's trade with East Asia have been studied in detail by Mizoguchi Toshiyuki.[12] His findings may be summarized as follows:

1 Japan's exports to China prior to the First Sino-Japanese War consisted mostly of marine products, mineral products, metals and metal products, chemicals, and textiles – in that order. Soon after the war, textiles became the dominant item and accounted for more than half of the total exports to China during 1907–26. Their share fell subsequently but contributed a quarter of Japan's exports to China even during the 1930s. Chemicals as well as metals and metal products remained important commodity export groups, no doubt structurally transformed. They were supplemented by processed foods and rapidly rising supplies of machinery as important categories.

2 Because textiles dominated among Japan's exports generally, their regional concentration ratio (RCR) was not high in the case of China. In fact, it was much less than unit value there as well as for Taiwan and Korea. But Japan's textile exports consisted mostly of raw silk which were shipped primarily to Europe and North America. Net of raw silk, therefore, the RCRs were higher in East Asia, but much above unit value only in China during 1907–26, when Japan rapidly replaced Britain as the principal supplier of imported cotton yarns and fabrics.

3 Other export groups with continuously high RCRs in all three territories were chemicals, metals and metal products, machinery, and other manufactured goods, for the reason that Japan protected the provision of such producer goods in its colonies and provided them increasingly to Korea and Manchuria, leaving areas outside East Asia with little more than one-third of all their exports from Japan. Exports of primary goods achieved high RCRs during the 1930s in the colonies but not in China, which remained a principal supplier of such products.

4 Japan's imports from China consisted at first primarily of agricultural products and secondarily of processed foods. Agricultural products retained their predominance, although their share fell from two-thirds to less than one-half of the value of all imports

from China. But their structure changed, textile raw materials being replaced by cereals as the predominant item. Processed foods lost their importance after the First Sino-Japanese War, when sugar from Taiwan had become a colonial product. In their place, chemicals appeared as the second most important category, chiefly in the form of imports of natural fertilizer, which eventually lost in relative terms while other chemicals, metals and metal products and mineral products gained correspondingly, especially during the 1930s.

5   The RCRs show continuously high values for Japan's imports of crude cereals from China, Taiwan and Korea. In addition, China was more than proportionately important at first as a source of textile raw materials and eventually as a supplier of other raw materials and producer goods. Taiwan provided other manufactured (consumer) goods to an extremely disproportionate degree as well. Otherwise the region tended to be under-represented among the suppliers of Japan's imports. In the case of China, Japanese imports of crude cereals, other raw materials and producer goods tended to come disproportionately from Manchuria.

THE GROWTH AND STRUCTURAL TRANSFORMATION OF CHINA'S TRADE

China's trade with the rest of the world is on record from 1864. It grew significantly over the years, though not nearly as rapidly as did Japan's foreign trade. The average annual changes in the value (measured in haikuan taels (HKT)) and the quantity indices of China's exports and imports, shown in Table 9.5, indicate the pace of change.[13] The rapid growth of imports relative to exports during 1895–1913 reflects the wave of mostly direct foreign investment that followed the First Sino-Japanese War. The difference between the 1913–29 and 1913–31 rates of change points to the effects of the depression and tariff reform.

China's international trade seems to have grown faster than its national income did, but for lack of adequate data the magnitude of this relation is in dispute. Aggregate real output increased, according to Perkins, at 1.4 per cent per annum during the period 1914–18 to 1933, and, according to Yeh, at 1.1 per cent per annum during the period 1914–18 to 1931–36.[14] Rawski has taken issue with both estimates, concluding instead that China's real gross domestic product grew probably more rapidly at 1.8 to 2.0 per cent and perhaps even at 2.3 to

Table 9.5 China's exports and imports: changes in value and quantity indices

Average annual change during	HKT values of Exports (%)	Imports (%)	Quantity indices of Exports (%)	Imports (%)
1868–95	3.2	3.8	2.5	2.2
1895–1913	5.9	6.9	2.3	4.4
1913–29	5.9	5.1	2.5	2.1
1913–31	4.6	5.3	1.8	1.5

2.5 per cent per annum during the latter period.[15] Rawski's revision tends to imply that the share of international trade in China's national income did not rise appreciably during those years. However, such a rise is indicated for the longer interval from the 1880s until 1933, and its relative magnitude appears to be consistent with the range of GDP growth rates derived by Perkins and Yeh. Chang Chung-li's GNP estimate for 'the 1880s' yields GNP shares of 2.8 per cent for exports and 3.3 per cent for imports during that decade. Feuerwerker's modification of Chang's estimate serves to reduce these shares to 2.3 per cent and 2.7 per cent, respectively.[16] The Liu-Yeh estimate for GDP for the Chinese mainland in 1933, which also accounts for Manchuria, implies GDP shares of 3.3 per cent for exports and 5.9 per cent for imports when the international trade of Manchoukuo (net of that with the Republic of China) is added to the international trade of the ROC (net of that with Manchoukuo).[17]

China's slower economic growth by any of the measures resulted in a more protracted structural transformation, which is evident in the three sets of output estimates as well. Rawski's findings do not differ much from those of Perkins and Yeh in this respect because his upward revisions of the sectoral growth rates affect all sectors but one, and the traditional ones relatively more than the modern components. The slower shift from primary production to 'manufacturing plus' reflected itself in turn in a similarly limited change of the composition of China's exports and imports, which is indicated by the percentage shares of Table 9.6. Like the Perkins, Yeh and Rawski estimates, these data cover the years since (the eve of) the First World War, when the effects of China's beginning industrialization became noticeable.

Prior to this period, China's exports consisted initially almost entirely of tea and silk plus silk goods. Their shares in total exports declined quickly while those of beans, bean cake, oil seeds, oil and a growing variety of other agricultural products rose to supplement them.

Table 9.6 China's international trade, by category[a]

Unit: Percent of total exports/imports

Year	Food-stuffs & beverages		Raw materials		Semi-manufactures		Manufactures		Other commodities[b]	
	Exp.	Imp.	Exp.	Imp.	Exp.	Imp.	Exp.	Imp.	Exp.	Imp.
1913	17.4	18.1	29.1	5.3	38.7	26.7	12.2	40.4	2.6	9.5
1916	16.9	22.5	24.7	7.7	43.2	26.2	11.0	40.5	4.2	3.1
1920	20.6	11.5	23.9	9.3	37.5	30.7	14.6	47.0	3.4	1.5
1925	13.9	23.3	31.3	15.4	38.9	21.8	13.8	38.1	2.1	1.4
1928	15.7	22.5	35.4	13.9	34.8	20.1	13.3	31.9	0.8	1.5
1931	15.0	22.6	37.7	21.7	32.5	19.7	13.6	34.4	1.0	1.6
1936	24.7	11.0	35.8	13.4	23.2	22.3	16.3	44.2		9.1
1937	21.4	13.9	37.7	8.2	24.7	22.8	16.2	55.1		
1938	21.2	23.9	40.9	7.3	18.6	17.7	19.3	51.1		
1939	23.7	28.8	34.4	19.2	16.8	16.1	25.1	35.9		
1940	21.2	30.7	33.5	20.0	15.9	16.3	29.4	33.0		

Notes

[a] 1936–40: excluding Manchuria

[b] Including live animals

Source: Yu-kwei Cheng, *Foreign Trade and Industrial Development of China*, Washington, D.C.: University Press of Washington, 1956, 35, 136.

Extractive materials such as coal, ores and metals accounted for relatively small shares at most times but gained significantly during the First World War and the Second Sino-Japanese War.[18] Until the loss of Manchuria, the export shares of foodstuffs and of manufactures tended to remain fairly stable, while that for raw materials grew and the one for semi-manufactures fell. After the formation of Manchoukuo, increases in the exports of foodstuffs (oil seeds, etc.) substituted for decreases in the exports of semi-manufactures (bean cake, etc.), and the export of manufactures (from Shanghai) increased on the eve of the Second World War.

Among China's imports, opium ranked first until the late nineteenth century, but gradually lost out to cotton goods, cotton yarn, and an increasing variety of other products, most of them consumer goods. During the period covered by Table 9.6, imports of cotton goods and yarn began to be replaced by those of raw cotton, and imports of numerous industrial producer goods (liquid fuel, transport materials, chemicals, metals, machinery) increased in value relative to other goods.[19] The data of Table 9.6 points to progress in import substitution more generally. The import shares of semi-manufactures and manufactures tend to fall while that of raw materials tended to rise. Deviations from those trends – and from the tendency of the foodstuff share to remain rather stable – occurred primarily during the period of military action at the onset of the Second Sino-Japanese War.

EAST ASIA'S CHANGING POSITION IN THE CHINA MARKET

East Asia's shares of these exports and imports are made evident in Table 9.7. The data, which include China's trade through Hong Kong and with Siberia among the 'others', thereby focusing on the emerging Japanese Empire, indicate that Japan's share of China's trade grew very rapidly from the 1880s until the period of the First World War, contracted somewhat during the 1920s, and declined more strongly during the 1930s, following the loss of Manchuria and the outbreak of the Second Sino-Japanese War. China's trade with Korea developed with a lag and at a much lower level on a similar pattern, but its balance was positive most of the time, unlike the one with Japan. China's trade with Taiwan, which was included in the trade with Japan from 1895 until 1930, appears to have been relatively small at all times. China's trade with Manchuria, which became international after the creation of Manchoukuo, decreased in response to the erection of tariff barriers and

Table 9.7 East Asia's share in China's international trade
Unit: Percent of exports/imports

Period	Japan Exp.	Japan Imp.	Korea Exp.	Korea Imp.	Taiwan Exp.	Taiwan Imp.	Kwantung[a] Exp.	Kwantung[a] Imp.	East Asia Exp.	East Asia Imp.	Others[b] Exp.	Others[b] Imp.
1864–65	0.6	3.8							0.6	3.8	99.4	96.2
1866–70	2.3	3.2							2.3	3.2	97.7	96.8
1871–75	2.1	3.7							2.1	3.7	97.9	96.3
1876–80	2.7	4.5							2.7	4.5	97.3	95.5
1881–85	2.4	5.1	0.1[c]	0.0[c]					2.5	5.1	97.5	94.9
1886–90	4.1	5.5	0.3	0.1					4.4	5.6	95.6	94.4
1891–95	8.0	6.0	0.5	0.1					8.5	6.1	91.5	93.9
1896–1900	9.7	11.3	0.5	0.4					10.2	11.7	89.8	88.3
1901–05	14.0	13.1	0.7	0.3					14.7	13.4	85.3	86.6
1906–10	14.9	14.2	0.8	0.4					15.7	14.6	84.3	85.4
1911–15	16.9	20.5	1.4	0.8					18.3	21.3	81.7	78.7
1916–20	27.6	34.6	2.9	1.6					30.5	36.2	69.5	63.8
1921–25	25.8	24.4	3.7	1.1					29.5	25.5	70.5	74.5
1926–30	24.0	26.7	5.1	1.2					29.1	27.9	70.9	72.1
1931–35	19.7	14.4	3.0	0.4	1.0	0.3	3.4[d]	1.0[d]	27.1	16.1	72.9	83.9
1936–40	9.3	20.9	0.7	0.8	1.0	1.1	4.3	3.8	15.3	26.6	84.7	73.4

Notes
[a] Kwantung Leased Territory representing Manchoukuo
[b] Including Hong Kong and Siberia
[c] Average, 1883–5
[d] Average, 1932–5
Source: Derived from Hsiao Liang-Lin, China's Foreign Trade Statistics, 1864–1949, Cambridge, MA: Harvard University Press, 1974, 22–4, 152–6.

Table 9.8 China's trade with Japan, 1919–36: regional concentration ratios (RCRs)

Imports from Japan	1919	1927	1931	1936
Manchuria	1.78	1.94	2.85	
North China	1.69	1.67	2.04	2.53
Central China	0.82	0.80	0.69	0.82
South China	0.07	0.19	0.20	0.39

Exports to Japan	1919	1927	1931	1936
Manchuria	1.95	1.54	1.63	
North China	2.41	1.66	1.27	1.88
Central China	0.60	0.60	0.59	0.90
South China	0.06	0.22	0.01	0.03

the territory's integration into the Yen bloc.[20] *In toto*, the share of Japan-dominated East Asia rose from about 2 per cent in the mid-1860s to one-third of China's entire foreign trade during the First World War years, when it peaked.

Trade relations with Japan did not develop similarly in all parts of China, and regional foci changed during the evolution of Japan's commercial policy. Its emphasis shifted from Hong Kong and south China during the pre-treaty power years to Shanghai and then to Manchuria and north China after the Russo-Japanese War. By the 1920s, more than 40 per cent of the Japan trade involved the north-east, close to 25 per cent the north, more than 30 per cent central China, and merely 2 per cent the south. The concentration ratios for these four regions indicate that on the eve of the creation of Manchoukuo, trade with Japan predominated in the north-east and north but not in central China and not at all in the south.[21] A comparison of the RCRs for exports and imports reveals in addition that during the 1920s Manchuria and north China tended to become more dependent on Japan for their imports but not for their exports (see Table 9.8).

The regional distribution of China's Japan trade was in large measure commodity specific. In terms of major export items, the reorientation from the south and central parts to the north and north-east involved shifts from (Taiwan's) sugar and from raw cotton to soya beans, bean cake, coal and pig iron, for example, whose production and marketing developed rapidly in south Manchuria under Japan's 'informal'

Table 9.9 East Asia's share in Manchuria's external trade
Unit: Percent of exports/imports

Year	Japan[a] Exp.	Japan[a] Imp.	Korea Exp.	Korea Imp.	USSR Exp.	USSR Imp.	Hong Kong Exp.	Hong Kong Imp.	China Exp.	China Imp.	East Asia Exp.	East Asia Imp.
1929	39.7[b]	42.1[b]	?	?	9.7	4.8	?	?	21.8	29.1	71.2	76.0
1930	29.4	37.9	10.7	3.4	12.8	5.1	1.7	4.2	26.3	32.6	80.9	83.2
1931	33.6	39.9	5.0	3.1	9.6	6.6	1.6	3.9	31.2	30.2	81.0	83.7
1932	30.7	54.0	2.9	4.3	5.5	2.3	0.9	2.7	27.5	18.3	67.5	81.6
1933	40.8	60.8	7.2	5.1	3.0	1.5	1.5	0.7	13.0	15.5	65.5	83.6
1934	38.4	64.6	10.4	4.3	1.9	0.8	1.5	0.8	14.6	9.7	66.8	80.2
1935	43.6	71.9	8.0	3.7	1.1	0.2	1.8	0.5	15.5	5.3	70.0	81.6
1936	39.4	73.3	7.2	3.9	0.3	0.0	1.4	0.7	21.3	6.9	69.6	84.8
1937	42.9	70.7	6.9	4.4	0.0	0.1	1.3	0.5	17.6	4.4	68.7	80.1
1938	57.5[b]	73.2[b]	?	?	0.0	0.0	0.5	0.1	18.6	5.5	74.8	78.8
1939	62.5[b]	84.8[b]	?	?	–	–	0.0	0.0	16.6	3.7	82.8	88.5
1940[c]	69.5[b]	88.8[b]	?	?	–	–	0.0	0.0	25.6	4.3	95.1	93.1

Notes
[a] Including Taiwan
[b] Including in addition Korea
[c] January to September
Sources: *The Manchuria Year Book*, 1931, 1932–3; *The Manchoukuo Year Book*, 1934, 1942; *The Japan–Manchoukuo Year Book*, 1935, 1939.

domination and management. Imports from Japan, which had consisted predominantly of textiles since the late nineteenth century, were more widely dispersed in terms of destination, as were other consumer goods. Investment goods, however, followed more clearly the directions of proprietary interests and flowed disproportionately into the Kwantung Leased Territory, the SMR Zone, and eventually other parts of northeast and north China.

China's trade with Korea and Soviet Siberia was concentrated even more on the north-east. The trade with Siberia, which consisted mostly of exports of soya beans, bean cake and grains as well as imports of coal, iron and steel, gunny bags, cotton piece-goods and sugar during the late 1920s, ceased soon after the creation of Manchoukuo and the Soviets' sale of the Chinese Eastern Railway, as indicated in Table 9.9. The trade with Korea, which at most times appeared statistically as part of the trade with the Japanese Empire, involved, in particular, exports of millet, bean cake and raw wild silk, as well as imports of cotton piece-goods and yarn, clothing and sugar during the late 1920s, attesting to Korea's more advanced industrialization as well as to its transit location in the trade with Japan.[22] The data of Table 9.7 would show increases during the 1930s if the transactions of Manchoukuo were added to those of the Republic of China. By implication, the declining shares of exports and imports indicate one of the consequences of the territorial loss.

MANCHURIA'S EVOLVING JAPAN TRADE

As a frontier region which was severely underpopulated as well as underdeveloped at the time of its opening, Manchuria grew rapidly in response to the immigration of labour as well as the importation of capital and the imposition of (Japan's) law and order, beginning with the colonization of the Kwantung Leased Territory and the South Manchuria Railway Zone and ending with the forcible creation of Manchoukuo as a satellite state. The quantitative dimensions of this development have been studied by Kang Chao, whose work will be the principal reference for the following observations.[23] His series of export and import values implies in addition that Manchuria's trade had already begun to accelerate significantly under Chinese rule and Russian domination (see Table 9.10).[24]

During Japanese times, Manchuria's trade expanded on the familiar cyclical pattern: very rapid growth from 1907 through the First World War, followed by stagnation in its wake, and renewed growth during

Table 9.10 Manchuria's trade: average annual change,
1872–1939 (%)

Average annual change	Exports	Imports
1872–1893	7.6	4.4
1896–1903	8.5	13.5
1872–1903	7.7	7.0
1907–1931	13.2	7.9
1931–1939	1.7	23.0
1907–1939	10.1	11.5

the later 1920s, terminated by the depression. In contrast with the rest of China, however, exports increased more rapidly than imports did at most times, exceptions being the initial railroad construction period from the late 1890s until the Russo-Japanese War and the years of intensive Japanese investment in Manchuria's industrialization during the 1930s. During that latter period, the rate of growth of exports fell to unprecedentedly low levels in current terms. In real terms, exports apparently peaked in 1931–2 and declined significantly thereafter.[25]

Prior to its separation from the rest of China, Manchuria thus contributed a rapidly increasing share of China's total exports, its percentage rising from 16.8 in 1913 to 35.4 in 1931. The share of imports, on the other hand, fluctuated around a fairly constant trend, changing from 11.3 per cent in 1913 to 10.7 per cent in 1931.[26] Exports also must have risen relative to Manchuria's gross domestic product, while imports may have accounted for a more constant share. After 1931, of course, these relations were reversed when the growth of imports accelerated dramatically and that of exports decelerated greatly, probably turning negative in real terms. Because these movements tended to offset each other, the GDP share of total trade apparently did not change much during the years 1924–41, while the territory's real output grew at 4.2 per cent per annum on the average. Yet it remained fairly stable at a surprisingly high level, exports accounting for 17 per cent and imports for 22 per cent of the territory's GDP in 1934.[27]

Until the 1930s, this rapid economic growth did not result in a significant structural transformation. Agriculture-plus (fishing, forestry, and subsidiary production) continued to contribute about 50 per cent of the GDP, and the share of manufacturing-plus (mining and construction) increased very slowly.[28] The composition of exports and imports remained correspondingly stable. Soya beans, bean cake and bean oil, which had supplied 87 per cent of all export value in 1872, still provided 60 per cent of this total on the eve of the separation,[29] supplementary export items of major importance by then being millet and raw wild silk as well as coal and pig iron.[30] Imports consisted of a larger and increasing variety of goods, yet textiles, wheat flour, sugar, alcoholic and tobacco products accounted for close to half of the total import value during the late 1920s, iron and steel, machinery and vehicles adding merely 15 per cent to it.[31]

Table 9.9 shows that this trade was heavily concentrated on East Asia, before as well as after the separation. It also indicates, however, that the East Asian trade partners' shares of exports and imports changed substantially in response to the establishment of Manchoukuo as a Japanese satellite state. Trade with Soviet Siberia, which had not been negligible, ceased. Trade with Hong Kong, which had been much less important, became practically insignificant. China's trade shares declined, especially on the import side. Accordingly, Japan's trade shares rose greatly also, in particular on the import side. Japan thus replaced China as a source of imports but not as a destination of exports, even during the years of war-related autarky. Japan's colony Korea apparently did not share much in this development and remained more important as a buyer of Manchurian products.

Table 9.11 shows, in addition, that during the mid-1930s, at least, Manchuria depended on Japan to a disproportionate extent for supplies of manufactured goods and disproportionately little for sales of raw materials, which China provided in comparatively large shares. On the export side, Japan appeared as a customer for larger than average shares of semi-manufactures, while Korea concentrated its purchases on foodstuffs and China on foodstuffs and manufactured goods. As a consequence of the territorial separation, the commodity structure of Sino-Manchurian trade thus changed significantly, China losing its established markets for manufactures to Japan. But Japan and its colonies could not meet all of Manchuria's requirements equally well, and countries outside East Asia therefore remained particularly important as buyers as well as sellers of raw materials.

The industrialization efforts of the 1930s accelerated the process of structural transformation of the Manchurian economy and its trade. Both import and export substitution progressed more rapidly than before:

In 1932, production goods imports constituted 22.3 per cent of

Table 9.11 East Asia's share in international external trade by commodity group
Unit: Percent of group total

Year	Exports to				Imports from				
	Japan	Korea	China	East Asia[a]	Japan	Korea	China	Hong Kong	East Asia
Foodstuffs, beverages, prepared tobacco									
1935	46.13	31.05	14.01	91.19	59.14	7.45	6.20	1.08	74.14
1936	34.49	37.11	25.16	96.76	57.36	7.81	12.86	2.65	80.67
1937	42.48	29.94	23.32	95.74	63.82	10.80	9.26	1.86	85.74
Raw materials									
1935	39.36	6.78	8.90	55.04	33.76	6.75	14.24	0.96	55.71
1936	27.59	5.97	8.70	52.26	34.04	5.01	17.69	1.13	57.87
1937	41.59	5.27	4.07	50.93	20.91	5.37	13.62	0.90	40.80
Raw materials for further manufacturing									
1935	57.36	4.23	13.11	74.70	65.20	1.89	5.12	0.64	72.85
1936	60.44	4.11	11.90	76.45	73.25	3.26	3.76	0.76	81.03
1937	61.20	3.57	9.08	73.85	62.60	2.82	2.05	0.81	68.28
Wholly or mainly manufactured goods									
1935	46.80	10.72	38.16	95.68	84.43	2.09	3.50	0.11	90.13
1936	46.31	7.31	43.15	96.77	85.73	2.61	3.58	0.07	91.99
1937	36.70	13.46	38.35	88.51	83.37	3.28	2.48	0.05	89.18

Note
[a] Note the omission of Hong Kong, which was the recipient of less than 2 per cent of Manchuria's exports during 1935–7. See Table 9.9
Source: Far East Year Book, 1941, 652.

total imports while imports of consumption goods amounted to 77.7 per cent of total imports. However, the percentage of production goods imports has increased gradually until in 1937 production goods amounted to 39.4 per cent and consumption goods to 60.6 per cent, a trend which indicated the increasing importance of production goods. In 1938, 1939 and 1940 this trend continued. This fact is a natural reflection of the internal activities in Manchoukuo, going on in the industrial, mining and construction fields.[32]

This change in proportions resulted first of all from the additional acquisition of large amounts of iron, steel and machinery. But it also involved decreases in the importation of wheat flour because of the increased milling of domestic grains, increases in the importation of raw cotton and raw jute as imputs for the growing textile industry, and so on. On the export side, the changes were less dramatic, but the exports of coal and pig iron decreased, for example, apparently because they could be used to a greater extent in domestic production.[33]

The progress in industrialization was achieved by very substantial external resource commitments, which Japan made in the form of the previously mentioned import surpluses. During the Manchoukuo period, in fact, Japanese investments in the territory varied closely with its trade deficit.[34]

THE REORIENTATION AND EXPANSION OF TAIWAN'S TRADE

The Manchurian experience resembled in many respects that of Taiwan during the initial phase of its colonization, when its economy and its trade were restructured to accommodate Japan's needs and interests. As indicated before, Taiwan's international trade was part of the foreign trade of China until the First Sino-Japanese War and part of the trade of the Japanese Empire thereafter. It has been studied and discussed in detail by Samuel P.S. Ho, among others, in the context of his work on the economic development of Taiwan.[35] The following statements are based mostly on this source.

During the pre-colonial period, Taiwan's trade grew rapidly until 1880, then fluctuated without any further gain until the outbreak of the First Sino-Japanese War, with setbacks especially during the Sino-French War of the early 1880s. Exports, whose volume apparently increased at close to 15 per cent per annum during 1868–80, consisted

Table 9.12 East Asia's share in Taiwan's external trade
Unit: Percent of exports/imports

| Year | Japan[a] | | China[b] | | East Asia | |
	Exports	Imports	Exports	Imports	Exports	Imports
1897	14.2	22.6	66.9	45.1	81.1	67.7
1900	29.5	38.2	52.3	27.3	81.8	65.5
1905	56.4	55.3	20.6	22.1	77.0	77.4
1910	80.0	59.5	6.2	11.9	86.2	71.4
1913	75.7	70.2	5.4	12.5	81.1	82.7
1915	79.6	76.0	6.6	15.0	86.2	91.0
1919	80.0	58.6	7.2	20.9	87.2	79.5
1920	83.7	65.0	5.5	19.3	89.2	84.3
1925	81.8	69.7	10.4	17.5	92.2	87.2
1929	87.8	68.5	6.9	15.5	94.7	84.0
1930	90.6	73.2	4.4	14.0	95.0	87.2
1935	89.6	82.9	5.0	11.6	94.6	94.5
1939	86.0	87.5	11.8	9.0	97.8	96.5
1940	81.1	88.4	16.6	8.3	97.7	96.7

Notes
[a] Including Korea
[b] Including Manchuria at all times
Source: Derived from Samuel P.S. Ho, Economic Development of Taiwan, 1860–1970, New Haven, Conn.: Yale University Press, 1978, 392–3.

primarily of sugar, a traditional crop destined for China and Japan, and tea, a new crop shipped mostly to America; tea replaced sugar as the dominant export during those years. Rice also appeared as an important item, but its shipments were not fully recorded. Imports, whose volume increased at more than 10 per cent per annum during the same period, consisted predominantly of opium from India and the Middle East and secondarily of textiles, initially from Britain and then from Japan. The relative importance of opium diminished, while that of a growing variety of other consumer goods increased. During the entire period, Taiwan's trade tended to be fairly balanced, its growth driven by the expanding overseas markets for tea.[36]

After Taiwan's colonization by Japan, the regional pattern, volume and composition of its external trade all changed greatly. Within a decade, Japan replaced the Chinese mainland as the principal trade partner and retained this predominant position until the end of the period, as Table 9.12 makes clear. Yet the trade with China remained important, whereas the trade with the rest of the world, widely

Table 9.13 Estimates of Taiwan's annual growth rates,
1905–35

NDP in 1937 prices, 1911–35	4.3
GNE in 1934–6 prices, 1905–35	4.5
Export volume index, 1905–35	7.4
Import volume index, 1905–35	6.0

dispersed as it was, became less significant over time, especially after the First World War. Likewise, within a decade of the takeover, the balance of Taiwan's total external trade and of that with Japan became notably positive while the balance of its China trade turned negative.[37]

Taiwan's incorporation and integration into the Japanese Empire induced a rapid economic expansion and transformation which became evident in the changes of its territorial income and trade. The estimates of average annual growth rates in Table 9.13 indicate the adaptation to Japan's pace.[38] The share of external trade in Taiwan's gross national expenditure increased rapidly as a consequence, to more than 50 per cent in 1935. After 1935, most aggregate indicators tended to stagnate or decline, thereby lowering the long-run average growth rates until 1940 by perhaps 1 per cent. At the same time, however, industrial production continued to spurt, as it did in Manchuria and in Korea, though without resulting in comparable balance of trade deficits.

Japan's principal economic objective was to turn Taiwan into its primary source of sugar and a major source of rice, tropical fruits, and raw materials – rather than of tea, which continued to appeal to Chinese and Westerners instead. The effective pursuit of this goal, which involved the development of agricultural production and productivity in those directions, of processing industries for those crops, and of an appropriate physical and social infrastructure,[39] is ultimately evident in the composition of Taiwan's exports and imports during the colonial period. The data in Table 9.14, which have been compiled and processed by Mizoguchi, show that exports consisted predominantly and increasingly of foods (sugar, rice and other products, in that order), which were destined mostly for Japan. Other consumer goods and raw materials for production (in particular alcohol) added relatively little to them. Exports of construction materials, machinery and equipment remained insignificant throughout the period.[40]

Taiwan's imports consisted mostly of manufactured products, the

Table 9.14 Taiwan's external trade by category
Unit: Percent of total exports/imports

Period	Food, processed and unprocessed		Other consumption goods		Raw material for production		Material for construction		Machinery, equipment	
	Exp.	Imp.	Exp.	Imp.	Exp.	Imp.	Exp.	Imp.	Exp.	Imp.
1896–1900	76.8	32.9	18.7	39.5	4.3	19.0	0.2	8.1	0.0	0.5
1901–05	74.1	27.7	21.2	41.6	4.4	17.1	0.2	12.4	0.0	1.3
1906–10	80.3	22.8	14.9	35.5	4.6	19.4	0.2	20.1	0.0	2.2
1911–15	77.3	30.2	12.7	28.7	9.7	23.7	0.4	14.9	0.0	2.6
1916–20	77.7	29.8	8.3	24.4	12.9	30.0	0.9	10.6	0.1	5.2
1921–25	82.9	32.2	6.6	26.6	8.2	27.4	2.2	9.6	0.1	4.1
1926–30	84.6	28.5	6.9	28.7	6.8	28.2	1.6	9.2	0.1	5.5
1931–35	86.5	21.8	5.4	29.6	7.1	32.4	0.9	9.4	0.1	6.7
1936–38	89.1	24.0	5.0	28.9	4.7	26.9	1.0	13.4	0.3	6.8

Source: Toshiyuki Mizoguchi, 'Foreign trade in Taiwan and Korea under Japanese rule', *Hitotsubashi Journal of Economics*, 14(2) (1974), 40.

majority of which came from Japan. The import shares of foods and of other consumer products (in particular textiles) remained relatively large and stable. The share of raw materials for production rose during the second decade because of the importation of agricultural inputs such as fertilizers, including bean cake from Manchuria. The share of construction material imports fluctuated, rising rapidly, first, when the infrastructure had to be developed during the first decade, and again on the eve of the Second World War. The share of machinery imports increased more steadily but remained relatively small even during the 1930s.[41]

To reorientate and develop Taiwan's economy and external trade as indicated, Japan committed substantial resources, especially during the initial years of the colonial period. Taiwan's balance of trade deficit with Japan during the first decade no doubt understated the magnitude of Japan's investment. Soon thereafter, however, this relation changed:

> Taiwan was an economic asset to Japan not only because it was a source of food and raw materials, but equally important, because Japan was able to obtain Taiwan's primary products without exchanging an equivalent value of manufacturing goods. Except for the first decade of its occupation, Taiwan exported substantially more than it imported. From 1916 to 1944 Taiwan's export surplus (here defined in the conventional manner) as a share of its export averaged 26 per cent. Because Taiwan's trade was mostly with Japan, the export surplus was essentially to Japan's advantage. The very large and persistent export surplus was made possible because in Taiwan the income distribution decision was largely in Japanese hands. The real wage in Taiwan was kept low, so total consumption as well as imports of consumer goods also remained low. Profit, on the other hand, was high. Part of the profit was reinvested in Taiwan, but much of it was transferred to Japan.[42]

The Empire-wide protection of agricultural products certainly enhanced this distributive effect, at the expense of the Japanese consumer.

KOREA'S EAST ASIA TRADE

Unlike the trade of Taiwan, Korea's external trade did not require much redirection towards Japan after 1910. Soon after the Meiji Restoration, Japan in 1876 pressured Korea into opening its borders and proceeded at once to pursue its commercial interests, in competition and conflict

Table 9.15 East Asia's share in Korea's external trade
Unit: Percent of exports/imports[a]

Period	Japan		China[b]		Other countries	
	Exports	Imports	Exports	Imports	Exports	Imports
1910–12	73.7	62.4	16.8	10.1	9.5	27.5
1914–16	79.9	67.5	13.0	12.9	7.1	19.6
1919–21	89.9	64.4	8.8	23.7	1.2	11.9
1924–26	93.1	68.0	6.6	24.3	0.3	7.7
1929–31	91.4	76.5	8.2	15.9	0.4	7.6
1934–36	87.7	84.8	11.6	10.8	0.7	4.4
1939–41	77.4	88.3	21.2	4.8	0.4	6.9

Notes
[a] Three-year averages based on current values
[b] Including Manchuria and areas in north China occupied by Japan
Source: Suh Sang-Chul, 'Growth and structural changes in the Korean economy since 1910', tables II-11 and II-14, as quoted by Paul W. Kuznets, *Economic Growth and Structure in the Republic of Korea*, New Haven, Conn.: Yale University Press, 1977, 10.

first with the Souzereign China and then with Russia. By the time Japan resolved these conflicts by force and colonized Korea, the composition of trade and Japan's preponderance as a trade partner were already well established. Information on Japan's involvement in Korea's foreign trade during the pre-colonial era appears, for example, in the decennial reports of the Chinese Maritime Customs for the treaty ports of Jenchuan (Chemulpo, now Inch'on), Fusan (Pusan) and Yuensan (Wonsan) during 1882–91.[43] The expansion and restructuring of this trade during the colonial period has been summarized by Paul W. Kuznets.[44] His work will serve as one of the basic sources for the following comments, together with Mizoguchi's previously cited article.[45]

During the triennium 1907–9, Japan accounted for close to 66 per cent of Korea's total trade.[46] Table 9.15 demonstrates that, during the following three decades, its predominance increased, though it dominated Korea's exports more than its imports. Korea's trade with China, which consisted mostly of trade with Manchuria, developed on an unusual pattern that needs to be considered in the context of changes in the composition of trade. The share of exports to China fell until the mid-1920s and rose thereafter, while the share of imports from China during the same periods first rose and then fell. Both changes are distorted by transit shipments (between Japan and Manchuria). The

Table 9.16 Korea's external trade by category
Unit: Percent of total exports/imports

Period	Food, processed and unprocessed		Other consumption goods		Raw material for production		Material for construction		Machinery, equipment	
	Exp.	Imp.	Exp.	Imp.	Exp.	Imp.	Exp.	Imp.	Exp.	Imp.
1911–15	72.3	19.1	4.5	47.0	22.4	21.3	0.8	7.1	0.0	5.5
1916–20	68.4	18.5	4.7	44.2	26.4	24.7	0.5	6.2	0.0	6.4
1921–25	67.8	21.7	4.4	41.5	25.6	24.4	2.2	8.8	0.1	3.7
1926–30	66.4	24.7	6.3	36.9	25.1	26.3	1.6	6.5	0.2	5.7
1931–35	61.1	17.0	7.7	39.8	28.7	29.9	1.8	6.4	0.7	7.0
1936–38	49.3	14.6	15.0	38.9	32.5	28.1	1.5	7.7	1.7	10.8

Source: Toshiyuki Mizoguchi, 'Foreign trade in Taiwan and Korea under Japanese rule', Hitotsubashi Journal of Economics, 14(2) (1974), 40.

shares of exports to and imports from other countries both declined very rapidly, the former to insignificant levels by the end of the First World War. The external trade of Korea thus appeared even more focused on the Japanese Empire than that of Taiwan and of Manchoukuo.

Korea's integration into the Japanese Empire, like that of Taiwan generated rates of growth of output and trade comparable to those of Japan. During the period from 1910–12 to 1939–41, Korea's net commodity product grew on average at 3.9 per cent per annum and the volume of its trade at 8.6 per cent per annum. The trade ratio therefore increased rapidly as well, and exceeded 50 per cent during the 1930s. Unlike the growth of Taiwan, that of Korea occurred primarily in the non-agricultural sector, so that manufacturing plus mining increased their share in the net commodity product from 8.2 per cent during 1910–12 to 36.9 per cent during 1939–41 while agriculture's share decreased from 84.6 per cent to 49.6 per cent.[47]

Changes in the composition of Korea's external trade, which also accelerated during the 1930s, reflected the changes in the structure of output, as Table 9.16 indicates. Among the exports, the share of foods, processed and unprocessed, decreased, while the shares of other consumer goods and of intermediate products both increased. Classified according to the Brussels Convention, the same data depict a very substantial shift from raw materials to semi-finished and finished manufactures.[48] Among the imports, the share of machinery and equipment and the share of raw materials for production both rose, while the share of other consumer goods fell. The share of food imports increased at first and decreased subsequently, like the share of imports from China. Varying imports of food grains from Manchuria, especially of millet, thus appear to explain both patterns.

Food grain imports became necessary to cover, at least in part, the deficit in the food grain balance which the rapidly growing exports of rice to Japan caused after the First World War. Together with Taiwan, Korea served as the principal supplier of rice for Japan but, unlike Taiwan's output, Korea's production of rice could not be increased fast enough to provide an adequate surplus, which was extracted in the form of rent and taxes. Rural impoverishment and food crises as a consequence contributed to rural–urban migration within Korea as well as to emigration to Japan and Manchuria.[49]

In addition to rice (and beans), Korea exported to Japan primarily an increasing variety of other raw materials and intermediate products. Exports of other consumer goods and especially of cotton textiles apparently went mostly to Manchuria, augmented by transit shipments from Japan. Conversely, Korea imported from Manchuria in addition to grains primarily raw materials for production (notably bean cake and raw silk). Japan provided mostly manufactured goods, which changed in composition gradually from consumer goods to producer goods, especially during the 1930s.

Throughout the colonial period, Korea experienced a balance of trade deficit which at times reached relatively large magnitudes. Until the later 1930s, however, its commodity account with Japan was fairly well balanced and even in surplus at times. The disproportionate provision of services by Japan may have tipped the balance in the opposite direction. The trade deficits with China and the rest of the world clearly were not covered by their investments and had to be met by exports of specie and bullion as well as by remittances from Koreans residing abroad. Japanese investments may have been financed in part internally. Balance of payments deficits appear to have been covered before the 1920s by government transfers and during the 1930s by long-term capital flows.[50]

CONCLUSION

The Japanese began their modernization efforts under duress, at a time when the major powers of the time reached the Far East in their quest to open up and carve up the less-developed areas of the world, imposing 'unequal treaties' on Japan as well as on China. Unlike China and virtually every other country at that time, Japan responded very effectively to this challenge. Within a generation, it had developed sufficiently through free trade, however manipulated, to emancipate itself from all restrictions on its sovereignty and to pursue instead openly protectionist and imperialist ambitions. Its integration of Taiwan, Korea, the Kwantung Leased Territory–SMR Zone and eventually Manchuria into the Japanese Empire and co-prosperity sphere accelerated the rates of dependent growth of output and trade in all these territories to Japanese levels, thereby assuring the metropolis of food and raw material supplies (without payments problems), as well as of markets for its not so competitive producer goods. The rest of China, which expanded and transformed its output and trade much less rapidly under an 'unequal' free-trade regime, also provided food and primary products but served in addition mostly as an outlet for cotton textiles and other consumer goods, with the opportunity to convert balance of trade surpluses into foreign exchange. The share of this China trade remained fairly stable, while that of the colonial trade increased significantly. As a result, East Asia's share of Japan's external trade, which became more and more coterminous with the Yen-bloc share, grew dramatically, especially during periods of imperial expansion.

In evaluating this experience, Lockwood, among others, has argued that Japan and its dependencies would have fared as well or better if instead of following the European powers' examples of empire building, Japan had continued to pursue comparative advantage commercially, through essentially unmodified free trade. He stresses in particular that the Pacific War was an inevitable consequence of Japan's confrontational strategy, that trade with East Asia was not so critical because Japan's comparative advantage did not depend on locational proximity or cultural affinity, and that commercial success in the East Asian market did not require political domination, whether formally through colonization or informally through participation in the treaty power system.[51]

The Pacific War no doubt was an exorbitant price, and a discussion of its inevitability goes beyond the scope of this paper. The assertion that Japan could have gone on trading after 1894, as it had done until then, assumes that the rest of the world, and in particular those principal powers which had colonized much of it, were sufficiently free-trade orientated to accommodate Japan's evolving trade interests. Yet with few exceptions and not by choice, Japan in fact exported less to the more-developed countries and their colonies than it imported from them, and it made slow progress in broadening the composition of its exports. It therefore had reasons to be concerned about payments problems which could constrain the pace of its growth as well as of its transformation.

The contention that Japan could have traded as much or more in East Asia without becoming imperialistic assumes that China and Korea as well as the Western treaty powers would have responded appropriately without the use of force, which was not the case. In particular, China did not grant most-favoured-nation status, which meant treaty power status, without military confrontation; and Russia, which had made great efforts to keep Japan out of the north-east, gave up its concessions in south Manchuria and its sphere of influence in Korea only after a lost war. Moreover, Japan's full-fledged treaty power status granted it equal access to the East Asian market but not necessarily the sought-after changes in trade, which were limited in particular by the slower pace of East Asia's 'semi-autonomous' economic development.

Japan's resort to colonization and Empire-wide protection appeared to be a solution to both problems. Political domination made it possible to export not only consumer goods or capital or labour but the entire system – Americans nowadays might say: of property and agency rights – which created the environment for accelerated growth. Protective tariffs added to the incentives to produce food and raw materials for the Japanese market and to use Japanese producer goods in the process, which thereby benefited more extensively from economies of scale in production. Securing food supplies internally – apparently a Japanese fixation to this day – in turn limited the payments problems to less-critical purchases abroad, at the expense of the Japanese consumer. Internalizing economic activities more generally helped to stabilize Japan's as well as its dependencies' growth, also at the cost of sacrificing some comparative advantage.

Throughout its colonial period, Japan thus traded off improvements in efficiency for more-rapid and more-stable development, with notable success especially during the 1930s. The increases in production and trade evidently benefited the Japanese,[52] no doubt more so as producers than as consumers. As a means to this end, the colonial development efforts may have had positive effects on the existential conditions there as well, the colonizers' exactions notwithstanding. But the evidence is not uniformly positive. In addition to infrastructure generally, public health and basic education seem to have improved in all dependencies. Real wages increased in Taiwan by more than 1 per cent per annum until the late 1930s, according to Ho.[53] Real wages were much higher in Manchuria than in north China (and in Korea), accounting for the immigration from both regions, but fell also during the inflation of the late 1930s.[54] A similar decline is indicated for Korea, according to Kuznets, who concludes generally that 'growth may not have brought substantial benefits to most Koreans during the colonial era' and that 'the average Korean did not benefit from industrialization and expansion of trade'.[55]

In comparison, average per capita consumption in China grew by 0.5 per cent per annum during the period from 1914–18 to 1931–6, according to Rawski's calculations, or stagnated during the same interval, as an implication of the Perkins and Yeh estimates,[56] followed by the same kind of decline which is evident for the other parts of China during the late 1930s. The similarity of the magnitudes suggests that, on average, people in the colonized areas did not fare any worse and perhaps somewhat better than those in the Republic, in spite of the impositions put on them. *Cui bono?*

NOTES

1. Bank of Japan, Statistics Department, *Hundred-year Statistics of the Japanese Economy*, July 1966, 32, 278–9.
2. William W. Lockwood, *The Economic Development of Japan: Growth and Structural Change, 1868–1938*, Princeton N.J.: Princeton University Press, 1954, 336.
3. Ibid., 325.
4. Mizoguchi Toshiyuki, 'The changing pattern of Sino-Japanese trade, 1884–1937', in *The Japanese Informal Empire in China, 1895–1937*, ed. Peter Duus, Ramon H. Myers and Mark R. Peattie, Princeton, N.J.: Princeton University Press, 1989, 13.
5. Ibid.
6. Ibid.
7. Bank of Japan, *Hundred-year Statistics of the Japanese Economy*, 290, 297.
8. Ibid., 278.
9. Mizoguchi, 'Changing pattern of Sino-Japanese trade', 12.
10. See note 7.
11. Yu-kwei Cheng, *Foreign Trade and Industrial Development of China*, Washington, D.C.: University Press of Washington, 1956, 48–9, 204.
12. Mizoguchi, 'Changing pattern of Sino-Japanese trade', 17–27.
13. Derived from Hsiao Liang-lin, *China's Foreign Trade Statistics, 1864–1949*, Cambridge, Mass.: Harvard University Press, 1974, 274–5.
14. Thomas G. Rawski, *Economic Growth in Prewar China*, Berkeley, Cal.: University of California Press, 1989, 272.
15. Ibid., 330.
16. Peter Schran, 'The minor significance of commercial relations between the United States and China, 1850–1931', in *America's China Trade in Historical Perspective*, ed. Ernest R. May and John K. Fairbank, Cambridge, Mass.: Harvard University Press, 1986, 238.
17. Derived from ibid.; Hsiao, *China's Foreign Trade Statistics*, 24, 156; and *Manchoukuo Year Book, 1934*, Tokyo: Toa-Keizai chosakyoku, 1934.
18. Cheng, *Foreign Trade*, 6, 19, 34; Hsiao, *China's Foreign Trade Statistics*, 74–124.
19. Cheng, *Foreign Trade* 6, 19, 34; and Hsiao, *China's Foreign Trade Statistics*, 30–70.
20. See Table 9.8.
21. Derived from Cheng, *Foreign Trade*, 48–9.
22. *Manchuria Year Book, 1931*, Tokyo: Toa-Keizai chosakyoku, 1931, 192–229.
23. Kang Chao, *The Economic Development of Manchuria: The Rise of a Frontier Economy*, Michigan Papers in Chinese Studies, no. 43, Ann Arbor, Mich.: University of Michigan Center for Chinese Studies, 1982.
24. Derived from ibid., 22–3.
25. *Manchoukuo Year Book, 1942*, 272, 313.
26. Derived from *Manchoukuo Year Book, 1934*, 579–80.
27. Chao, *Economic Development of Manchuria*, 14, 17.
28. Ibid., 16.
29. Ibid., 22–6.

30. *Manchuria Year Book, 1931,* 192–211.
31. Ibid., 212–29.
32. *Manchoukuo Year Book, 1942,* 317.
33. Ibid., 318–19.
34. Nakagane Katsuji, 'Manchoukuo and economic development', in Duus *et al.* (eds) *The Japanese Informal Empire in China, 1895–1937,* 153.
35. Samuel P.S. Ho, *Economic Development in Taiwan, 1860–1970,* New Haven, Conn.: Yale University Press, 1978.
36. Ibid., 13–16.
37. Ibid., 392–3.
38. Derived from ibid., 27.
39. See ibid., chs 3–6, for an analysis of the policies and their effects.
40. Ibid., 30–1.
41. Ibid.
42. Ibid., 31–2. Note 8 omitted.
43. China, Imperial Maritime Customs, *Decennial Reports, 1882–91,* Shanghai, 1893, Appendix II, Korea, xxxivff.
44. Paul W. Kuznets, *Economic Growth and Structure in the Republic of Korea,* New Haven, Conn.: Yale University Press, 1977, ch. 1.
45. Toshiyuki Mizoguchi, 'Foreign trade in Taiwan and Korea under Japanese rule', *Hitotsubashi Journal of Economics,* 14(2), (1974), 37–53.
46. Kuznets, *Economic Growth ... in ... Korea* 9–10.
47. Ibid., 10, 19.
48. Ibid., 12.
49. Ibid., 14, 17.
50. Mizoguchi, 'Foreign trade in Taiwan and Korea', 40, 50.
51. Lockwood, *Economic Development of Japan,* 402–4.
52. Ibid., 144ff., esp. 146.
53. Ho, *Economic Development in Taiwan,* 93.
54. *Far East Yearbook, 1941,* Tokyo: Far East Yearbook Inc., 1941, 850–1.
55. Kuznets, *Economic Growth ... in ... Korea,* 22–3.
56. Rawski, *Economic Growth in Prewar China,* 280, 341.

INDEX